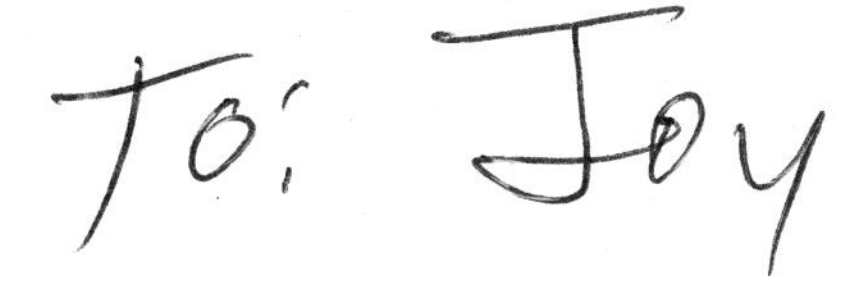

YOU'VE GOT HIS WORD ON IT

DR. LENNY WISEHART

Lenny Wisehart

2 Cor. 4:16–18

ISBN: 9798767466979

Independently published

To my precious wife Joy who is indeed my best friend.
She has taught me much about the Word of God through her
preaching, teaching and her intimate walk with God.
I see Him in her every day. Without her love, support and
encouragement this book would not have been possible.

Introduction

Would you like to know God better—to explore scriptural truths each and every day of the year? *You've Got His Word On It* includes 493 separate scriptures with a scripture index to help you find specific passages in your personal study. All of these devotionals can be read in five minutes or less, but it could be the five minutes that impacts you for years to come.

2 Corinthians 4:16-18 is my life verse and the first passage I memorized as a new Christian at the age of 13.

> "Therefore we do not lose heart. Even though our outward man is perishing, yet the inward man is being renewed day by day. For our light affliction, which is but for a moment, is working for us a far more exceeding and eternal weight of glory, while we do not look at the things which are seen, but at the things which are not seen. For the things which are seen are temporary, but the things which are not seen are eternal."

Many people today (even in the church) focus on the things they can see and touch rather than on the things that are unseen and eternal.

I'm praying *You've Got His Word On It* will help you focus on the hidden things of God, the inner life with God. This will not happen just by reading a book, but by making a conscious effort to enter in to a deeper knowledge of God through His Holy Word. I pray you will allow His Word to be such a daily part of your life that you naturally think, "What does the Bible say about that?"

> "All Scripture is God-breathed and is useful for teaching, rebuking, correcting and training in righteousness, so that the man of God may be thoroughly equipped for every good work."
>
> 2 Timothy 3:16–17

As you pour over Scripture, you should keep seeking to understand those great biblical clues that enable you to interpret life as a Christian. How much happier and how much more effective all of our lives would be if we were thoroughly biblical in our outlook and orientation. Scripture is the key to the interpretation of reality.

If you read this book for 30 days and feel it does not feed your spirit and influence the way you think, email me (lennywisehart@yahoo.com) and I will refund your money.

The more you become quiet before His Word, the more intimate your relationship with Him will become. If you truly want Him, He will meet you somewhere today. Look for Him.

To you dear reader I would say: I am blessed just knowing you are interested enough in the Word of God to seriously consider reading these daily devotionals and applying them to your life.

There are two primary reasons I wrote this book. First, to help us think biblically each and every day. These scriptures have deeply touched my heart and have impacted the way I think; I pray they will touch your heart as well.

Secondly, they are designed to carve out space in our lives for God to reveal Himself to us.

The fact that you are reading *You've Got His Word On It* is an indicator of your hunger to know Him better. Jesus said (Matt. 5:6) "That those who hunger and thirst for righteousness would be blessed and filled." May this book help to bless and fill you with God's Word.

"Lord, I pray for everyone who reads these pages. May your Holy Presence be made manifest in their lives."

Lenny Wisehart

JANUARY 1

Jesus and the Power of the Word

It's interesting to note how Jesus, the greatest person who ever lived, handled Satan, the greatest foe who ever lived.

It's recorded in Matt. 4:1–11 that Jesus simply quoted the Scriptures when confronted by Satan. Three times He said, "It is written." Where was it written? In Deuteronomy—that's where.

Jesus was simply quoting Deuteronomy, but why? He who could speak worlds into existence, silence storms, and raise the dead; He who had power over demons and could call ten thousand angels, maybe ten million angels—what was it He did when facing the foe of all foes? He simply quoted the Word of God as written by Moses over fourteen hundred years before. Jesus knew there was power in the quoted Word of God.

What about you? What have you been using to fight the foe these days? New Year's resolutions? Intestinal fortitude? Maybe at your house it's positive thinking, or perhaps simply the determination not to give up. They all sound good to contemporary society, but they were not the Master's method for spiritual survival. No, He used what Paul calls the Sword of the Spirit, the Word of God. I doubt we can improve on Jesus's method. As a matter of fact, I don't *want* to try improving on it. I just want to get *in* on it. How about you?

Remember: Jesus was the great model for us all! And He resisted the evil one with the Scriptures. Go back in your memory. Resurrect some of those passages you used to know. Write them down. Quote them to your family. Keep them near you. Commit them to memory.

I don't know about you, but I feel better already knowing that I'm using the Master's method for spiritual survival. He's promised to bring you through, you've got His Word on it.

JANUARY 2

Jesus Is Always with Us

Do you ever feel at a distance from Jesus? Ever wish that you could see Him with your eyes? I mean, do you ever feel that He is not around when you need Him? He tried to address this issue with His disciples. In Matthew 28:20 He said, "I will be with you always, to the very end of the age." Jesus was trying to assure them that He would never be out of their reach. It is interesting to note that after His resurrection and prior to His ascension, forty days had transpired.

Acts 1:3 says that during this time Jesus appeared to His followers and gave them many proofs that He was alive and well. It was at this time that He told some fisherman to throw their nets on the right side of the boat. After they obeyed, they caught so many fish that they could not bring the net in. It was during this time that He appeared to Thomas, who finally believed after seeing and touching the Christ.

At first you might think that for forty days He should have fellowship with them every waking moment. But such is not the case. His appearances to Simon, the Emmaus Road travelers, the disciples as a group, more than five hundred brothers at the same time, to James, and even (after His ascension) to Paul on his way to Damascus—all these contacts had one common factor: they were all brief encounters.

He gave evidence that He had been with them even when they could not see Him. For example, Jesus knew of Thomas's doubts about His resurrection.

I wonder why Jesus did not stay within eyesight the entire forty days. It was no doubt to teach them that even when He was not visible, He was still very much with them. In fact, He would be with them to the end of the age.

In John 16:7 Jesus told them it was for their good that He was going away. What strange words these must have been! How could it be good when the best person they had ever met was going to a place they had never been?—confusing to say the least. The facts are, He left them physically so He could fill them spiritually. What a privilege, to have not only the Savior *with* you but actually living *within* you as well!

Jesus's words in Matthew 28:20 are as true today as they have ever been. Jesus is with you, my friend—whether you see Him or not. And He is going to be with you to the end of the age.

JANUARY 3

Miracles

John 2:1–11 records the first miracle of Jesus as He changed water into wine. In numerous Scripture references Jesus came and before He left, a miracle had occurred. Have you had any miracles in your life lately? Sometimes I'm sure we hinder the miracle-working power of God by not doing our part. God does not perform a miracle out of the blue just to impress everyone. No, He works after we have done something ourselves.

Before Jesus turned the water into wine, He instructed the servants to get some vessels, fill them to the brim, and start pouring. That's when the miracle came. The fisherman had worked all night and had caught nothing. But Jesus said, "Launch out into the deep and let down your nets"—and then the miracle came. The blind man in John 9 had to go to Siloam to wash the mud from his eyes and—then the miracle came.

The point is this: there's always a human factor in every miracle. What is the human factor in the miracle *you* need today? What is it you're to do to help bring this miracle to pass? Mary told the servants, "Do whatever Jesus tells you," and that's the key to any miracle. Stay in the Word of God, saturate yourself with it, pray the Word of God—stay with it long enough until He speaks to your soul. Simply do what He says. Then your miracle will come.

JANUARY 4

Lukewarm: Worse than Cold

I bring to you a word of caution from Revelation 3:14–16, written to the pastor of the church at Laodicea: "I know your deeds, that you are neither cold nor hot. I wish you were either one or the other! So because you are lukewarm and neither cold nor hot, I'm about to spit you out of my mouth."

The Message says, "I know you inside and out, and find little to my liking. You're not cold, you're not hot—far better to be either cold or hot! You're stale. You're stagnant. You make me want to vomit." These would be sobering words indeed if they were directed to people who made no spiritual profession. But here they are directed to a church. These are people who had walked with God. More than sobering, they are a stern warning. You see, Laodicea was known for at least three things.

1. It was a very wealthy city. In a day when other cities had gone to neighboring friends and borrowed funds to save their economies, Laodicea had been destroyed and later rebuilt itself with its own resources. It was indeed wealthy.
2. It was known as a medical center throughout the entire country and was especially known for eye salve. People would come from miles around to have eye salve from Laodicea placed upon their eyes that they might see again.
3. It was known as a clothing center. People would make the needed sacrifice to get to Laodicea to purchase the city's fine material.

Isn't it interesting that the three things that should have been their strengths became their greatest needs? Verse 17 says, "You do not realize, Laodicea, that you are poor, blind and naked." How could this be? How could it ever happen to the church at Laodicea? Those who had wealth—God called poor. Those who had the eye salve—God called blind. And those who had been distributers of fine cloth—God called naked. And wonder of wonders, verse 17 says that they did not realize their own condition.

Here we find a warning we would be wise to heed. We live in a day when our wants have been disguised as needs. Our over-indulgence has been disguised as the "good life." Laodicea was neither cold nor hot—they were just so lukewarm they were about to make God sick.

Being lukewarm is worse than being cold. If you're cold, you don't care about the things of God; you're your own boss. But if you're lukewarm, you're kind of in and kind of out—and the sad thing is that you can think you're *in* but be *out* all the time.

Let's make up our minds to fight lukewarmness just as much as we would fight cold, dead religion!

JANUARY 5

Jesus Has a Higher Plan

In John 11 Jesus receives the news that Lazarus is sick. Now you would think Jesus would run to the side of His sick and hurting friend. But the Scriptures are careful to state that Jesus stayed where He was two more days. How unlike the caring Christ we know! But He waited until Lazarus was dead to go to the family.

Martha, one of Lazarus's sisters, said to Jesus, "If you had been here my brother would not have died." And you know, no doubt she was correct. But verses 38–44 reveal that Jesus had a higher plan, for He was soon to raise Lazarus from the dead. If Jesus had responded immediately after hearing the news, He would have raised Lazarus simply from a sick bed. Although that would have been good, by waiting He did a greater miracle with a higher plan—raising Lazarus from death itself.

Do you ever wish Jesus would come to your situation right now? You wanted Him immediately, but He waited two days, maybe two weeks, or two years—perhaps you're still waiting this very moment.

Why would a good God allow us to go on and on and on in our struggling situations? Why doesn't He help when our plans are hindered, when our health is faltering, when all kinds of bad things are happening to us? Could it be, as with Lazarus, He has a higher plan? We must never forget that God's delays are not God's denials. The Lord simply has a higher plan.

JANUARY 6

Balcony People

Years ago I came across an interesting concept I want to pass on to you. Keith Miller had a film series in which he quoted Sigmund Freud: "Our mind is divided into two basic areas. One third is conscious and the remaining two thirds is unconscious."

The conscious mind is the upper level; you might call it the tip of the iceberg. The unconscious mind is the lower level, the iceberg below the surface. These are like two separate worlds in which people we have met continue to influence our lives.

The people who live in our lower level are those living or dead who continually reach up and try to pull us down. Freudian psychologists call them "basement people."

Do you have any basement people in your life?

Basement statements are pronouncements and questions like "You're never going to change." "Can't you do anything right?" "What's the matter with you?" Sometimes parents even communicate basement statements to their children with comments like "Not now—I'm too busy" or hurtful names like "You're weird" or "You're lazy." It has been observed that we Christians are different from people of the world because although we do have basement people, we have the advantage of "balcony people" who speak the things of God into our minds.

Some characteristic balcony statements are "I love you," "I'm so proud of you," "I know you can make it—I believe in you." Do you have any balcony people in your life? Let me ask you another question: Are you a balcony person or a basement person in someone's life? Whose balcony are you in? I hope you're the best balcony person your spouse, children, or friends ever have.

Hebrews 11 is known as the great faith chapter of the Bible. In it we have a list of faith heroes from the Old Testament; you might call them "Bible balcony people." Then Hebrews 12 begins with the word *therefore.* Whenever you see the word *therefore* in the Bible you know that whatever is going to be said after that word bears directly on what was said before it. Hebrews 12:1 reads, "Therefore since we are surrounded by such a great cloud of witnesses, let us throw off everything that hinders and run with perseverance the race marked out for us."

The word *surrounded* paints the picture of a crowd towering above the race. These faith heroes are in your balcony. They are smiling and encouraging, beckoning you to keep on. Think of it: Paul, Simon Peter, James, along with Abraham, Moses, and Elijah with thousands of others have joined Jesus in your balcony. Do you see them? They are there.

The Scriptures indicate that Jesus is seated at the right hand of God. An amazing statement is made in Acts 7. Stephen has just given his great testimony to the Sanhedrin. The people listen to his words and are cut to the heart. They lash out at Stephen and begin stoning him. But in verse 56 Stephen says, "I see heaven open and the Son of Man standing at the right hand of God." It is as if Jesus has sat in the balcony long enough and now stands in support of one of His who is going through a life-threatening trial.

I'm not sure what you're going through, friend, but it could be that Jesus has sat in the balcony long enough and is about ready to stand to His feet in support of the faith you have in Him this very day. Hold steady!

JANUARY 7

Choose Peace

Colossians 3:15 says, "Let the peace of Christ rule in your hearts." The word for *rule* here is an athletic term that could be rendered "umpire" or "arbitrator." An arbitrator is one who settles the differences between two people. An umpire is one who settles the disagreements on an athletic field. The peace of Christ is to be the umpire of our hearts, forcing us to evaluate our decisions and attitudes on the basis of whether or not they will maintain peace in our lives. Whatever is not of peace is not of God.

The New Testament word translated "*peace*" carries in it the idea of wholeness or health. In other words, God's plan is for peace. It's the healthy thing to have. It's as if the Creator is saying, "Keep things as the architect has planned and the house fits together." Operate your life according to His plan and you'll have the natural, normal, healthy, balanced life that God intended.

One way to describe peace of heart is a sense of spiritual warmth. I know that when something brings warmth to my spirit it is most often in the direction of God's will for me. When something brings coldness to my spirit it is always a sign that I'm moving in the wrong direction.

If you're trying to make a decision and you want to be sure that it's God's will, ask yourself this question: As I move in the direction of doing this thing, do I feel the peace of Christ, the warmth of His Spirit? Or does it bring coldness to my spirit, a sense of separation from the peace of Christ?

Note: the passage begins with the word *let.* In other words, God doesn't force His peace—we must *choose* peace. Doesn't it sound strange to say that we must *choose* peace? Wouldn't anyone rather have peace? Wouldn't anyone rather have a healthy, balanced, complete life? Yes, of course, but the problem is Satan. He tells people that peace comes from pleasures, possessions, or prestige. But remember: he is the father of lies; you can't trust him.

Always move in the direction of the peace of Christ and you're always moving in the direction of God.

JANUARY 8

The Trap of Comparison

My wife, Joy, wrote a devotional that I want to pass on to you. In Galatians 6:4 we read, "Each man should test his own actions, then he can take pride in himself without comparing himself to somebody else."

Some people say, "If I only had her looks," or "If I only had his talent." Does that sound like you? Do you ever fall into the trap of comparing yourself to someone else? It's a deadly game.

What does comparing do?

First, *comparison causes conflict.* If I'm always comparing my weaknesses or my strengths to that of others—will I ever be free to give, love, and accept others? At this point seeds of jealousy, resentment, and hate germinate. Don't ever entertain such thoughts.

Second, *comparison cancels faith.* My mindset determines my emotions. If I constantly fill my mind with self-doubts and negative qualities instead of the power and possibility of God—in other words, if I focus on problems instead of the problem-solver—my faith will be short circuited. Self-doubt and negative thinking are not faith builders.

Third, *comparison camouflages confidence.* As I set my mind on the thoughts of Christ and spend time in His Word, something happens in me. His idea of me and how He perceives me begins giving me the true value and identity He has for me. I begin seeing myself as He sees me. As a result, my self-esteem begins growing and I'm encouraged.

What if David had compared himself to Goliath? Would he have marched on in faith? What does it matter if you're physically more attractive or have more material things? That's not where your true value comes from anyway. It's a subtle trap that you must fight with all your strength. The Bible says, "Test your own actions"—then, my friend, you can take holy pride in yourself without comparing yourself to others.

Don't let comparisons cause you conflict, cancel your faith, or camouflage your confidence. Take these thoughts captive in Christ and see your worth through His eyes and not the eyes of others.

JANUARY 9

Fighting the Good Fight

In 2 Timothy 4:7 we have some familiar words from Paul: "I have fought the good fight, I have finished the race, I have kept the faith." Paul was soon to die. But as he looked over his life, he thought of the Olympic games, the competition involved. He pictured the athletes, the excitement, and the energy of that historic time.

Paul imagined the discipline of the participants. The excruciating fight of it all—the fight to train, stick to a proper diet, maintain a positive attitude—and as he looked back, he remembered his own fight and called it a "good fight."

Think of it: Paul had been stoned, shipwrecked, beaten with rods and whips, mistreated, and misunderstood, but he said it was a "good fight." The key to seeing the good in the fight must be from the perspective of the future. Paul said in Romans 8:18, "I consider that our present sufferings are not worth comparing with the glory that will be revealed in us." Friend, whatever fight you're in today, ask yourself this question: How big does your problem look from heaven? I encourage you to try the "heavenly perspective"—I'm convinced it's always the best.

Paul continued: "I have finished the race." Now that's one of the hard things in any test of endurance—simply to finish. How about at your house? Do you have some jobs you started but as of yet you've not completed them? Without a doubt, Paul had many opportunities to quit, to simply give up. There were some who had serious doubts about him. They questioned his conversion story and his literal vision of Jesus. It was just too much for them to believe. So Paul repeatedly began his epistles by writing things like "Paul, called to be an apostle" or "an apostle by the will of God." He was testifying to what had happened to him in a life-changing moment—a divine moment , a great moment—when God touched him on the road to Damascus.

Now there's a key for us all, a realization, a reminder, a refocusing on our great moments with God. Do you remember when you last were touched by God and knew He was real? At that moment perhaps you made some decisions, set some goals, plotted a new direction for your life. The question is this: Are you continuing in that direction, continuing to trust your great moments?

Finally Paul says, "I have kept the faith." He wants us to see the Christian life as a trust. The Greek literally says here, "guard the deposit." What is the deposit? It is the gospel, the good news about Jesus. That's the deposit Paul was entrusted with, and that is the deposit we are now entrusted with—the good news of Jesus!

It's interesting to note that in Paul's familiar words he says, "I have fought… I have finished… I have kept." There are clearly some things Paul had done; granted, there were many things God had done—He sent Jesus and the Holy Spirit, gave us the Scriptures, and at this moment He is preparing a place for us in heaven.

But there are some things *we* are to do. God will give us the grace and strength to do them—I'm sure. But the choice, the follow-through, is our decision. God has given you the ability to choose to fight the good fight, to finish what you have started, and to guard the deposit He has entrusted to you.

Friend, since God believes in you so much, doesn't it just make good sense to believe in yourself today? We are all in a battle. Make up your mind to see it through to the end.

JANUARY 10

Eat All You Want—No Calories Here

We are so diet conscious these days that *calories* is a negative word in most people's vocabulary. But I'd like to paint a sign that says, "Eat All You Want—No Calories Here." Then I would take that sign and hang it on everyone's Bible.

I'm reminded of Psalm 119:78, which reads, "I will meditate on your precepts." Verse 97 reads, "How I love your law. I meditate on it all day long." And then in verse 103 we read, "How sweet are your promises to my taste, sweeter than honey to my mouth."

The word *meditation* at times gets a bad rap, but basically in this context it's "focused thinking.'

Physicians indicate that the flavor of food is not properly savored until it has been thoroughly chewed, and, of course, chewing helps digestion as well. What chewing does to food to make it useful for our physical bodies—meditation does to the Word of God to make it useful to our spiritual bodies. God's promises can be, to quote the psalmist, "sweeter than honey to our mouths."

The Word of God is not just to be swallowed in large gulps without savoring its deeper meanings. At times we need to live with a verse, sometimes all day long (as the writer said he did). Then there are times we need to think on a single passage for many days.

How long has it been since you spent a day, half of a day, or even an hour thinking about some passage from God's Word? Our devotional time should not end after we have read a few verses and prayed a short prayer. We need to think, we need to meditate on what we have read, perhaps all day long. I challenge you to take your favorite verse, maybe one you memorized years ago, think on it, meditate on it, chew on it all day today.

If no particular verse comes to your mind, then think on Psalm 23:1—"The Lord is my shepherd, I shall lack nothing." Now think about a shepherd watching over, guiding, protecting, caring for his sheep, and then think about Jesus, the good shepherd. Think about how He watches over you, guides you, protects you, and cares for you.

Remember that in Matthew 4:4 Jesus said, "Man does not live on bread alone, but on every word that comes from the mouth of God." The way to live spiritually is to take healthy bites of God's Word and chew them thoroughly.

Yes, go ahead, friend—eat all you want. There are no calories here.

JANUARY 11

Our God Has No Equal

Jesus says in 2 Corinthians 12:9, "My power is made perfect in weakness." How long has it been since you reminded yourself that Satan is no match for God? I mean, it's no contest.

I love to play ping-pong. I guess I've played it since I was about ten years old. What would you think of me if I said, "I beat a five-year-old boy in ping pong today?" You'd probably say, "So what? The boy couldn't even reach the top of the table, let alone play the game. That's not a win for you, Lenny, because it was 'no contest'!"

Listen, my friends—there is no counterpart to God. It is not true that Jehovah is the "good God" and Satan is the "bad god." I mean, God has no counterpart, no opposite. There are no other gods. God is high and lifted up there is no one else like Him. Satan is a fallen angel. And angels are no match for Jehovah God. I guess you could say that it's "no contest." So think of it. In our lives God gets no real glory by defeating Satan head on—it's *no contest.*

While Satan is no match for God, we as individuals in our own strength are no match for Satan. As a result, God gets the glory when Satan is defeated by our dependence upon Almighty God. Go ahead, friend—give God glory today by overcoming the evil one in the power of Jesus Christ. His "power wants to be made perfect" in you today.

JANUARY 12

A Useful Yoke

In Matthew 11:30 we have some familiar words from the lips of Jesus: "My yoke is easy and my burden is light."

I have no idea how many times I have read that scripture. Many times it has brought comfort to my heart to realize that the yoke was not designed to be pulled by one animal, but two. The load was never to be carried alone but with a partner, a helper. I have found comfort in that verse from the standpoint that whatever I'm facing, I'm not facing it alone. The Lord is with me; He helps me carry my burden.

But to be totally honest with you, there are things I face in my life that do not *feel* very easy. And then I read, "My yoke is easy and my burden is light." I say it again: some things just don't seem light, and for sure they're not easy. How am I to understand this passage?

While studying the passage in the Greek, I came across a very interesting truth I want to pass on to you. The word translated "easy" does have that meaning and can also mean "comfortable" but it can also be translated "useful." When I saw that, a light went on in my mind and spirit. There are many things I have faced as a Christian that did not seem very easy and often were not comfortable—but *every* time they have been very, very *useful.* Yes, I would say a loud amen to the useful work of God in my life, even through adversity.

These things may not be desired, but they have always taught me a needed lesson. They have stretched me in some areas of personal growth, or they simply have drawn me closer to Jesus. My yokes have always been useful.

How about you, friend—what is your yoke today? It may not seem very easy. What is it you're going through? What is it that God has allowed to impact your life? Is it a physical problem, a financial crunch, or maybe it's just that you feel at a distance from God? Cheer up, friend. God is working in your situation—and He's not just working in it but also working in it *for good.* God causes all things to work together for good for those who know Him.

Whatever you're going through, it's for a purpose, for developing spiritual character in your life. Yes, what you face may not seem very easy, but mark it down—it's going to be *useful.* You Got His Word on it!

JANUARY 13

There Is Always a Way Out

In 1 Corinthians 10:13 the Bible says, "No temptation has seized you except what is common to man. And God is faithful; He will not let you be tempted beyond what you can bear. But when you are tempted He will also provide a way out so that you can stand up under it."

In the first ten verses of 1 Corinthians 10 Paul reminds his hearers of Moses and the children of God who were in Egyptian bondage. Moses led thousands of captive Jews to their anticipated freedom. Miracle after miracle spotted their journey. They had everything from miracle food to miracle water. Then a miracle cloud took them to the edge of the Red Sea. You would think with all that God had done for them that there would be tremendous gratitude. Some words of thankfulness would have been in order, but such was not the case.

Rather than seeing what God had done, all they could think of was the Red Sea before them and the Egyptian army behind them. I can hear them cry out to God's man, "Moses, why did you bring us out here to be slaughtered? We're all going to die! There's no way for us to escape the crushing hand of the Egyptians?" But then something happened. God did the unexpected. He parted the waters right before their eyes.

All they could see was the water and the enemy, but God saw more—He *always* sees more. They thought that time had run out but found out God was running the time. When the children of God were safe on the other side and the enemy had been destroyed, then they saw that when God does things, He does them just right.

That's what verse 13 is all about—God is faithful. He will not let you be tempted more than you can handle. That means once you give your life to Jesus, you need never go back to sin again. The scripture continues: "He will also provide a way out." If there is always a way out, then there's always a way for me to be victorious.

The Israelites could see no way out—but God did, and He parted the waters. At this point in your life you may not see a way out either. The crushing enemies' hoof beats are approaching and a raging sea lies before you. What should you do—stand still and be stampeded, or maybe jump for it and be drowned? What should you do?

I'll tell you what to do. Get your eyes off the enemy, off the barriers, off the situation, and onto the Savior. Focus your attention on Jesus, and when the time is right, the waters will part. God has promised. You can count on His Word, and you can count on it today.

JANUARY 14

Answers to Prayer

In 1 Kings 16–17 the Bible paints a very wicked picture in the life of Israel. Ahab was king and was perhaps the vilest king they had ever known. Elijah was God's man. He was to come and reveal the sins of the people and to confront the godless Ahab.

James 5:17 tells us of a time when Elijah prayed that there would be no rain—and the rain stopped for three and a half years. I'm sure the drought got the people's attention. In 1 Kings 17 we hear Elijah proclaiming to Ahab that there would be no rain in the land except at his word. After Elijah's thundering testimony, God told him to get out of there. He was instructed to go down to a stream where he would find water to drink. The ravens, God said, would bring him bread and meat in the morning and again in the evening.

Elijah was alone with God. There he was, all alone, listening, talking, eating, drinking, and having fellowship with the Almighty. Elijah was right where God wanted him. I guess you could say he was "in the center of God's will." But then something strange took place. There was bread and meat for sure—but there was no water. The river had completely dried up. Elijah must have asked himself, "How can *no water* be God's will?"

Now get the picture: Elijah is obedient to God, he confronts the evil king Ahab, he's right in the center of God's will—and no water. I can almost hear Elijah asking, "God, why have you brought me out here to a place with no water?" Then it hits him. "Now I know why there's no water—*I prayed that there would be no rain!*"

Friend, if you cut off the rain long enough, pretty soon you'll run out of water. The facts are that the lack of water was an answer to Elijah's own prayer.

Maybe today you feel as if you're sitting by a stream but there's no water. It's very dry. Maybe you made a decision, you prayed about a job you've taken, and there were other accompanying decisions that you took to the Lord in prayer. After you prayed about the job, it seemed right—but it's not working out as you anticipated. Perhaps your friendships have evaporated and your emotional strength is gone. Perhaps like Elijah, you're in the center of God's will but it's awfully dry. How can *no water* be God's will?

Just as the lack of rain was an answer to Elijah's prayer, maybe your parched tongue is an answer to your own prayer. Perhaps a while back you prayed that God would stretch you spiritually, that He would teach you to go more deeply into the things that count most—and now He's doing it in answer to your own prayer.

Yes, a "dry stream" is sometimes God's way of helping us on the journey. I challenge you to look back. Look at your situation from God's perspective. Look at the lessons He's trying to teach you—and then get your umbrella. The showers are on the way!

JANUARY 15

Take a Nap

In 1 Kings 18 we read about Elijah's famous challenge to Ahab and the prophets of Baal. The stone altar was covered with wood; an animal sacrifice was then placed on top. Normally at that time they would ignite the wood as an offering to their false god Baal. But this time Elijah challenges them to do everything as usual except lighting the fire. "Just pray, and the God who sends fire, Baal or Jehovah, we'll let him be God." The four hundred fifty prophets of Baal had yelled and danced and even cut on themselves trying to get Baal to set the sacrifice on fire. Nothing happened. Finally as evening rolled around, Elijah came forward. He prayed to the true God and fire descended like rockets from the sky. It was a testimony to the people that Jehovah was alive and well.

In 1 Kings 19 Ahab's wife, Jezebel, received the news of Baal's defeat and was infuriated. She sent a messenger to Elijah informing him that in twenty-four hours he would be dead. I would like to say Elijah called her bluff, but such is not the case. He ran like a scared rabbit. How could this be? The prophet who had just expressed great faith now fell flat on his face. Elijah was feeling sorry for himself, getting his eyes on the wrong thing.

Think for a moment: Elijah was a man. He was flesh and blood, a person just like us. He had just won a significant victory over Ahab and the prophets of Baal. It had been a long ordeal and his physical strength was gone. There was no record that he ate anything that day. His emotional energy was depleted as well. I'm telling you—the man was worn out. Finally he said, "Lord, I've had it." In my mind I can hear him say, "This is too much for me; I'm turning in my prophet's badge today." He then laid down and fell asleep under a tree.

What happened next is one of the most practical helps in all the Bible. An angel came and provided some fresh bread along with a jar of water. He touched Elijah and said, "Get up and eat." He ate and drank, and then went to sleep again. The angel came a second time and repeated the catering service for the worn-out prophet. The Bible says, "He got up and went on the strength of that food for forty days and nights."

What is the point of it all? It is this: some of our spiritual battles are not really spiritual issues at all. They are physical. It could be that what you need is a good night's rest—maybe you need an entire day of rest. Perhaps it's a good meal you need. Maybe you need to do something that has no deadline attached to it at all.

God made our bodies in such a way that they give us signals when they are overloaded. Perhaps this is a day for you, friend, to give your spiritual life a boost and go take a nap.

JANUARY 16

Hearing the Voice of God

In 1 Kings 19:11–13 we read, "The Lord said, go out and stand on the mountain in the presence of the Lord. For the Lord is about to pass by." And as Elijah stood there, "a great and powerful wind tore the mountains apart and shattered the rocks. But the Lord was not in the wind. After the wind there was an earthquake. But the Lord was not in the earthquake. After the earthquake there was a fire, but the Lord was not in the fire. And after the fire came a gentle whisper. When Elijah heard it he wrapped his face in his cloak and went out and stood at the mouth of the cave." Elijah's previous dramatic "fire-falling" incident with the prophets of Baal was not to be viewed as God's normal way of dealing with people.

As God was about to pass by, isn't it interesting that when the wind tore the mountains and shattered the rocks, God was not in the wind? Isn't it interesting also that when the earthquake came next, God was not in the earthquake? Next came the fire, but God was not in the fire (I'm beginning to see a pattern here). Then came the gentle whisper—and *that* was the voice of God.

I don't know about you, but many times I long for the God of the wind, the God of the earthquake, the God of the fire to exert His great power. I want to "see" His power at work, but generally He speaks in a gentle whisper. If I'm not careful I can miss His voice because I'm looking for the spectacular.

The psalmist said, "Be still and know that I am God." Friend, if you are too busy to be still, chances are that you'll never hear His voice.

JANUARY 17

How to Know You Are Right with God

Remember how you prepared your vehicle for your last vacation? It was as if you had an automatic checklist. I mean, you wanted to be sure your tires were okay, the oil had been changed, the air conditioning was operating properly—everything seemed to check out, and you were finally ready for the trip.

Did you ever wish you had a *spiritual* checklist, one that could bring assurance to you that you're ready for your *spiritual* journey? Let me give you a six-point checklist that could help give you assurance for your journey forward.

This checklist will center around one question: How do I know I am right with God?

1. I know I am right with God because of the Bible.

In 1 John 1:9 we read, "If we confess our sins, He is faithful and just to forgive us our sins." Now that I have confessed my sins and turned from them, on the authority of God's Word I know He has forgiven all my sins. First John 5:13 adds, "I write these things so that you may *know* you have eternal life" (emphasis added). You see, because of what God's Word says and because we have acted upon His Word, we *know* we have what the Word says. This is not a hope-so situation or a maybe-so or a good-chance-so—but a *know-so* relationship.

2. I know I am right with God because of the Holy Spirit.

First John 4:13 says, "We know that we live in Him and He in us because He has given us of His Spirit." In Romans 8:16 we read, "The Spirit Himself testifies with our spirit that we are God's children." I know I am right with God because the Holy Spirit gives me an inner witness, an inner assurance, an inner awareness in my soul that what I accepted by faith has been witnessed to by the Holy Spirit. A sense of peace grips your heart as you know all is well with God. It is not that you force yourself to think you are a Christian—rather, there is a rest, a relaxation with His Spirit's presence in you.

Of course there is something for us to do—we must pray, we must be faithful to God's Word, faithful to God's house, faithful in stewardship—but there is a sense in which there really is a rest to those who have totally trusted in God.

3. I know I am right with God because of the blood.

Hebrews 9:22 states, "Without the shedding of blood there is no forgiveness." Yes, because of the fact of Calvary, I mean the historical fact that Jesus gave Himself for the sins of us all, we have assurance of our salvation. And the fact that this has been personally accepted in our lives gives us a reason for the belief that our sins are forgiven.

4. I know I am right with God because of my new life.

In 2 Corinthians 5:17 we read, "If anyone is in Christ he is a new creation. The old has gone, the new has come." We are different than we used to be, we are different than we were before we found Christ. The burden of sin is gone, the guilt is gone and the peace of Christ has come. Without doubt, one way you know you are right with God is because of the new life you have in Him.

5. I know I am right with God because I love the brothers and sisters.

If people say they're Christians but do not love each other, they don't love God, according to God's Word.

First John 3:14 says, "We know we have passed from death to life because we love the brothers and sisters." In John 13:35 Jesus said, "Your love for one another will prove to the world that you are my disciples."

The special love that followers of Jesus have for each other is evidence that they are truly born again.

6. I know I am right with God because of my concern for others to know Him too.

Proverbs 11:30 says, "He who wins souls is wise." At first when we hear that proverb we usually think it means, "He who wins people to the Lord, he who causes people to turn from their sins is wise." And though that is true, there is another point in this passage that can be missed. Simply stated, it would be "He who wins souls to himself is wise." In other words, there are some people we may never win to Jesus until we win them to ourselves, until they have confidence in us.

The person who wins people to himself finds it a short step to win them to Christ.

JANUARY 18

Don't Forget Your Cross

In Matthew 16:24 Jesus said, "If anyone would come after me he must deny himself, take up his cross and follow me." I have read that verse for years and have felt direction from it for my own discipleship. But all too often the verse is interpreted as if our daily problems were the cross being mentioned. For example, I've heard people refer to their sickness, their jobs, or unsaved loved ones as their cross. But none of these are at the heart of Jesus's words. The focus here is upon personal sacrifice willingly accepted.

What the Lord commands here is that each Christian should take up not Jesus's cross but his or her own cross. The crucified Leader is to be followed by crucified followers. But how is that to be lived out in everyday life? To put it simply, it means there are times when you give up the comfort of the fireplace or the pleasure of entertainment in order to give that time in ministry for Jesus's sake. It may mean you do not buy something you can well afford because you want to give that money to someone in need.

I'll never forget what a wealthy man once said to me: "Lenny, I don't buy all I can afford because my church may have a special financial need and I want to be able to respond to that need immediately."

Taking up our cross is basically sacrificing for the cause of Christ. It is a sacrifice of your time, your talents, and your treasures for the advancement of the kingdom of God. As simply as I know how to say it is this: cross-carrying is basically what you do on purpose for Jesus—everything from teaching a class to calling on a needy person to telling someone of Jesus and His love for them.

In Luke 9:23 an added dimension is seen as we read we are to "take up our cross daily." Yes, cross-carrying is a daily deliberate decision. As you prepare today for the responsibilities ahead of you, don't forget your cross.

JANUARY 19

The Power of Praise

In 1 Thessalonians 5:18 we read, "Give thanks in all circumstances for this is the will of God." Notice the second part of that scripture: "this is the will of God." It would seem from this passage that there is no debate concerning our giving thanks to God. If we know that something is God's will, then we are expected to do it. No need to wonder if you are to give thanks today in whatever situation you face. The Bible is very clear on this point.

Now look at Ephesians 5:20—"Giving thanks to God the Father for everything in the name of our Lord Jesus Christ." In this verse we have an added dimension. In 1 Thessalonians 5:18 we see it is God's will for us to give thanks *in* everything. But in Ephesians 5:20 we read we are (as believers) to give thanks *for* everything.

Commentators are divided on this passage. Some say it means to give thanks for good things. For the scripture is given in the context of singing, making music in your heart to the Lord, and giving thanks for all things. But other respected scholars say yes, it means that but also means more.

Regardless of what happens in the life of a believer, God has allowed it and since God allowed it, there must be a purpose in it. It must be a part of the things God works together for good for those called according to His purpose.

In Acts 16:25–26 Paul and Silas have an earth-shattering experience. They've just been beaten for their preaching about Jesus and find themselves thrown into prison. I can imagine it being a stinking, filthy, depressing place to be—all because they were preaching the truth. What do you think you would do if you were them? They prayed. I think I would have prayed too. The apostles did what most of us would do under similar circumstances. It seems that when we are in severe trials we often do turn to prayer. But wait—the apostles were not just praying but were beginning to sing as well. And they were not just singing any old song—they were singing a song of praise. Do you think you would be singing a song of praise after being beaten and thrown into prison? As they sang, something began to happen. The walls began shaking, the floor began moving, the doors came open, and everyone's chains fell off. Praying and praising had released the power of God.

I'm convinced that every Spirit-filled child of God has the power of God within, but it lies dormant in many people because they don't choose to praise God. They don't release His power through praise.

I want you to think of the best church service you've ever been in. Picture it in your mind. Now answer this question: How much praising of the Lord went on? The best services I can ever remember have been services filled with verbal praises to God.

Note one final thing about Paul and Silas. After their beating, how do you think they felt? Imagine how we would feel: misunderstood, hurt, and rejected. Notice that they sang praises anyway—obviously not because they felt like praising, but they had just made a decision to praise regardless of the circumstances.

Today, friend, you are going to have a chance to be hurt, rejected, misunderstood, or a hundred other possible things. Why not plan now to choose praise today and see God's power released in a new dimension in your life?

JANUARY 20

How to Resist the Devil

In James 4:7 we have these words: "Resist the devil and he will flee from you." What do you think is the best way to resist the devil? Should we simply try avoiding those places that are potential temptations for us? Not a bad idea. Should we try guarding our attention to be sure our thought life is always pleasing to God? Again, that would be a good thing to do. What if we decided to memorize scripture to help keep our focus on spiritual things? Without doubt, God's Word in our hearts does bring strength.

All these things seem to be good—they make sense. But what about those times when it's too late to avoid the temptation? I mean, we're in the middle of the battle. What can we do then? Here's something that makes biblical sense and has been a help to me.

Think with me. Who is the devil? Satan, yes. Lucifer, yes. But I mean—who is he really, or perhaps I should ask, *What* is he? Satan is an angel, a fallen angel to be sure—but still an angel.

I know of no record in the Bible in which angels know our thoughts. And I don't believe Satan knows our thoughts. He can give us thoughts, and so can I. I can say to you, "Elephant," and as a result I implant a thought into your mind. Do you see it now? A big, grey, floppy-eared, long-trunked animal? But just because I can put a thought into your mind does not mean that I know all your thoughts. Satan and his demonic forces are busy placing all kinds of temptations in our paths. The Bible says, "Resist the devil and he will flee."

Now the point is this: I need to learn to resist the devil as Jesus did, using my most powerful weapon, Scripture, as Jesus verbally did. Then I need to say it out loud as Jesus did. You see, if Satan does not know my thoughts, then he doesn't hear the scriptures I have memorized until I say them.

Friend, I challenge you today to verbally resist the attacks of Satan with the scriptures that apply to each situation. You won't need to shout them—his hearing is very keen. Sometimes even a whisper will do. Again, I challenge you to try it today; it will make a difference in your life and the battle you face with Satan or any other demonic force.

JANUARY 21

Do You Know the Truth?

The Word of God in Psalm 119:130 says, "The entrance of your word gives light." Isn't it a privilege for us as believers to be able to spend time with the Word and thus spend time with Jesus and sense the light it gives us? Jesus said in John 8:32, "You will know the truth and the truth will set you free." Now answer this question: What is it that sets people free? Now, if you said *truth,* listen again. "You will know the truth and the truth will set you free."

Across America every Sunday truth echoes through live streaming on computers, through television sets, from churches, and yes, from pulpits—the message of Jesus and full salvation in Him alone. But let me ask you: Do you think America is a free country spiritually? Oh, yes—we have freedom of worship, but I mean are the majority of Americans who hear the truth actually free in their spirit? No, hundreds and thousands are bound by the power of sin.

The truth is being preached across the country but obviously many are not free. Why? Because it is not *truth* alone that sets people free but rather the truth they *know* that sets them free. Look at Jesus's words again: "You will know the truth and the truth will set you free." You can hear the truth over and over but still not *know* the truth. Only those who *know* the truth are free.

What encouragement that is to me as I study the Word of God! Every day as I read a passage, as I memorize a verse, I'm finding the truth that sets me free. And when the Lord sets you free, you are truly "free indeed."

We hear it said that it's important to know the right people. Well, the important thing is to know the right person, Jesus, to know what He says, and to know His truths. Be sure that in all you know, you really *know* the truth.

JANUARY 22

Wash Your Mind with the Word

In Ephesians 5:25 the Word of God talks about husbands loving their wives just as Christ loved the church and gave Himself for her. But then it says, "cleansing her with the washing of water through the word." "The washing of water through the word" is an interesting expression to say the least. Do you ever read the Bible and find a verse jumping out at you—I call it a "zinger"—that jumps out and seemingly has your name written on it? That's a great thing when it happens in your devotional life. Although zingers may not happen that often, the Bible is always good for us.

The verse that talks about "the washing of water through the word" has a couple of different applications. I'm sure it has implications relative to water baptism, but there's something I have found in my own life that I draw on from this scripture, and it's simply this—the place you work, people you're around, even jokes you hear all impact you at some level. Things that are negative, things that at times are just downright filthy, though they are not things you yourself would say or do—because you are around them at school, work, or even home, they impact the way you think.

There used to be a time when you could watch television and seldom ever hear someone using foul language—but not today. It's everywhere. It's even on national news broadcasts. Do you ever go to a professional sporting event? The language and conduct are often vulgar and undesirable. When I leave situations like that, I need to have my mind washed just because of what others have said or done. We might as well face it—through all these situations, our minds are infiltrated by evil. Satan tries to bring things into our minds every day, so every day we need to have our minds cleansed. Whether you have a zinger or not, through your time reading the Bible every day, you will have your mind washed by the Word of God.

Whenever I read the Bible—whether I get a zinger or not—something happens in my mind: a washing of my mind by the Word of God occurs.

Let's take time today to "wash our minds" in His holy Word.

JANUARY 23

Jesus Has a Reputation

One of the most popular areas of Scripture in the entire Bible is the Psalm 23. Let its words rest on your heart today.

> The Lord is my shepherd, I lack nothing.
> He makes me lie down in green pastures,
> He leads me beside quiet waters,
> He refreshes my soul.
> He guides me along the right paths
> for His name's sake.
> Even though I walk
> through the darkest valley,
> I will fear no evil,
> for You are with me;
> Your rod and Your staff,
> they comfort me.
> You prepare a table before me
> in the presence of my enemies.
> You anoint my head with oil;
> my cup overflows.
> Surely Your goodness and love will follow me
> all the days of my life,
> and I will dwell in the house of the Lord forever. (NIV)

There's an insight in verse 3 that I missed for many years. It's wrapped up in the words "He guides me along the right paths for His name's sake." What does the phrase *name's sake* bring to your mind? If you do something for the name's sake of your family, it means you do what enhances that name. You lift up your family name. You do not do what might discredit that name. It has to do with reputation. As a matter of fact, you could substitute the word *reputation*: "He guides me along the right paths for His *reputation.*" The way we respond to the world shapes their view of Jesus.

What kind of a view of Jesus are you giving to the world? Oh, I know you may have been wronged and shouldn't have to bear that certain problem you're facing now. But can you bear it for Jesus? Can you take it for His reputation's sake?

I know your employer may not do things just as you would like. I know there may be stuff at school that should not be happening. At times even Christians may be part of the problem you face—but can you take it? Can you just take it for Jesus?

I've heard it said that we as Christians are the only Jesus the world really sees. We could also say that at times we Christians are the only Jesus other Christians see as well.

Today, face life as God's representative. You are a part of His "name's sake."

JANUARY 24

God's Directions

Proverbs 3:5–6 says, "Trust in the Lord with all your heart and lean not on your own understanding. In all your ways acknowledge Him and He shall direct your paths" (NKJV).

Are you trying to find God's will for some area in your life? There are many who say that this passage is the greatest passage in all the Bible concerning God's will for one's life.

Four key words are found in these verses: *trust, lean, acknowledge* and *direct.*

First, "Trust in the Lord with all your heart. *Trust* means "to feel secure, to confidently reside in something." It is a relaxed abandonment. Did you ever have a child go to sleep in your arms? The child does not have a care in the world as he or she lies limp in your arms. Likewise, we are not to be tense or filled with anxiety about what God wants us to do. No, we are to relax in God's arms. That is trust.

Second, "Lean not on your own understanding." The word *trust* is a positive word—it is the "what to do" part of the verse. Next we have the negative, the "what not to do" part. We are not to lean on or trust in our own perspective of the situation. How many times have you been frustrated because things didn't seem to be working out? Then to your amazement things turned out better than you ever dreamed.

Third, "In all your ways acknowledge Him." The word *acknowledge* means to recognize the authority of someone. In all our ways we are to recognize God's authority in our lives. It's like saying a daily yes to the will of God, whatever it may be.

That brings us to the fourth and final phrase: "He shall direct your paths."

If you're trying to find God's will in some area of your life, follow these admonitions in Proverbs 3:5–6. First, trust the Lord; feel secure in Him. Second, lean not on your own view of things. Third, acknowledge Him as the authority in your life. And fourth, have confidence not only that He will direct you but recognize He is directing you this very moment.

JANUARY 25

Jesus Witnesses to Us

What comes to your mind when you hear the phrase *the witness of the Holy Spirit*? I think most generally we think about knowing God, having an assurance in our heart and mind that He is real in our lives. The Bible says in Romans 8:18, "The Spirit Himself testifies with our spirit that we are God's children." In other words, God the Holy Spirit communicates to our human spirit that we have indeed had an encounter with the divine.

There is also what is known as "the witness of the Word." I'm sure in the broadest sense it is a witness of the Spirit as well, but it is more directly related to what the Bible says. In other words, if I have met the conditions of the passage of Romans 12:1, "I urge you, brothers and sisters, in view of God's mercy, to offer your bodies as a living sacrifice," I can proceed with the confidence that God will perform the work He wants to do in cleansing my heart. As I submit myself to His Word, I can have confidence that His Word is working in my life. The Holy Spirit can "breathe" on that passage, making it come alive in my heart and spirit.

Various factors—poor health, financial pressure, loss, hurt, misunderstandings, to mention a few—can impact what our human spirit is sensing from the Holy Spirit. Sometimes our peace of heart is threatened, but one thing we can all find as a constant is the witness of the Word. That's why the Bible is so very important. Memorizing the Word has great power in our lives, because when our hearts are disturbed within us, when our inner peace seems gone for a while, we can still come back to what the Bible says as a fact that we can stand on at all times.

One final thought, another witness, is our changed lives. We can see that we are different on the inside by the way we react to life's pressures. Perhaps you used to react in anger, desiring to get back at someone—but praise the Lord, those feelings are gone. You're different than you used to be. And that's because of the working of God in your life.

So we have at least three witnesses in our lives: the witness of the Holy Spirit to our human spirit, the witness of the Word of God, and the witness of a changed life. Be encouraged today by His witness to you of His abiding presence.

JANUARY 26

Jesus Is Knocking

In Revelation 3:20 we have a familiar verse from the lips of Jesus: "Here I am! I stand at the door and knock. If anyone hears my voice and opens the door, I will come in and eat with that person, and they with me."

The Message paraphrase says, "Look at me. I stand at the door. I knock. If you hear me call and open the door, I'll come right in and sit down to supper with you."

This verse has been used multiple times admonishing nonbelievers to respond to God's knock at their hearts' doors. Though I'm sure He does want all people to invite Him into their lives, there is another aspect of this scripture that's sometimes overlooked.

Who is Jesus talking to in Revelation 3? He's talking to a church, to those who have been born again. To them Jesus said, "Here I am! I stand at the door and knock."

Before I come back to that passage, answer this question concerning prayer: Does prayer begin with us or with God? Who initiates prayer? Usually we think of some need or some word of praise, or we take something to the Lord in prayer, all the time assuming that the thought had originated in our hearts and minds. But Isaiah 65:24 says, "Before they call I will answer; while they are still speaking I will hear."

I'm beginning to see in my own life that prayer begins with God. This verse in Revelation 3:20 applies not only to Jesus knocking at the door of a nonbeliever's heart but also at the door of the believer's heart. Jesus is knocking, desiring fellowship with the believer. Note: it is not the believer who is knocking, but it is Jesus knocking at the heart's door. Why? To have fellowship with us. Jesus literally wants to sit down and have supper with us. Sometimes because of schedules and previous commitments a busy person may be heard to say, "I'm sorry, but I have to eat and run." And that's exactly the opposite of Jesus's words. He wants to eat and stay. He wants us to wait in His presence, to enjoy His fellowship as He enjoys ours.

I used to think that prayer was primarily talking, but God showed me the listening side of prayer that I had overlooked. I know that silence can be uncomfortable, but the fact is that we often get what we expect. Do we expect God to speak to us when we listen? Does He speak a language our hearts can understand? When was the last time God spoke to you?

As you go about your day today, take some time, time to sit down and fellowship with Jesus. Let Him have lunch with you today. Listen—I think I hear Him knocking now.

JANUARY 27

God Remembers You

In Genesis 6–8 we have the familiar story of the flood. Can you imagine what it must have been like? Year after year Noah worked on the ark. His neighbors thought he was crazy. How could a flood happen? It had not even rained at this point in history. The earth was simply watered by light dew. I wonder what Satan said to Noah. It must have been something like "Why don't you just give up? Has anyone ever done this before? You are embarrassing your family. What will people think?"

Regardless of what Satan said, the Scriptures tell us that Noah did everything just as God commanded him. And finally the eventful moment came when all the animals were gathered into the ark. Noah's family were the crew as the rains began falling and falling and falling, for forty days and nights. So much water fell that the highest mountain peaks were covered with twenty feet of water. The entire earth was covered with water for one hundred fifty days.

Noah had been obedient to God, and God had allowed him to have a front-row seat to one of the greatest miracles of all time. There was the miracle of building such a huge vessel, four hundred fifty feet long, seventy-five feet wide, and forty-five feet high. He saw the miracle of all the animals coming into the ark and the miracle of the deluge of rain. Literally, Noah was riding on a miracle!

Get the picture. Every living creature on the earth, except those in the ark, had been destroyed. Noah and the ark crowd were the only ones alive in the entire world. If God was going to watch anyone, He would watch Noah and his family, right? There was just no one else to watch, but I can hear Satan speaking to Noah: "God has brought you out here to die with your family and all the animals. Noah, you're a fool. You've done all this work for nothing and God has forgotten all about you." But the Bible simply and powerfully says in Genesis 8:1, "God remembered Noah."

Friend, that's what I want to say to you today—*God remembers you.* He knows your name, He knows where you live, He knows the color of your toothbrush. "Resist the devil and he will flee from you. Come near to God and He will come near to you" (James 4:7–8). Always remember: regardless of what Satan says to you, God remembers you!

JANUARY 28

Being with Jesus

The first four chapters of Acts contain some of the most exciting and yet practical truths in the entire Bible. Here Peter and John (with others) hear the Master say in Acts 1:4–5, "Do not leave Jerusalem...in a few days you will be baptized with the Holy Spirit." They were promised power from God to do the work they were called to do.

In Acts 2 they experience this baptism of the Spirit at Pentecost as the power of God came upon them mightily. They witnessed one of the greatest days in all of church history.

In Acts 3 they touched a man who was over forty years old and had been crippled since birth. The healed man jumped to his feet, found himself walking, and then began to run. As he ran he began praising God for what He had done. You talk about exciting, you talk about a thrill—all the World Series and Super Bowls wrapped together couldn't match the genuine excitement of that moment. Everyone knew that a miracle had taken place. They had observed this man unable to walk for years—yet now they saw him standing, jumping, and running as he praised God.

In Acts 4 the religious leaders became concerned because Peter and John were teaching the people about Jesus and proclaiming He had been raised from the dead. The leaders could not handle that report, so they threw Peter and John into jail. The religious leaders were scared to death and could not condone this preaching about Christ, for He was the very one they had condemned to death. And now this healed man was standing right in front of them. They could not deny that a miracle had taken place. Indeed, these leaders were in a dilemma.

The next day the leaders gathered together to cross-examine Peter and John. A wonderful truth is illuminated in Acts 4:13: "When they saw the courage of Peter and John they took note that these men had been with Jesus."

I can imagine a couple of men from the Sanhedrin Board talking to one another: "Do you remember that Jesus Christ fella' who stood before us a while back?" Another would say, "Oh, yes—I remember Him. I had nightmares about that man for weeks." Another might say, "Do you remember the quiet strength that surrounded the man called Jesus?" The answer could come back, "Yes, I remember there was a presence, a power about Him." And then the reply went something like this: "Well, whatever was in Jesus, I see it in Peter and John also. These two men have been with Jesus."

Friend, that's the great need of our day. We need men and women who have been so much around Jesus that when others see us, somehow they will see Him. Ask yourself—when people come away from me, do they ever sense they have been with a person who has been with Jesus? Or are you a person who is so consumed with your job that you exude your vocational interests? Are your kids and grandkids the main thrust of your life? Do they come away from you feeling they have been with a sports commentator? Or do they say, "I've been with a person who has been with Jesus"?

Let's take time to be with Jesus today. There is a person you will meet today who will be in need of seeing someone who has been with Jesus.

JANUARY 29

An Appetite for God

Proverbs 22:6 says, "Train a child in the way he should go and when he is old he will not turn from it."

We all desire the best for our children. We want the best health, the best education, the best spouse, and the best relationship with Christ they can have. It is just natural to desire these things for those we love so much. But sometimes our children do not make the best decisions. As a result, we are tempted to be filled with anxiety over the direction they are headed.

This passage has an encouraging word for us today. It tells us what parents are supposed to do. They are to "train a child in the way he should go." Is this passage a guarantee of our child's salvation? I mean, if we do everything right, can we be guaranteed our child will serve the Lord? Unfortunately, there's nothing that can be done to guarantee anyone's salvation. It is a matter of personal choice. The Bible indicates that Jesus prays for everyone and that there are some people who still do not get saved.

But this verse still stares us right in the face. What does it mean? It says, "Train a child... " The word *train* is very important. Its root word is a *mouth* word, a *palat*e word, a *taste* word. The suggestion here is definitely about appetite. We are to live before our children in such a way that we create in them a desire for God's Word, a desire for prayer, a desire for faithfulness to God's house. We are to create an appetite for things that are spiritual.

How do we do that? By being excited about the things God is excited about. Parents must take time to talk about the Bible, prayer, and God's house, and even more important, they themselves must model what all of that looks like.

What is the result of training a child in the way he or she should go? The scripture continues by saying, "He will not turn from it." Here we have no guarantee of salvation but rather a guarantee of *appetite.* The child will remember the spiritual examples from his or her past. A picture is worth a thousand words; we might add that an example is worth a thousand words also.

Ask yourself: Is my life creating an appetite for God in others?

JANUARY 30

The Movement of the Holy Spirit

One night Jesus received an interesting visitor named Nicodemus, a Pharisee, a teacher in Israel. The focal point of their conversation was the new birth. The educated Pharisee could not understand how someone could be born a second time. He could not squeeze that concept into his fact-filled mind. Jesus's response is found in John 3:8: "The wind blows wherever it pleases, you hear its sound but you cannot tell where it comes from or where it is going. So it is with everyone born of the Spirit."

Nicodemus had felt the brush of the wind upon his face and indeed had no idea of where it came from or where it was going. Jesus was trying to tell this confused Pharisee that there are workings in the Spirit world that are real but not always explainable. We can be sure of the wind even though we cannot explain it, and we can be sure of the spiritual winds even though we cannot explain them.

For centuries people have tried to explain faith. One biblical definition is Hebrews 11:1: "Faith is being sure of what we hope for and certain of what we do not see." At times our attempts to harness a definition of faith seem like trying to catch cottonwood seeds on a windy spring day. All too easily they elude our grasp. But *we know that we know that we know* God—for one time we took a step of faith, choosing to trust in God's inner dealings with us. We confessed and turned from our sins, while also turning to our Savior.

There are times we break through to a deep spiritual awareness, but much of our walk is simply trusting God for our salvation. We must never be discouraged over our inability to understand some things. Think of it: a child can speak long before knowing the alphabet. And we can operate in the spiritual realm without understanding how the Holy Spirit's activity is carried out.

At times Satan seems to whisper, "If God is so loving, so kind, so good, why doesn't He make Himself more real to people?" Why does the Christian life seem so confusing? At those times we need to remind ourselves of who Satan is. The Bible calls him the accuser. We could also add that he is the "confuser."

In those times we need to think of the changes in our lives since meeting Christ. Where is the crushing load of sin we used to carry? It's gone—it's really gone. Where is the aimless life we used to know? It's gone—t's really gone. Where are the habits we used to have that enslaved us? Praise the Lord! They are gone—they are really gone! Why do we now desire to be with God's people? It's because we are changed—we are really changed!

Why does God's Word bring so much comfort to our souls? Because when *He* is alive in us, *His Word* is alive to us! Think of it, my friend—we are really His. Why is it that we see things we never saw before? Because once we were blind and now we see!

JANUARY 31

God's Days

Have you ever heard a song so old that it was new? Some truths in the Bible seem like that. I want you to be sure to have your Bible by you right now. I'm going to give you a scripture that I guarantee you can find in five seconds. Ready? Now turn to page one—yes, the very first page of the Bible. Chapter 1 of Genesis tells us of the events of the great creation story. Look at the last part of verse 5: "There was evening, there was morning, the first day." Verse 8 says, "There was evening, there was morning, the second day." A pattern is developing here. Do you see it yet? Look at verse 13: "There was evening, there was morning, the third day."

I want you to see something that has blessed my heart many times. Notice that these verses do not say, "There was evening and there was night." No, they say, "There was evening and there was morning." The implication is that God's days in Genesis always ended in the morning. Regardless of how long a day was, Genesis says each day ended "in the morning."

You may be facing something now in your life that's gone on and on and on. It's like the light of your day has gone out. You're going through a nighttime experience.

In Psalm 30:5 the psalmist wrote, "Weeping may last for the night but a shout of joy comes in the morning" (NASB). Perhaps you have shed some tears in the midnight hours, friend, but God is working and a shout of joy is on its way. Yes, a shout of joy is coming in the morning. God has not forgotten about you. You're going to be a better person when your nighttime experience passes than you were beforehand.

God takes the "nighttime" experiences in our lives and works on them, and they become part of something good. As Romans 8:28 states, "We know that in all things [yes, *all* things] God works for the good of those who love Him." He is working in your situation not just to help you exist—He is working to see that things turn out better than you ever dreamed possible. Romans 8:28 has been stated this way: "God is able to orchestrate everything to work toward something good."

Hold steady. God is up to something, and it will be good. It may be nighttime now—but morning is on its way.

FEBRUARY 1

The Prayer Window

Daniel is one of the greatest characters in the entire Bible. A Hebrew, he rose to prominence in a foreign empire. He was admired and promoted by a pagan monarch, yet he never wavered from his faith in God.

Daniel 6:10 says that he went to an upstairs room with the windows open toward Jerusalem and there, three times a day, he fell on his knees and prayed. He was known for his prayers of praise and thankfulness to God. Jerusalem represented to him the faithfulness of Almighty God as well as His embodiment of truth. Daniel kept his window open toward this great city.

The king in that day was named Darius. He was a powerful man who held in his hands the life or death of his people. He was persuaded to make a decree stating that no one could pray to any god in the next thirty days. The only acceptable prayer would be one directed to the king himself.

This passage in Daniel records his response to the Darius's decree—he simply went upstairs with his window opened toward Jerusalem and continued praying as he had always done. Daniel was committed to God and nothing anyone could say would alter the direction of his life. Most of us know of Daniel's miraculous deliverance from the lion's den. But how many of us stop to think of why he was there in the first place? It was simply because he had such a vital prayer life; he just couldn't stop praying to God. The threat of the lion's den could not deter him from intercession.

Answer this question: What does it take to deter you from praying? What does it take to stop you from opening your "window toward Jerusalem"? For you it's probably not a lion's den but something far more subtle. Could it be television, the Internet, or your iPhone? Think over your last week. How much time did you spend in front of the TV, or on the Internet or your iPhone? How much time did you spend in prayer? Or could it be your hindrance is your job? Some people seem to spell the word *job* L I F E. Friend, your job is not your life. If it is, I guess you'll die if you lose your job.

Perhaps your window is shut toward Jerusalem because of a problem that stares you in the face. Maybe you've had a great loss or you're filled with anxiety about the future. But the greater your need, all the more reason to keep the window open.

If we would have strength in the lion's den we must keep the prayer window open all the time.

FEBRUARY 2

In What Direction Are You Going?

According to 2 Peter 2:7–8, Lot, who escaped the destruction of Sodom and Gomorrah, was a righteous man. However, he made a very foolish decision. His story is recorded in Genesis 13:11–12, where we learn that he chose for himself the Jordan plains and pitched his tent toward Sodom. He was definitely moving in the wrong direction.

This righteous man was troubled by the lifestyle of the Sodomites, for they were filled with great wickedness. He became a prominent man in the community, probably the mayor of the city. When judgement came to Sodom, Lot lost his land, his wife, many of his children, and perhaps even his grandchildren. It was a terrible price to pay; it was a price he never planned on paying. He just went in the wrong direction and it cost him greatly.

Many Christians today have no desire to turn their backs on Jesus, yet they are compromising some of their beliefs, doing things and going places they never dreamed would be a part of their lives. They are not living in "Sodom" but are pitching their tents in that direction. It is a fact of life that some things are wrong not in themselves but because they lead in the wrong direction.

Ask yourself: In what direction am I going? If I live the next five years the way I've lived the last five years, will I be closer to God or farther away? The tragedy of it all is that not only are you hurting yourself, but your influence is impacting your family and friends as well.

Have you ever stopped to think that a sunrise and a sunset both look alike? The difference is in the direction they're going. I challenge you not to just look at where you are but also to be honest about the direction in which you're heading.

Leave Sodom while there's still time.

FEBRUARY 3

Doing What You Know to Do

Naaman was a gifted captain in the Syrian army. He was in good standing with King Ben-Hadad, but he had a terrible problem—he had leprosy. When he took off his military garb and looked at his decaying flesh, he lost his commanding status.

Naaman humbled himself one day and came to a man of God, the man Elisha. But the prophet was not impressed by the officer's high rank. As a matter of record, he didn't even go out to meet this prestigious soldier—he simply said, "Go and wash in the Jordan seven times" (2 Kings 5:10). The austere captain lost his temper and said, 'I don't want to dip in the Jordan, that dirty creek. We have superior waters right here in Syria." But Naaman's friends influenced him to give it a try.

The stately officer walked into the Jordan and went under the water. Once, twice, three times, then four, five times and six, but nothing was happening. His flesh was still decaying from the dreaded leprosy. Those looking on, as well as Naaman himself, no doubt wondered if the prophet was making a fool out of this high-ranking captain. But on the seventh dip—his flesh was a clear as a child's. Naaman experienced a miracle.

The miracle happened at the end of complete obedience. Now there's a point for us all to consider. Faith must always be followed by obedience. The blind man in John 9 did not have his vision restored when Jesus put mud on his eyes. The miracle came after he went to the pool in Siloam and washed his eyes. When God says, "Dip in the Jordan," or "Wash at Siloam," you can count on it that victory will be found at the end of your obedience.

Whatever your miracle need is today, my friend, remember: doing what you already know to do allows God to do what only He can do.

FEBRUARY 4

No More Sea

Revelation 21:1 says, "And there was no longer any sea." I remember looking out over the Atlantic Ocean with its glistening blue water and its never-ending caps. To me it's a thing of beauty. But strange as it may seem in a day when we can split an atom, walk on the moon, and fly at supersonic speeds, the ocean still contains unsolved mysteries. Many vessels and thousands of lives have fallen prey to the depths of the ocean.

I'm reminded of the apostle John, who wrote the last book of the Bible. He was the last living apostle and was now exiled to a lonely island called Patmos. This desolate island was surrounded by the surging waves of the Aegean Sea.

Throughout the Bible the ocean is used to symbolize many negative and threatening things. In Psalm 77:16, 19, the sea is a symbol of mystery. In your life and mine we also experience many mysteries, unanswered questions we would like to have the answers for. I wonder what we would find if we drained the ocean dry. I wonder what continents would show up, what canyons and craters, what mountains and valleys would appear.

The sea is indeed a symbol of the mystery we call *life.* We are so ignorant, we know so little—only a tip of the iceberg rises above the surface. As the Bible says, "We see through a glass darkly and we know only in part," but one day the mystery will clear and there will be no more "sea."

The sea is also a symbol or evil and unrest. In Isaiah 57:20 we read, "The wicked are like the tossing sea which cannot rest." Does anyone question that description for the day in which we live? Every day and in a thousand different ways the turbulent waters of evil roll across America. We are in a restless time in our country as well as in our world. Tranquilizers sell in record proportions, suicides in our global population take nearly a million lives a year, one every forty seconds. God's map of the new heaven and new earth reveals no turbulent oceans, no evil, and no unrest.

More than anything else, the sea is a symbol of separation. How lonely John must have been on Patmos Island! Gone were the other disciples, gone was the fellowship with other believers. He was separated from everyone. No matter which way he looked—north, south, east, or west—all he saw was ocean. Deep in his heart he longed for the time when there would be no more separation.

In a very real sense we as believers are exiled here on the earth. We are separated from the saints in previous ages, also from believers who have gone to heaven during our lifetime. But John in Revelation 21:1 said, "I saw a new heaven and a new earth and there was no longer any sea." Mark it down, friend: whatever the sea symbolizes for you—mystery, evil, unrest, or separation—in the new heaven and earth there will be no more sea. All will be peace.

FEBRUARY 5

Prayer Tools

The Bible points out that Jesus was a gifted teacher, but His disciples never asked Him to teach them to be teachers. He was a great preacher, but they never said, "Teach us how to preach." And, of course, He was a great healer, but they never said, "Teach us how to heal." However, in Luke 11:1 we have these words from the disciples: "Lord, teach us to pray." Note that they did not say, "Teach us *how* to pray," but simply "Teach us to pray."

Without a doubt, this is the greatest need of believers today. The greatest power we possess is released when we call upon the Lord. In Luke 18:1 we read, "Men ought always to pray." In 1 Thessalonians 5:17 Paul said, "Pray without ceasing." These admonitions seem like tremendous challenges in a day when prayerlessness is so common.

Here are five tools that can help you as you move through the prayer journey.

1. *Pray regularly every day.* There's something about regular praying that has clout and influence with God that a hit-and-miss prayer life does not have.
2. *Pray at the start of your day.* Whenever your day begins, let that be one of your times of prayer. If you work all night, then your day begins differently from mine, but whenever your day begins, let that be one time you connect with God in prayer.
3. *Don't feel you can pray only on your knees.* Sometimes you need to walk around with your eyes wide open. Sing to the Lord, talk to the Lord, read scripture to the Lord. Don't get bound to a posture or position.
4. *Get alone.* Privacy is a very important ingredient in an effective prayer life.
5. *Use paper and pencil or pen.* Do you try to pray and find your thoughts wandering? One of the greatest tools I have found in prayer to keep me on track is writing down the stray thoughts. When a stray thought comes into my mind, I stop praying, write it down, and then go back to praying. Sometimes a sermon seed thought will come to mind while I'm praying, or an appointment that's coming up. By stopping and writing it down, I clear my mind so that when I pray, I really pray.

Use these prayer tools as you daily call upon the Lord.

FEBRUARY 6

A Prayer Pattern

In Matthew 6:9–13 and Luke 11:2 we have the prayer commonly known as "The Lord's Prayer"—

> Our Father in heaven, hallowed be your name, your kingdom come, your will be done, on earth as it is in heaven. Give us today our daily bread. And forgive us our trespasses, as we also have forgiven those who trespass against us. And lead us not into temptation, but deliver us from the evil one.

Jesus gave it as a pattern for prayer. Do you have a pattern for your own prayer life? Let me give you one I use at times. It has been around for a long time but it's worth revisiting. It is easy to remember when you think of the word *acts:*

A = adoration

C = confession

T = thanksgiving

S = supplication

The first letter, *A*, for *adoration*, reminds us to begin our praying with praise to the Lord for who He is. Glorifying our great God opens the way to communication with Him.

C is for *confession.* We need not only to recognize our dependence upon God but also to confess it to Him. Additionally, if there is any failure in our lives, we should confess it to God and turn from it.

T is for *thanksgiving.* Here is where we give the Lord thanks for the specific things He has brought into our lives: the families we have, our jobs, our health, and the strength He has given us. Thank Him for all the answers He has blessed us with.

S is for *supplication.* What is it we want to talk to God about in an area that concerns us right now? We are invited to tell Him.

A = Give adoration to God.

C = Confess your need of Him.

T = Thank Him for what He has done in your life.

S = Make supplication for your needs right now.

Whatever pattern you use, do it every day. It's hard to believe that God actually has more of a desire to communicate with us than we do with Him. He's listening and ready to answer.

FEBRUARY 7

You Never Really Pray Alone

When you pray, what image do you see in your mind? Perhaps you see God "up there" someplace and you down here trying to get His attention. The Bible says in Romans 8:26, "The Spirit helps us in our weakness; for we do not know how to pray as we ought, but the Spirit Himself intercedes for us with sighs too deep for words" (RSV). In other words, when I pray it is not just me praying, for the Bible says the Holy Spirit is interceding as well. So that means while I am praying the Holy Spirit is praying and that means *two* of us are praying.

But that's not all. Romans 8:34 says, "It is Christ who died, and furthermore is also risen, who is even at the right hand of God, who also makes intercession for us" (NKJV). This passage tells us that another personality is involved in our praying. When we pray as individual people, not only are our minds involved, but also the Holy Spirit and Jesus. That's *three* of us praying at the same time.

Do you see the tremendous power available to every believer? It is any wonder that Satan would go to any length to get a person not to pray? For when I am praying, not only is my mind involved, but that of the Spirit and of Jesus Himself!

Don't cheat yourself today. Take time to call upon the Lord and in your mind see that the Holy Spirit and Jesus our Savior are both interceding to the Father on your behalf. They are helping you as you pray. Visualize God seeing you and hearing you. Think of it—*you never really pray alone.*

FEBRUARY 8

Rules for Answered Prayer

Boundaries are important. Can you imagine a football player taking the ball, running off the playing field out into the parking lot and suddenly ending up at the opposite end of the field acting as if he had scored a touchdown? No one would think his actions could ever be counted as a legitimate scoring drive. The reason? He went out of the boundaries—he did not play by the rules. Prayer works within boundaries and rules as well. Here they are:

First, *the will of God.* In 1 John 5:14–15 we read, "This is the confidence we have in approaching God: that if we ask anything according to His will, He hears us. And if we know that He hears us—whatever we ask—we know that we have what we asked of Him." When God reveals His will to you about a situation, you can pray with confidence. Many times our first prayer needs to be "God, what is Your will in this matter?"

Second, *obedience.* Obedience is a boundary within which prayer works. Jesus said in John 15:7, "If you remain in Me and My words remain in you, ask whatever you wish, and it will be done for you." In verse 10 He said, "If you keep My commands, you will remain in My love." A key to remaining in His love is keeping His commands, for then you can pray with power. Obedience to what you already know is basic to having your prayers answered.

Third, *determination.* In Luke 11:5–8 Jesus gives a parable concerning persistence. A guy goes to his neighbor in the middle of the night and says, "I've had some friends come to my house tonight. They're on a journey, they're hungry, and I have no food." The neighbor responds, "Man, it's midnight—we're all asleep! I can't help you tonight." But the man continues knocking on the door, saying, "I've *got* to have food for my friends!" The Bible says that the neighbor does not want to disturb his sleeping household. Nevertheless, he does get some food for his neighbor's guests, not because he is friends with his neighbor (though they *are* friends) but rather because of the man's persistence. And it is given as a boundary or rule within which prayers are answered.

Fourth, *faith.* Hebrews 11:6 says, "It is impossible to please the Lord without faith. For those who come to God must believe that He is and that He is a rewarder of those who diligently seek Him."

Answer these questions: Do you really believe God is going to answer your prayer? Do you have confidence that God has shown you what His will is? Have you made up your mind to be obedient? Are you willing to be persistent? Do you have faith that God is going to answer what you pray?

As a football game has to be played within the boundaries and rules of the game, so prayer must be made within the boundaries and rules God has set up.

FEBRUARY 9

Barriers to Prayer

Yesterday we looked at the boundaries or rules within which effective prayer takes place. Let's look at some of the barriers that can get in the way of effective prayer.

First: *sin.* Isaiah 1:15 says, "When you spread out your hands, I will hide My eyes from you; Even though you make many prayers, I will not hear." The context reveals God would not hear them because of their sins. In Psalm 66:18 the psalmist writes, "If I have iniquity, if I have sin in my heart, the Lord will not hear me." Sin is a barrier to effective prayer and must be confessed and turned from.

Second: *selfishness.* James 4:2–3 tells us, "You do not have because you do not ask God. When you ask, you do not receive, because you ask with wrong motives, that you may spend what you get on your pleasures." Why we pray and what we pray for are very important when it comes to answered prayer. Ask yourself, "Why am I praying this prayer? Is it a selfish prayer? Will it bring glory to God? What is my motive behind this prayer?"

Third: *an unforgiving spirit.* In Matthew 5:23–24 Jesus talks about a person who comes to pray and while praying remembers he or she has had a falling out with someone (a fellow believer). The person is told to stop praying and first be reconciled to the individual. After that, the person is free to bring his or her prayer concerns to the Lord. An unforgiving spirit is a barrier to anyone's prayer life. If there is someone you have an unforgiving spirit against, you must first make it right with him or her before you will ever be able to pray effectively and touch God.

Fourth: *failure to take time.* Isaiah 40:31 says it's "they that wait upon the Lord" who will renew their strength. They are the ones who mount up with wings as eagles. Have you had any waiting time before the Lord, when you just listen for God's voice?

We have looked at four barriers to prayer: sin, selfishness (wrong motivation), an unforgiving spirit, and the failure to take time. The greatest power we possess is released in the time of prayer.

FEBRUARY 10

Thank God for the Church

Nearly half of the Psalms were written by King David, described by God in Acts 13:22, as "a man after My own heart; he will do everything I want him to do." Sometimes when I read the Psalms I feel as if I need to close the book because it is too personal, like a private diary. Other times it is a mirror of my own life.

In Psalm 38:4 David thinks about sin and what it had done to his life. He writes, "My iniquities have gone over my head; they weigh like a burden too heavy for me" (NRSV). The Amplified Bible reads, "My iniquities have gone over my head like the waves of a flood." David's sins seemed like a tidal wave, drowning him in his guilt. In Psalm 38:5 he says, "My wounds grow foul and fester" (NASB). Here he gives us a picture of the results of his sin.

Do you remember the burden of sin you used to carry? David went on to say in verses 10–11, "My heart pounds, my strength fails me; even the light has gone from my eyes. My friends and companions avoid me because of my wounds; my neighbors stay far away."

Sin took his strength, it took the light out of his eyes, and it took his friends away. Sin has a way of doing that to everyone: weakness, darkness, and loneliness are sin's great gifts. But the paradox of it all is that when Jesus comes, He gives strength, He turns the light on, and He becomes your best friend. And He often does His work through the church.

How long has it been since you thanked the Lord for your local church—your church friends, your pastors, your Sunday School teachers, your small-group leaders? I encourage you today to take time to thank the Lord for the church in which He has led you to serve and grow. In the church of Jesus Christ you will find strength for your weakness, light for your darkness, and fellowship that dispels the loneliness that sin brings.

I'm thankful that Christ gives strength, light, and fellowship and uses the body of Christ to be channels of His presence to our lives. Thank Him today!

FEBRUARY 11

Rest for God's People

Yesterday we looked at what sin had done to David. Now let's look at what David did. In Psalm 38:17 he wrote, "I am about to fall, my pain is ever with me." Sin had been the great betrayer of David. It was as if he were taking a ride on a roller coaster that was up and down on the thrills of life until he finally ran out of track. That's the way sin is—it seems to be filled with thrills for a while but then leads to the way of death.

In verse 18 David writes, "I confess my iniquity, I am troubled by my sin." Do you remember when you confessed your iniquities, when you were so troubled by your sins that you not only confessed them but also turned from them?

In Psalm 39:7–8 we read, "Now, Lord, what do I look for? My hope is in you. Save me from all my transgressions; do not make me the scorn of fools."

We learn in Hebrews 4:9 that "there is a rest for the people of God." If we are not careful, we as Christians can forget the burden of sin we used to carry. It might be a good thing, even now, to remember the guilt you used to feel, to remember the load of sin you used to carry. Of course, you don't want to go back to that condition but to be alert to Satan's tactics. He wants you to look at the pressures of this moment and forget the heavy load you used to carry.

Thank God, friend—there is a rest, even in this life, for the people of God.

FEBRUARY 12

Doing What Comes Naturally

Yesterday we saw what David did with his sin. Today let's look at what *God* did with David's sin. In Psalm 40:1–3 David writes, "I waited patiently for the Lord. He turned to me and heard my cry. He lifted me out of the slimy pit, out of the mud and mire; he set my feet on a rock and gave me a firm place to stand. He put a new song in my mouth, a hymn of praise to our God." What a powerful picture of being changed by the working of a gracious God! No doubt that kind of change, in all of us, inspired song writers to express things like—

My heart was distressed 'neath Jehovah's dread frown,
And low in the pit where my sins dragged me down,
I cried to the Lord from the deep miry clay,
Who tenderly brought me out to golden day.

He brought me out of the miry clay;
He set my feet on the rock to stay.
He puts a song in my soul today—
A song of praise, hallelujah!

'He Brought Me Out' —Henry J. Zelley. Refrain: Henry L. Gilmour

Isn't it something that when the Lord comes into your life and forgives your sins, the birds seem to sing better, the sky seems bluer, and people seem different? It's not that anything on the outside has actually changed, but you are different on the inside, and that changes everything.

Many people reject the idea of keeping the law but in verse 8 David says, "To do your will, O my God, is my desire. Your law is within my heart." It is not a burdensome thing to serve the Lord, for He places His law and His love deeply within our hearts. Doing God's will becomes the natural, normal thing to do because He lives within us.

FEBRUARY 13

Thank God for Temptation

Some people are converted, serve the Lord, and then turn their backs on Him—they backslide. They may still basically believe the Bible and believe in God, but what happened? They had not planned on falling away, but temptation came and they were defeated.

Everyone everywhere deals with temptation. If you haven't faced temptation today, hold on—you will. The Bible tells us that we are to anticipate a battle, a spiritual battle against the evil one. In Ephesians we are advised to "put on the whole armor of God." We are in a conflict, not against flesh and blood (people) but against "the powers of this dark world and against the spiritual forces of evil in the heavenly realms." Don't be surprised when your battles come repeatedly to the same spot in your life.

Temptation is a kind of "proving ground" for our faith. By definition, a temptation is a test designed to strengthen or corrupt. God allows it to strengthen, but Satan brings it to corrupt. Ever wonder why temptation is even possible? It's a part of what it takes for a person to have free will.

When I was a little boy I used to play, by the hour, with plastic cowboys and Indians. They were just toys, plastic people. They didn't do much—except when I was pretending they were riding horses and interacting with each other. But when I put those little people into a shoebox and onto the shelf, they didn't move, they made no noise—they waited patiently until my boyish mind once again brought them to life.

I guess God could have made us like plastic people, like ornaments hanging on a Christmas tree called "Earth." But plastic people can't love, they can't pray, they can't live. God made us so we can love, pray, and live. The fact is that there is no real victory without the possibility of defeat.

I used to practice playing ping pong against a wall. I'd push the ping pong table up against the basement wall and for hours hit the ball fifty times without missing. I would then try to beat my own record, hitting the ball one hundred times without missing, and then one hundred and fifty times, and I thought it was fun. But the real test came when I played *someone else* in ping pong. The real victory came when there was a possibility of defeat.

Temptation brings the possibility of defeat but also gives us the possibility for new strength in our lives. Why is temptation possible? Because God has given us free will and we can use it every day to become stronger in Him. I thank God for temptation because He has allowed it for a purpose. Always trust His purposes even though you may not figure out what good can come from your temptation.

FEBRUARY 14

Three Steps in Temptation

We've been examining temptation and why it is possible, but today let's see how it works, what stages it goes through. The two greatest examples of temptation are in the first book of the Old Testament (Genesis) and the first book of the New Testament (Matthew).

In Genesis 3:1–6 we have Eve and her desire for food. She is an example of great failure. In Matthew 4:1–11 we have Jesus after His forty days of fasting and His desire for food. Satan had said to Him, "Turn these stones into bread," and it had ended in great triumph. It is important to note that both these temptations came to innocent and holy individuals. Adam and Eve were created holy and Jesus, of course, was without sin—He was holy. So these temptations came to holy individuals. There are at least three steps or three progressions that accompany temptation: attention, desire, and choice.

Attention: Eve looked at the fruit. Jesus was asked to turn the stones into bread. Attention is a very important factor in temptation. That's why there is potential danger in the friends we choose, the movies we watch, the games we play, and what we look at on our computers. All these things put our attention somewhere. It has been said, "You are what you read." Proverbs 23:7 says, "As he thinks within himself, so he is" (NASB). Be careful what gets your attention—there's a good chance it will get you.

Desire: We move from attention to desire. In James 1:13–15 we read, "Let no one say when he is tempted, 'I am tempted by God'; for God cannot be tempted by evil, nor does He Himself tempt anyone. But each one is tempted when he is drawn away by his own desires and enticed. Then, when desire has conceived, it gives birth to sin; and sin, when it is full-grown, brings forth death" (NKJV). Eve desired the fruit, Jesus desired food—He was hungry. Both of them had natural desires and those natural desires were not sinful in themselves. That brings us to the third step in temptation.

Choice: Choice is simply the decision to act. The question is "How will you deal with the desire you are experiencing?" Will you fulfill it in a wrong way or will you fulfill in a right way? Will you follow Satan or God? It is important to keep it clear in our minds that although temptation has within it the element of desire, the desire itself is not necessarily sinful. Sin enters at the third point, the point of choice. When the will is used to fulfill a desire in a way that is not pleasing to God, it is called sin.

We have the freedom to choose sin or to resist sin. The choice is ours to make. Make the choice you can live with for eternity—because that is exactly what you will do.

FEBRUARY 15

How to Resist Temptation

Let's think about how to resist temptation.

First you must guard your attention, your thought life. What have you been thinking about these days? Think ahead about how you will deal with possible temptations. You know where your weak areas are and so does Satan. You know there are some places you shouldn't go. You know some people who are not a good influence on you. Guard your attention; guard who you are around and where you go. As much as you can, plan to avoid anything that makes you vulnerable to temptation.

Second, make up your mind that you will never give up—*never.* If you fall a hundred times over the same test, get up a hundred and one times. See yourself victorious—and one day you will get up for the last time. God can make you strong in your weak places.

Third, resist temptation in its early stages. In 2 Timothy 2:22 we read, "Flee youthful passions and pursue righteousness, faith, love, and peace, along with those who call on the Lord from a pure heart" (ESV). This is directed not only to young people but also to all people who have had these strong desires from their youth. In various translations the word *flee* is rendered "run away from," "stay away from," "keep away from," "turn away from," "avoid." And the admonition is to do it *right now.* We must resist temptation at its first sign. We are to make a choice to flee from temptation. You might ask, "How do you flee temptation?" The answer is to pursue what helps and avoid what hinders—seeking fellowship with other believers, praying with them, praying by yourself, searching the Word, and being honest with God in all your searching.

Finally, we are to resist the devil directly. James 4:7 reads, "Submit yourself to God. Resist the devil and he will flee from you." *Submit* literally means to put yourself under the authority of another. Keep yourself under the authority of God. *Resist* means to stand up against. The thought behind the Greek here is that when you take your stand against the devil, he will flee from you.

Friend, stand up today, not by your own power but by the power of the Spirit and the Word of Almighty God. Quote James 4:7, pray it, believe it—and watch Satan flee from you.

FEBRUARY 16

Jesus Is Praying for You

In Luke 22 we have the familiar record of the Last Supper. Jesus has gathered the disciples, He has talked to them about His body and blood, and then in verse 31 He says, "Simon, Satan has asked to sift you as wheat, but I have prayed for you, Simon, that your faith may not fail. And when you have turned back, strengthen your brothers."

Not long after this, as a matter of fact that very night, we have the record of Simon Peter's denial of Jesus. It must have been a comforting echo in his mind to replay the words of Jesus: "I have prayed for you."

As you think of these words, I have some good news for you. Jesus has prayed not only for Simon, but also for you. I have some more news that is even better—Jesus not only *has* prayed for you but *is* praying for you.

I'm not sure how He does these things, but whatever you're facing, as hard as you're praying about it, I want you to be reminded that you are not praying alone, but Jesus Christ Himself—think of it—Jesus right now is praying for you. Keep trusting Him. The Lord never promised that living the Christian life would be easy—but that it would be worth it.

FEBRUARY 17

The Holy Spirit Is God

Who is the Holy Spirit? Over 1,600 years ago the church tried to decide who the Holy Spirit was by writing the Nicene Creed. Here is what it says about Him: "We believe in the Holy Spirit, Lord and giver of life which proceeds from the Father and the Son and together is worshiped and glorified." What is that saying? Among other things it proclaims that the Holy Spirit is God. In Psalm 139:7 the psalmist asks, "Where can I go from your Spirit?" He's talking about the Holy Spirit, who is everywhere at the same time.

In Hebrews 9:14 He is called the "Eternal Spirit." The Holy Spirit had no beginning and will have no ending. Men and angels all had a beginning, but not the Holy Spirit.

In Matthew 28:19 we have the familiar water baptism formula: "Baptizing them in the name of the Father, the Son, and the Holy Spirit." Who is the Holy Spirit? The Holy Spirit is God. Right now, right here God is with us, and more than that, He actually lives within us. Whether you are at home, in your car, at school, or at work, wherever you are there is an unseen deity present, the Holy Spirit of God. He is so inseparable from the Father and the Son that if you were transported to heaven itself, in a very real sense you would be no closer to God than you are right now. Oh, I know when you are transported to heaven your sensitivities will be greater and you'll be more aware than you have ever been. But think of it—if we know God, through His Holy Spirit He is with and in us this very moment. Talk to Him today. He's listening and He's praying.

FEBRUARY 18

What Is the Holy Spirit Like?

At the end of Jesus's earthly ministry the disciples became concerned that Jesus was going away. In John 14:16 He said, "I will ask the Father, and He will give you another Helper (Comforter, Advocate, Intercessor, Counselor, Strengthener, Standby), to be with you forever" (AMP). He was telling them they would not be alone because the Counselor (the Holy Spirit) would soon be there.

What is the Holy Spirit like? Before I answer that question, here's another: What is God the Father like? We find out what God the Father is like by looking at who? At Jesus—that's who. And it's the same with the Holy Spirit. The Holy Spirit is not some weird ghost who moves around in our world from place to place. I think sometimes we get a picture in our minds of Pentecost and the rushing mighty wind and end up thinking of the Holy Spirit as just an influence and not a person. The Holy Spirit is the actual Spirit of Christ.

If Jesus suddenly opened the door and came into your house, what do you think you would do? Would you run to the neighbors as fast as you could? I know you would be awestruck but I have a feeling that when you saw Him you would feel as if you had seen Him before. It's not unlike being in a doctor's office or some other waiting room, sitting across from someone you've never met. You engage in conversation with this person and begin feeling a oneness with him or her. You find out very soon that the oneness you feel is because he or she is also a Christian and loves the same Lord you love. Immediately you are a part of the same family because you both have the same Father, Almighty God, and His Son, Jesus Christ.

When our eyes see the Christ we will feel that we have seen Him before, because we have many times. The Holy Spirit is not someone to be feared but someone to be loved. He can be grieved, He can be quenched, He can be resisted, but the Holy Spirit can also be warmed and blessed by our love and faithfulness. In Luke 24:29 Jesus commanded His disciples, "Stay in the city until you have been clothed with power from on high." And the Father's promise was fulfilled in Acts 2:4.

The Holy Spirit is God, yes. What is He like? He is like Jesus: loving, kind, and compassionate. Aren't you glad for the warm presence of the Holy Spirit inside you?

FEBRUARY 19

The Witness of the Spirit

Let's think today about what the Holy Spirit can do in our lives. As you go back in your mind to Pentecost, answer this question: What is it, aside from cleansing, that took place at Pentecost that had never happened before? It seems to me there was a new evidence for the disciples' faith.

Previously Christ gave evidence of His Messiahship in at least three ways. First, He said in John 5:39, "You search the Scriptures because you think that in them you have eternal life; it is these that testify about Me" (NASB). Jesus was saying the very Scriptures they were reading were speaking of Him. Second, He said to listen to John the Baptist, who pointed to Him and said in John 1:29, "Behold! The Lamb of God who takes away the sin of the world!" (NKJV). And third, He said in John 14:11 they should believe Him "because of the work you have seen me do" (NLT). Searching the Scriptures, listening to John the Baptist, and observing the works that Christ did were all external evidences of who Christ was.

But now, through the Holy Spirit, God was bearing witness in a new and fuller dimension than ever before. The Holy Spirit was giving believers an internal witness of His living presence.

Today advertisers are quick to look for endorsements for their products. An athlete will tell us how good a certain car may be. A movie star will brag about a hair product that makes her hair beautiful. Endorsements from well-known people impact the sale of many products.

Today the Holy Spirit is the greatest endorsement we have for the presence of Christ in our lives. There is a personal knowledge, an inner witness to the soul by the Holy Spirit that testifies of God's presence. That's what the disciples had never had previously and that is what too many Christians lack today.

Acts 15:8 states, "And God, who knows the heart, bears witness giving the Holy Spirit." The word *witness,* in the language of the New Testament, Greek, means "confirmation." The Holy Spirit confirms in us the presence of God within us.

Ask yourself, "Do I have this inner assurance? Do I have this inner confidence of God's presence?" I challenge any seeker after the fullness of the Spirit to allow the Holy Spirit to bring into your own heart this inner assurance, this inner confidence, this inner knowledge. You accept His presence by faith and experience His presence by the witness of the Spirit.

You might ask, "What do I do in the meantime?" Stay close to the Word, be faithful to what God says, and the witness, the assurance, will come in God's own time.

FEBRUARY 20

Be Filled with the Holy Spirit

To any person who is a seeker after the fullness of the Holy Spirit, I want to give you some items that will help you in your journey. To the person who is a seeker—

1. *You must know you are born again.* Jesus talked about giving the Holy Spirit to His disciples. He said in John 17:9, "I pray for them. I am not praying for the world, but for those you have given me, for they are yours."

In John 14:17 Jesus is speaking to His disciples about the Holy Spirit: "The Spirit of Truth, whom the world cannot receive because it does not see Him or know Him, but you know Him because He (the Holy Spirit) remains with you continually and will be in you" (AMP). Jesus prays for believers because the unsaved cannot receive the fullness of the Spirit. The fullness of the Spirit is reserved for those who are born again. So to any person who is a seeker after the fullness of the Spirit, you must be sure that you're born again.

2. *You must be sure that this is a need in your life.* You must be convinced that the Holy Spirit's fullness in your life is not simply some special, deluxe edition of Christian living but rather a part of God's total plan for all believers, here and now. Pardon and purity have always been God's will for His children. In John 17:17 Jesus prays for His disciples with the phrase "Sanctify them." In verse 20 He continues: "I pray also for those who will believe." Jesus has prayed for your sanctification as well.

3. *You must genuinely want to be filled with the Spirit.* Not only must you be born again, and not only must you feel the need to be filled with the Holy Spirit, but you must also have the desire. You may say, "Of course I have the desire. I'm reading this devotional, I read my Bible—isn't that evidence enough?" Not necessarily. Are you sure you want to be possessed by the Holy Spirit? Are you willing to give Him control of your life? If you are, if you are willing to scoot over and give Him the controls of your life, if you know you're born again, right now you can be filled with the Spirit—and filled "through and through." Romans 12:1 tells believers to "present your bodies as a living sacrifice." Give yourself unreservedly to God and you too can know the fullness of the Holy Spirit.

FEBRUARY 21

How to Be Filled with the Holy Spirit

Did you ever wonder how a believer could be filled with the Holy Spirit? Here are four things that might help you:

First, Romans 12:1 talks about believers ("brothers") giving themselves in total surrender. So we begin, as saved people, by giving ourselves to God. He can't fill what He can't have. Galatians 2:20 talks about being "crucified with Christ"—that's what giving myself is all about. I totally submit myself to His complete control.

Second, Luke 11:9-13 says, "Ask and it shall be given." Later on in that passage it reads, "He gives the Holy Spirit to them that ask." If you're going to be filled with the Spirit, you're going to have to be specific. In other words, we're not talking about simply turning over a new leaf. We're not talking about some kind of self-improvement or just doing better. We're talking about being truly filled with the Spirit of God. Can you specifically pray, "God, give me the fullness of Your Holy Spirit"?

Third, Acts 5:32 says, "The Holy Spirit is given to those who obey Him." Are you willing to obey God? What's that? That means when God's Word says no, you say no, and when God's Word says yes, you say yes.

Finally, we read in Acts 15:8–9, "God, who knows the heart, bore witness to them... giving them the Holy Spirit... having cleansed their hearts by faith" (ESV). Faith in what? Faith in what God has said. Are you willing to trust what God has said? Are you willing to trust the Word of God? Are you willing to accept it personally, right now? I guarantee you on the authority of God's Word that His Spirit will give witness to your spirit that you are not only a child of God but also a *Spirit-filled* child of God.

FEBRUARY 22

Are You Filled with the Holy Spirit?

Ephesians 5:18 says, "Do not get drunk on wine, which leads to debauchery. Instead, be filled with the Spirit."

God's people across the country are lacking something. They are hungry for something. They are thirsty for something. Many Christians are struggling for existence. Many are living lives of spiritual anemia or deficiency. Some indicate that the Christian experience is not all they thought it would be. Defeat seems to recur in cyclic fashion. Little growth is occurring in their lives. Instead of going from victory to victory, they seem to go from defeat to defeat—no joy, no thrill, no excitement, and no power. Some have lost the sense of His presence deep within their hearts.

The Bible commands us, "Be filled with the Spirit." This Spirit fullness is not optional—it is a command—and it is given to those who already know Christ as Savior. In Ephesians 1:1 Paul calls these people "saints" and "faithful in Christ Jesus."

The first part of verse 18 says, "Do not get drunk on wine." What do you think would happen at your church next Sunday if a member of the church, a leader, came to church drunk? I'm sure you would try to find out what's happening in the person's life and help with his or her problem. But what if this person came to church drunk *every* Sunday? Something would have to be done about his or her leadership role, right? Until the person could get help and restoration, someone else would have to step in.

Let me ask you this: Do you strongly express your concern over those who come to church but are not filled with the Spirit? The same verse that says, "Do not be drunk with wine" also says, "Be filled with the Spirit." I wonder if we are as concerned over people not being filled with the Spirit as we are over people being drunk. How much time do you spend praying for your family members that they might be filled with the Spirit? How much time do you spend praying for other believers to be filled with the Spirit? Are *you* filled with the Spirit? I challenge you to pray for Spirit-filled living for your family members, spouses, children, aunts, uncles, and then the people of your church.

Let's do what the Bible says: "Do not be filled or drunk with wine, but be filled with the Holy Spirit."

FEBRUARY 23

His Breath in You

In Ezekiel 37:1 we read, "The hand of the Lord was upon me, and He brought me out in the Spirit of the Lord and set me down in the middle of the valley; and it was full of bones" (AMP).

In Ezekiel 37:4 we find a message concerning the Spirit: "Prophesy to these bones." Ezekiel was to say, "Dry bones, hear the word of the Lord." In verse 5 the Lord says, "I will make breath to enter you." In the Old Testament the word *breath* is sometimes translated "wind" or "spirit."

The Wesley Bible makes this comment concerning Ezekiel 37:9, 14: "*Breath, wind,* and *spirit* all come from the same Hebrew word. Without breath or spirit, the bodies were still only corpses... The nation would be restored...but until the Spirit of God came upon them, there was no hope for them.... This promise was fulfilled at Pentecost."

Here is symbolic language directed to a people who should have already been a mighty army for the Lord. That's the picture of many church people today. The bones are in place, the organization is well oiled, and the machinery is running fast. We have our boards, our committees, and all the planning we need, but there is little vitality. Bones, tendons, flesh, and muscles are all in place. Blood vessels, eyes, hands, feet, ears, nose, and hair—but no breath. That is the picture of too many Christians. They have everything but the breath of God.

You will remember in Genesis that it was when God breathed into Adam that he became a living soul, and so it is today. It is as the Holy Spirit breathes into us that we find life for our souls. At Pentecost one hundred twenty believers were in an upper room, afraid and nervous, trembling because many people were outside milling around, some waiting to persecute and maybe even kill them. But suddenly the Holy Spirit came in His fullness. The same people who were so afraid were now ready to go out and change their world.

They had very little power until the Holy Spirit came upon them. That is exactly what Jesus said in Acts 1:8—"You will have power when the Holy Spirit comes upon you." It is not more organization we need, but more of the Spirit of God anointing and leading us as we follow Him.

There is little power where there is little dependence upon the Holy Spirit. The Bible challenges all believers to be filled with the Holy Spirit. I challenge you today as you go out into your world: be a voice that helps the world see there is a

Spirit-filled person in their midst. May the Spirit of God, who has touched you, touch others because of you.

FEBRUARY 24

The Cutting Edge

In 2 Kings 6:1 we read, "The sons of the prophets said to Elisha, 'Please notice that the place where we live under your supervision is too small for us'" (HCSB).

Verses 4–7 tell us,

> So he went with them, and when they came to the Jordan, they cut down trees. As one of them was cutting down a tree, the iron axe head fell into the water, and he cried out, "Oh, my master, it was borrowed!" Then the man of God asked, "Where did it fall?"
>
> When he showed him the place, the man of God cut a stick, threw it there, and made the iron float. Then he said, "Pick it up." So he reached out and took it.

The young man was chopping down trees with an axe when the axe head flew off into the stream. Of course, he didn't continue trying to cut down the tree with the handle. No, he stopped and went to Elisha to tell him what had happened. Elisha went with him to the stream, threw a stick into the water, and the iron floated for easy retrieval.

The fact is that some people try to do the work of God without the power of God. Some time ago they lost the head of the axe, they lost the cutting edge of their relationship with the Lord. They have been trying to chop with just a handle. They are trying to win souls, trying to be Christians, trying to produce the fruit of the Spirit with just the old axe handle. The iron head is gone.

If God has ever been real to us, He can *always* be real to us. We must take time to keep the cutting edge of our walk with God sharp and intact. Beware of anything that tries to crowd in. Avoid anything that causes the axe head to fly off the handle of your life. Get it back on. Whatever and wherever you were when the head fell off needs to be dealt with, confessed, and surrendered to God. Whatever the problem was, settle it and you will find that the axe head is back on the handle—and once again you will have the "cutting edge" of God back in your life.

FEBRUARY 25

The Holy Spirit, Our Teacher

In Galatians 5:22 we read, "The fruit of the Spirit is love, joy, peace, patience, kindness, goodness, faithfulness, gentleness and self-control." We all desire the fruit of the Spirit in our lives. Many people are frustrated that they do not see more of the fruit in their lives. It's somewhat like Paul in Romans 7—they want to do good but evil seems to be present with them. Their struggle and conflict smother their hope for victory. Why? Because the fruit of the Spirit cannot be manufactured; it cannot be brought about by human endeavor. It is impossible to produce the Christ-like life without the fullness of the Holy Spirit.

In addition, some are trying to do supernatural things without the power of the Holy Spirit. In Matthew 28:18–19 Jesus said, "All authority has been given to Me in heaven and on earth. Go therefore and make disciples of all the nations" (NASB).

In other words, the Christian life—living, witnessing, and winning the lost—are supernatural endeavors, not something we can do in our own power. We must *have* the Holy Spirit if we would do the *work* of the Spirit. Sometimes people feel that the prayer meeting is kind of dull, not very exciting. Bible reading can also lose its life and attraction—but why? Could it be that the prayer meeting is dull because we are dull to the Spirit? Could it be that our Bible reading is dull because the Spirit is not witnessing to our souls of its living truth?

Do you know who is the most neglected teacher in the universe today? It's not John Wesley, it's not the great theological minds of our day—the most neglected teacher in all the world is the Holy Spirit. Why not ask the Holy Spirit to turn some lights of understanding on in your mind today? He may want to talk to you about the fruit of the Spirit. It could be that He will want to turn the light on in area you have not thought about in a long time.

I challenge you to ask the Holy Spirit to be your teacher today.

FEBRUARY 26

Keep Your Eyes on Jesus

In 1 Peter 1:15–16 we read, "Just as He who called you is holy, so be holy in all you do; for it is written: 'Be holy, because I am holy.'"

What does the holy life mean to you? What would the holy life be in one word? It could be described by a word that does not appear in most dictionaries. And that would be the word *yieldedness.* Often your point of yieldedness or surrender comes to a key area in your life. Your job, your family, your future—it could be someone who is very special to you. Satan wants to confuse us and divide our loyalties.

I remember seeing a very interesting painting in Dallas. It was probably two and a half feet wide and three feet long, a large facial picture of the artist's idea of the face of Christ. In the lower right-hand corner was a round, black spot, probably three inches in diameter, that seemed to have nothing to do with the rest of the beautiful painting. I looked at the picture of Jesus—it was magnificent—and then I would glance down at the black spot. It seemed so out of place in the painting.

Three or four times I looked at the face of Jesus and then my eyes were drawn to the out-of-place black spot. After a few moments my eye caught a caption at the bottom of the painting, which said, "Notice that you cannot keep your eyes on Jesus and on the black spot at the same time." Then it added, "What is it in your life that is represented by the black spot?" I would ask this question: What is it in your life that tries to take your eyes off Jesus?

If we would be holy people, we must keep our eyes focused on Jesus. Ask yourself: Is there anything in my life that is threatening my clear view of Jesus? Is there any area in which Satan is trying to hinder my loyalty to serving the Lord? Is there anything that's becoming a "black spot" in my life?

Take it as a word of warning—make whatever correction you need to make and keep your eyes on Jesus.

Walk in Him and Be Filled with the Spirit

Colossians 2:6 says, "As we have received Christ Jesus the Lord, so walk in Him." How did you receive Jesus? Did you work it up? Did you pray it up? Did you make it up? How was it you received Him? It was by faith one day in what Jesus said. It's the same thing with being filled with the Spirit, or what Colossians calls "walking in Him." We can have confidence as we walk in the light that God will direct us to this Spirit-filled existence. How can I know I'm filled with the Spirit? Let me give you three ways you can know:

First: The Spirit-filled person has courage to witness. The book of Acts is the historical recollection of the Spirit's fullness in the church. Twenty-six times in that book observations such as "They spoke the word of God boldly" are included. There was something about the Spirit's fullness that gave them boldness in their witness. Courage to witness is an evidence of the fullness of the Spirit.

Second: The Spirit-filled person demonstrates the fruit of the Spirit, which is basically Christlikeness of character. Galatians 5:22 talks about the fruit being love, joy, peace, patience, kindness, goodness, faithfulness, gentleness, and self-control. Some people feel guilty because they do not have more patience and they doubt that they are filled with the Spirit. Let me ask you a question: Do you have all the gentleness you wish you had? How about your level of self-control—is it the way you desire it to be? In 2 Corinthians 7:1 we are told we should be "perfecting holiness." Literally that means we are to have a continual advance in holiness as we "walk in Him." It is an ever-growing experience. After a believer gives himself or herself in total surrender to God and is sanctified "through and through" (1 Thessalonians 5:23), there is continual growth in the Spirit. How can you know if you are filled with the Spirit? You know it if you are producing the fruit of the Spirit and are witnessing for Christ.

Third: The Spirit-filled person has a special place for Christ in his or her life. Ask yourself these questions: Does Jesus have first place in my life? Is He preeminent in all I say and do? Is He considered first in my decisions? Do I honor Him with all my resources? Here's the bottom line: If a person is walking in the power of the Spirit and has the fullness of the Spirit, he or she will have power to witness, will be producing the fruit of the Spirit, and Christ will have first place in his or her life.

FEBRUARY 28

The Will of God

Ephesians 5:17 says, "Do not be foolish but understand what the Lord's will is." The New Living Translation says, "Don't act thoughtlessly, but understand what the Lord wants you to do." First John 1:5 says, "God is light; in Him there is no darkness at all." God's very nature is to illuminate, to reveal, to make known. He wants to give His followers direction. Although that is true, it is not always easy to know what He is saying. One of the reasons is that sometimes He is simply saying, "Wait," and waiting is often not a pleasant experience.

I want to give you four points that will help you in your desire to know God's will. They are easy to remember—they spell the acrostic W O R D.

The *W* stands for "Word," the Word of God. In Psalm 119:130 the writer says, "The entrance of your words gives light." When you're trying to find God's will, the first thing to do is to check the Bible and see what the Bible has to say to you. The fact is that no one is really serious about God's will until he or she is serious about God's Word.

The *O* stands for "opportunity." If it is an opportunity from God, you won't have to force the issue or make it happen. When it's God's will, there is a timing that is right, a sense of rightness about the entire issue.

The third letter is *R* and stands for "reasonable." When you are trying to make a decision about God's will in your life, ask yourself: "Is this situation a reasonable thing for me to consider?" For example, if you want to be a singer but you can't carry a note, it's probably unreasonable for you to consider. If something is reasonable, it will be strengthened by evaluation. Get a piece of paper and make two columns. On one side write all the reasons you *should* do a certain thing. On the other side write all the reasons you *shouldn't* do it. Evaluation will only make the decision stronger, so reasonableness is a very important part of God's will. (Continued February 29)

FEBRUARY 29

The Will of God (Continued)

The last letter is *D* and stands for the question "Does it bring peace?" Listen to Colossians 3:15: "Let the peace of Christ rule in your heart." The Amplified Bible says, "Let the peace of Christ [the inner calm of one who walks daily with Him] be the controlling factor in your hearts [deciding and settling questions that arise]."

God's pattern of leadership is generally not to get into a hurry. If you have to rush to make a decision, chances are it's not of God. Psalm 23:1–2 says, "The Lord is my shepherd, I shall not want. He makes me lie down in green pastures; He leads me beside quiet waters" (NASB). The ESV says, "He makes me lie down in green pastures. He leads me beside still waters." Rushing waters scare sheep. In Hebrew the word for *quiet waters* or *still waters* means *restful waters.* Our Shepherd wants to lead us peacefully into a place of rest and calm. He wants to quiet our spirits as we follow His will.

Again, these four questions can help us when we are trying to discern God's will:

W – What does the Word of God say?

O – Is this an unforced opportunity, a genuine open door?

R – Is this a reasonable choice? Does it fit my gifts?

D – Does it bring peace?

On a fishing rod the line passes through round metal circles attached to the pole, called "eyes." Often a fishing pole is made so it will pull apart, making it easier to pack and transport. When the pole is assembled, the eyes on the pole need to be lined up so the line will flow freely through them as you cast the line to its intended destination. In our lives we must not just take one of our four points and build a decision on it. It's not just "Is it an opportunity?" "Does it bring peace?" or "Is it reasonable?" Rather, it's all four: the Word, the opportunity, the reasonableness, and the peace that come with the decision. All four of these are lined up like the eyes on a fishing pole so that the "line of your life" can be straight, headed toward the proper destination.

In any situation look at Jesus, look at His life, do the most Christlike thing—and you'll never go wrong.

MARCH 1

Prison or Platform?

Paul was a gifted, intellectual, and dedicated Christian. He was a man of action, constantly doing, going, and working. I mean he was just busy all the time. Then something came into his life that—well, it could have defeated him. He was arrested and placed in confinement. I can hear Satan speaking things like "Well, that's just great. After all you've done for God, He let you get arrested—can you beat that? Wouldn't it be a lot smarter for God to keep you free—couldn't He even do that?"

The fact is that we have been given some of Paul's most inspired thoughts during these four years in prison. It was during this time that Paul wrote Ephesians, Philippians, Colossians, and Philemon.

Recall that in Ephesians 5:20 Paul said that "we should all give thanks to God the Father for everything in the name of our Lord Jesus Christ." Now if Paul uttered those words from the temple or at the banquet table, we wouldn't be so surprised. But here they are coming from a prisoner—a prisoner for the Lord.

What about you today? What's *your* prison? Is it your job, your boss, your health, your failures? What is your reason for wanting to give up? I wonder if God is doing something special in the midst of your difficult situation. Think of it. As with Paul, some of your greatest thoughts and experiences lie within the confinement of your prison situation.

Many people have found a hospital experience to be a blessing in disguise. You know what? Paul's prison became a platform from which to witness for Christ. Could it be that your prison situation is really a platform in disguise? Choose today to turn your "prison problem" into a "platform of proclamation" for the Lord.

MARCH 2

God's Will for Today

In Ephesians 1:1 Paul said he was "an apostle by the will of God." Paul knew that God had a plan for his life. He was convinced that God had him on the earth for an expressed purpose. Let me ask you a serious question: When did you last think about God's purpose for you? When did it last cross your mind that God was thinking about you?

It's easy for us to imagine that God cared about Paul because he was somebody; but an interesting insight is found in Ephesians 3:8, in which Paul says, "I am less than the least of all God's people." The name *Paul* in Latin actually means "small." The implication here is that Paul actually coins a brand new word when he says, "I, small Paul, am the 'leaster' of all God's people." I'm not sure how small "leaster" is, but I think it takes a magnifying glass to find it.

What is the point? If Paul sometimes felt dejected, rejected, and misunderstood, and yet he was an apostle of God, do you think you will be exempt from such temptations? You mark it down. The God who knows when a sparrow falls, the God who knows the number of hairs on your head—that God is not only watching you right now but also has a specific plan.

Do you ever ask God to show you what His plan is for your life? How about His plan for today? Do you ever allow His Word to be a signpost, a directive in your life? Paul was sure that he was where he was by the will of God.

Friend, if you are a Christian you are where you are on purpose. You are here by the will of God. Now—what are you going to do about it?

MARCH 3

Where Is the Real Battle?

Paul said in Ephesians 1:3, "We have been blessed in the heavenly realms with every spiritual blessing in Christ." The phrase "heavenly realms" appears five times in the New Testament, all of which are found in Ephesians. It refers to the arena in which the spirit world moves. It is the unseen world of spiritual activities—good or evil.

You may recall the familiar passage of Ephesians 6:12: "Our struggle is not against flesh and blood, but against the powers of this dark world and against the spiritual forces of evil in the heavenly realms." What is the point? It's simply this—if we know where and with whom our battles are, we are better equipped to win the battles.

The Bible says our struggle is not with flesh and blood but rather with spiritual forces of evil. In all honesty, if you were to ask someone, "What is your greatest point of conflict?" you would likely hear responses like "It's my teenager," "It's my in-laws," "It's my spouse," "It's my boss," "It's my neighbor," and so on. But these are flesh-and-blood conflicts, and the Bible says no, it's not flesh and blood we struggle with.

Could it be that we spend so much time focusing on the physical world and so little focusing on the spiritual world that we've not been aware of the location of the real conflicts in life? Our battles are won a long time before we go to work, before we go next door, or before we visit our family members. Our battles are always won or lost at the place of prayer. Yes, the real conflict is spiritual. It's with spiritual weapons that we must fight. That's it! There's our problem—we've been fighting spiritual battles with physical weapons. No wonder we're getting nowhere fast. We must choose to access our spiritual arsenal.

Prayer and the Word of God become our primary allies. Quote God's Word, apply the appropriate scripture to the corresponding trial, pray, fast, and pray again. Let it be a warning to you that when you think of your conflicts in terms of flesh and blood, you need to refocus—you're looking in the wrong place. Be sure to win the spiritual conflicts, and everything else falls into place.

MARCH 4

Glorifying God—On Purpose

I want to ask you a question today: What is the purpose of your life? For what reason do you exist? When I was a boy, I used to hear people say, "The purpose of my life is to win souls." Let me ask you—Is soul-winning the purpose of every Christian's life? I mean, when you get right down to the very basis of your existence, what is it? That question is very simple, isn't it? There are many noble causes in which to invest our energies: our families, our churches, our country, just to mention a few. But what is the main reason for which we were created?

In Ephesians 1:6 Paul writes, "We are to live to the praise of God's glorious grace." In 1 Corinthians 10:31 he writes, "Whether you eat or drink, or whatever you do, do it all for the glory of God." When did you last think about your responsibility to bring praise to God? The Bible clearly says that we are to live for the glory of God. In Matthew 5:16 Jesus said, "Let you light shine before men that they may see your good deeds and praise your Father in Heaven." I want us to see that although there are many worthy causes in each of our lives, there is but one main purpose for our existence—and that is to bring glory to God.

This point could be a great help to us in finding God's will in various circumstances. For example, if something you're about to do does not bring glory to God, it is not for you. When deciding between two or three good options, ask, "Which one of these brings the most glory to God?" Move in that direction.

I challenge you today, whether you eat or drink (for you, that might be lunch or coffee break today), whatever you do (that could be at work, at the office, at home, or at school—anyplace you do anything), whatever you do, be sure to glorify God—on purpose.

MARCH 5

The One Who Knows You Best Loves You Most

Do you remember when Christ came into your life? Were you a child, a teenager, or maybe an adult? Whenever it was, in many ways it was the greatest day in all your life. At that moment of conversion you were called out of your sins and called into Christ. The New Testament has a word that refers to those who are "called out"— it's the *church*. Yes, the church consists of those who have come out of the world and joined a new order, that of the born-again ones.

Ephesians 1:4 says that born-again people are to be "holy and blameless in His sight." There's an encouraging word for any believer. Note that this verse says we are to be blameless *in His sight*. If you followed me around long enough, I might do something you wouldn't understand, that would disappoint you. I guarantee you that I wouldn't do it on purpose, but in all honesty, you may not like something I say or do. And, of course, it works both ways—I may not like something *you* say or do.

But note the verse again. We are to be "blameless in His sight." Praise His name! You see, I may not know about the pain that wracks your body, but He does. I may not know about the injustices that surround your place of employment, but He does. I may not know about the battle you're going through right now, but He does. When God sees you, He *really* sees you. I see only what appears to be, but He sees what *really* is.

We all have faults, we all make errors in judgment, but note that God's Word does not say we are to be faultless but rather *blameless*.

Friend, I encourage you to take heart. The one who knows you best loves you most. And He believes in you.

MARCH 6

Little Boat Twice Owned

The name of the story was *Little Boat Twice Owned.* I remember it to be one of the very first stories we taught our son, Brady. It was about a little boy who had taken a piece of wood, attached a pencil-like structure to the top, and then added a piece of cloth. It became his first sailboat. How excited he was!

There had been a heavy rain, so the curbs had become rapid channels of water. The little boy launched his vessel into the miniature river. How delighted he was that his homemade sailboat weathered the storm! His delight soon turned to dismay, however, when the rapid current carried his boat out of reach and soon out of sight. He couldn't believe this happened and was extremely disappointed, to say the least.

A day or two passed, and to his wondering eyes what should appear but in the window of a pawn shop—his very own sailboat! What a surprise! The owner explained how it had been found by someone and that he (the shop owner) had purchased it. Now the sailboat had a price tag of $1.00.

The little boy was so happy to see his boat that he ran home and got $1.00 from his piggy bank and bought back the very boat he had made with his own hands. Yes, it was a boat twice owned.

In Ephesians 1:7 we read, "In Him [that is, in Christ] we have redemption." Without using the word *redemption,* that is what *Little Boat Twice Owned* is all about. God, the creator, made us with His own hands. We were rightfully His, but we turned to our own ways. The current of sin carried us on a rugged journey, away from our maker. One day He sent His Son to die on a cross—a terrible, humiliating execution—but Jesus bought us back. We are the vessel that was twice owned.

Think of it, friend. You have been redeemed; you have been bought back by the precious blood of God's Son. God loves you so much that He gave the best He had.

MARCH 7

When the Time Is Just Right

In Ephesians 1:9–10 the Bible indicates that God made known "the mystery of His will" in the "bringing of all things together in Christ." What is being said is that Christ is the source of all unity. What I want you to see today is that this coming of Christ happened, according to verse 10, "when the times had reached their fulfillment."

In other words, when things were just right, that's when Jesus came. Think of it. At the coming of Christ there was one government—the Roman Empire was in charge. Language was no barrier, for all people understood a common tongue. Can you imagine how difficult it would be to travel and communicate if every state in the United States had its own language? What a barrier that would be! At the time of the Roman Empire, roads were built that made transportation the best of its day. Yes, when Jesus came it was exactly at the right time.

If I had been in charge of the Messiah's coming, I'm sure I would never have thought of a baby in a manger, would you? No, I would have sent Him in on a white horse encircled by an army of angels. But you know, when you look back at the way God did it, it was just right.

We can devise all kinds of theories about the Second Coming and how it's all going to work out, but you know, when the Lord does come, it may not be exactly as we thought it would be—but it will be just right.

It could be that you're in a situation that appears should be different. You're tempted to ask why God doesn't do something—"Can't He see the mess I'm in?" Yes, friend—God sees the mess you're in. He knows what's going on. He knows exactly where you are and what you're facing, and He's going to do something all right, but He'll do it when the time is just right. Trust Him now. He's working on your situation right this moment.

MARCH 8

The Deposit of the Holy Spirit

Ephesians 1:13–14 says, "The Holy Spirit is a deposit guaranteeing our future inheritance." If you've ever purchased a house, you know what a down payment is. It's an initial payment by which you insure the seller that you intend to follow it up with more of the same. The down payment is often a small percentage of the entire purchase price.

The Scriptures note that the Holy Spirit is a deposit, sort of a down payment, indicating to us some of what lies ahead of us.

I want you to think of the time when the Holy Spirit has been nearest to you. It might have been in a time of crisis in your life. It could have been a revival in your own spirit brought on by prayer and the Word of God. Remember the peace of those moments? Remember the wholeness that seemed to grip your being? Remember how the entire world seemed different to you?

Friend, that's just the deposit of God's presence. That's simply the down payment, a sample of what is yet to come. It's a very encouraging thing to me to realize that this world at its best is simply a foretaste of what God has in store for us in eternity.

It used to be said that a person could be so heavenly minded that he or she was no earthly good. I guess the suggestion was that you can think about heaven so much that you lose touch with the real world. I don't think that's happening much these days. On the contrary, we are so bombarded with earthly matters that we are not nearly heavenly-minded enough.

Today why not spend some moments thinking on the next life? Think about heaven. Think about loved ones we'll see, and, of course, think about Jesus and the many others we've read about in the Bible. Remember—the Holy Spirit in your life right now is an internal witness of the good that is yet to come.

MARCH 9

What We Are to God

In Ephesians 1:18 Paul prays that we Christians would have the eyes of our hearts "enlightened in order that we may know the hope to which God has called us, and the riches of His glorious inheritance in the saints." Note the phrase "His glorious inheritance in the saints." This is a humbling thought to my mind, that God should look at me and you as a part of His great inheritance.

Let me ask you a question: Do you spend more time thinking about what God is to you or what you are to God? Do you ever think about what you mean to God? Our tendency is to think about what we need from God rather than what we can be to God. Think back to the creation story. Why did God make man in the first place? One of the reasons must have been simply an overflow of His love—a desire for further fellowship with one made in His image.

God desires our fellowship, our attention. The Bible says it is possible for us to grieve the Spirit of God, to quench Him and resist Him. The opposite of that is possible as well. We can bless, we can love, and we can draw near to God if we choose to.

The word *inheritance* in Ephesians 1:18 underscores the fact that God will not enjoy the fullness of His future glory until we are there to share it with Him. We are a part of His future eternal inheritance.

Today why not consciously think of what you are to God? How valuable you are to Him! Think of what you can be *to* God and not just what you need *from* Him.

MARCH 10

The School of Dependence

Listen to Ephesians 1:17: "I keep asking that the God of our Lord Jesus Christ, the glorious father, may give you the spirit of wisdom and revelation so that you may know Him better." Paul is praying that these Christians might know God better. Can you think of any prayer you would rather have prayed for yourself than this one—that you might know God better?

Answer this: When have you known God best? When has it seemed that He was most near to you? Sometimes new Christians seem to be in closer contact with God than those who have walked with Him for years. Is this an inevitable part of Christianity? Is Paul's prayer just for new Christians? No. Paul is writing to a church—young and old alike are a part of the crowd.

What, then, is our problem? Why do seasoned believers sometimes fail to sense the nearness of God? Part of the answer lies in Jesus's words in John 5:30: "By myself I can do nothing." Undoubtedly one of the reasons Jesus repeatedly got away to a solitary place, a place alone with the Father, a place of prayer, was because He felt such a dependence upon the Father.

You see, Jesus was convinced that by Himself He really could do nothing. He knew that if the Father did not enable Him, He was powerless. Ask yourself: How dependent was I on the Lord when I first found Him? Didn't it seem that every waking moment was shared with His presence? Did I not find myself talking with Him under my breath? It seemed I prayed about everything. It didn't matter if the situation was simple or complex—I knew I needed God in everything.

Ask yourself another question: How dependent am I on the Lord at this moment? Do I talk to Him about everything? Or have I progressed to the point at which I no longer trouble Him over some issues? I mean, some things I can handle myself, right? Wrong! If Jesus could do nothing by Himself, who are we to think that we have graduated from the school of dependence?

Yes, one of the keys to knowing God better is to come back to a daily dependence upon Him.

MARCH 11

Jesus Sees You Right Now

In Ephesians 1:20 Paul writes that "Christ has been seated at God's right hand." Do you remember when this event took place in biblical history? It was at the ascension. Do you ever think about the ascension of Christ? Does it have any meaning for us today at all? Generally when I think of Christ, I think about the times He talked to the disciples or when He healed the sick and raised the dead. I think of the Christ who fed the five thousand and taught in parables. Mostly when I think of Christ, it's during the time between His birth and resurrection. It seems I seldom think about Him in His ascended position.

You may recall His words in Luke 24:49 when He told the disciples to tarry in Jerusalem until they would be endued with power from "on high." Where do you think this "on high" was that Christ talked about? It's the "on high" that He went to at His ascension.

It is from this position at the right hand of the Father that Jesus now moves His Spirit throughout the universe. It is from this "on high" that He now watches His children in their daily pursuits. When Jesus walked upon the earth, He was in one place at one time. But now He is everywhere at the same time.

Wherever you are today, Jesus is there. Wherever you're going today, Jesus will be there. Whatever you do, Jesus sees you from "on high"' As a matter of fact—think of it—He's looking at you right now.

MARCH 12

We Are the Body of Christ

We read in Ephesians 1:22–23, "God placed all things under Christ's feet and appointed Him to be Head over the Church which is His body." Now here is a basic, biblical concept that impacts every believer. You, friend, are a vital part of the body of Christ. This metaphor was used to describe how Christ carries out His work in the world today.

As Christians, we are not only part of a local fellowship, but also a world fellowship called "the church," the body of Christ. Christ is the head—He is in charge. Everything flows from Him. But He has set it up so that He is not complete without the church, the body who carries out His mission to the world.

When did you last see yourself as a part of the task force, the actual working unit that carries out the purposes of Christ in the world today? We've heard it said that Christ has no feet but our feet, no hands but our hands, no eyes but our eyes, and no tongue but our tongues. You know what? It's the truth.

I challenge you to let Christ live behind your eyes today. See things as you think He would see. Do things you think Christ would do. Treat your spouse, your neighbor, your boss—everyone—as Jesus would. That's what the body of Christ is all about.

MARCH 13

You Are a Masterpiece

Ephesians 2:10 tells us, "We are God's workmanship." The word *workmanship* is literally translated "work of art." We are a sample of what God, the great creator, can do with us, the new creation. If you can draw a beautiful picture, you have a gift that many do not possess— and I'm one who does not possess it. But I can imagine what it must be like to spend time drawing or painting beautiful pictures and then to step back and see the canvas come to life. What a thrill that must be!

I do remember a few paint-by-number masterpieces I did as a boy. Multiply that by the infinite nature of God, and then imagine the thrill of His heart as He looks at you—His work of art. I can almost hear you laugh as you read these words, thinking something like "Huh, me—a work of art? Forget it!" Hey, friend: remember—it wasn't me who said you're a work of art. *God* said so.

Today, just like years ago, men and women you meet every day suffer from deep feelings of inferiority. They feel like anything but a work of art. Satan has a heyday causing Christians to be hindered by their poor self-image.

Why do we suffer so when God says we are His work of art? Feelings of inferiority come basically from two common causes. First is an unfair comparison of yourself to somebody else. It's unfair because you see only the outside of the other person. You cannot accurately judge what's going on in a person. You may have no idea of how he or she really feels on the inside. God says we're supposed to look at Him and not at others.

Second, feelings of inferiority result from unrealistic expectations placed upon ourselves. We're warned not only against looking at others but also against looking at ourselves. Again, we're admonished to look at the Lord.

Friend, God made you and He thinks you're very special. As a matter of fact, He says you are His work of art. I guess you could say you are *God's masterpiece.*

MARCH 14

Christ Is the Chief Cornerstone

In Ephesians 2:20 we read that "Christ is the chief cornerstone." Literally it is translated "binding stone." The picture is as follows. Two walls have been erected. They are brought together forming a corner. To give them support, a footing is made. A stone is placed into the corner to support and hold together the two walls.

Paul is saying that Jesus Christ is our footing. He is the one who holds us together. He is our sure foundation.

In Paul's day two "walls" that were brought together in Christ were the Jews and the Gentiles. These were two people groups who many thought could never dwell together, but in Christ they could. Have you found anyone lately you did not think you could have oneness with? It could be someone right in your church, or maybe right in your own home. What Christ did years ago with the Jews and Gentiles He is still doing today for those who will give Him a chance. And that's the key, to really give Christ a chance.

What is it that Christ would have you do to get your foundation in order? Do you need to tell someone you're sorry? Do you need to be obedient to something God has already told you to do? Do you simply need to wait? Whatever it is that God wants you to do, do it and be confident that God is doing His part to bring support to the whole structure.

Remember: it is Christ who is the chief cornerstone.

MARCH 15

We Are Temples

In Ephesians 2:22 we read, "In Him [Christ] you too are being built together to become a dwelling in which God lives by His Spirit."

I want you to picture in your mind your local church on a normal Sunday morning. Imagine the songs of praise to Almighty God. See the pastor behind the pulpit preaching the sermon as the congregation listens intently to the message. And then to your surprise, a group of young adults in the back of the sanctuary start passing donuts down the pew! Back and forth they go, and then cartons of milk come out of the sack secretly brought in by the irreverent instigator of the entire donut-and-milk affair. The noise from the back pew becomes an obvious disturbance, not to mention the impropriety of such an act in the first place.

Now you have the picture. You see the situation. Tell me honestly: How do you feel about what you've seen? Would you be troubled by the irresponsible conduct of these young adults? I imagine that if you were on the board of that church, you would hear about it at the next meeting, if not sooner.

But wait a minute. Though I'm not condoning the situation just described, think about it. Where is the sanctuary anyway? The Bible says in 1 Corinthians 6:19, "Do you not know that your body is a temple of the Holy Spirit?"

In Ephesians 2:22 we read, "We are a dwelling place in which God lives by His Spirit." What about your temple, your body? Yes, what about you? How are you treating the sanctuary you walk around in? Are you as careful about what you eat? Are you as careful about the rest you get and the exercise you take part in? Are you as concerned about your temple as you would be about the donut-and-milk episode? Think about it.

MARCH 16

How God Deals with His Followers

In Ephesians 3:2 Paul writes, "Surely you have heard of the administration of God's grace." The word I want us to look at today is *administration*. What does that word bring to your mind? When you think of the administration of a college, you usually think of the authority structure of the school. When you think about how a business is administered, you think about how the work is carried out. What did Paul mean here in Ephesians when he talked about *God's* administration?

In the Greek this word is literally translated "law of the house." I guess you could say it means the way we do things now. Have you ever noticed that at times it seems we have two different Gods in the Bible? We have the one in the Old Testament, who cracks the whip bringing severe judgment down upon men and women; and then we have this one in the New Testament, who is personified by love.

Now we know there's only one God, but why this difference in the way He administers His work? Let me ask you: Do you explain things to a teenager as you do to a first-grader? Do you deal with a college senior the same way you do an eighty-year-old individual? No, we try to deal with people in the context of their lives.

That is what God has done through history and is doing right now. He deals with people where they are in their lives. In the Old Testament God established authority and power. That is what the people needed, much as an informed parent must do with a young child today. The child must sense love, yes, but there must be a definite communication of who is in charge.

In the New Testament God gave complete expression of His love as He sent His Son to save us. Where are you in your journey? Do you sometimes wonder why God expects you to have more faith today than He used to? Well, you are at a different place in your journey now. God knows you are growing and He treats you accordingly.

MARCH 17

It Is Always Too Soon to Quit

Ephesians 3:13: "I ask you, therefore, not to be discouraged because of my sufferings for you, which are your glory."

NLT: "So please don't lose heart because of my trials here. I am suffering for you, so you should feel honored."

In Acts 21:27–33 Paul was accused of bringing an Ephesian Gentile into the Jewish temple in Jerusalem. This was totally unacceptable to the Jews. As a result, Paul was placed under house arrest. He wanted the Ephesians not to become discouraged when they heard of his struggles. He did not want them to "lose heart."

"Losing heart" conveys the idea of becoming weary or discouraged to the point of having no hope. "Not to lose heart" may be expressed in a number of ways, for example, "not to give up," "not to run away" or "not to think that all is lost."

It is worth noting that every New Testament use of the expression "lose heart" is preceded by the word *not*. Do not become discouraged. Do not lose your enthusiasm. Do not lose heart. Do not grow weary or tired. Do not despair. God's Spirit might use this passage to stimulate you to keep on fighting the "good fight," remembering that until we see Him face to face, it's always too soon to quit. Paul could have given up, but he didn't because Christ was with him. The same Christ is with you this very day.

May God grant that you will be "strengthened with power through His Spirit in your inner being" (Ephesians 3:16 ESV), so that at the end of your life you will have lived out Paul's words of 2 Timothy 4:7: "I have fought the good fight, I have finished the race, I have kept the faith."

Indeed, it is *always* too soon to quit!

MARCH 18

Coming into His Presence

You may recall that when Paul wrote Ephesians he was under arrest. He was often chained to a soldier. In Ephesians 3:14 note what Paul says just before he starts to pray, "I kneel before the Father." The most common posture for prayer in the New Testament was standing—perhaps rocking back and forth from toe to heel. But not here. No. This man of God falls to his knees to bombard heaven. Usually we would think of how uncomfortable a person would be to be chained to a soldier. But can you imagine what the soldier must have thought being chained to this distressing individual named Paul?

I guess today for many of us, standing, sitting, or walking have become common positions for prayer. Do you ever pray in the shower or in bed? Oh, I know we can pray anywhere and anytime. But I also know our posture communicates something. Many books have been written on the subject of body language.

I challenge you to try something today. Plan now, when and where, you can get fifteen minutes alone with God. I know we talk about bowing our heads and praying, but today let's not only bow our heads but also bend our knees. Let's come to God as reverently and as humbly as we know how.

Yes, today spend fifteen minutes—at least fifteen minutes (time yourself)—on your knees in prayer. Like Paul, let's kneel before the Father. (P.S. If you can't kneel, sitting will work just fine.) The issue is humbling yourself before the Lord.

MARCH 19

God Gives According to His Riches

What is the greatest need you face today? Is it something financial? Physical? Emotional? If you could walk right up to Jesus, face to face, what need would your bring to Him? In Ephesians 3:16 Paul prays that "out of God's glorious riches He may give you strength in your inner being."

Today I want you to notice something about God's giving. The literal reading says that God gives "according to" His riches and not just "out of." What's the difference? If I'm a millionaire and you present a financial need to me, and I give you $100 to help you with your need, I have given to you *out of* my riches. But if I respond to your financial need by giving you $100,000, I have given to you *according to* my riches.

You see, whatever your need is today, come confidently, come expectantly, for God desires to give to you not *out of* His vast resources but *according to* them. No wonder God's Word in Hebrews 4:16 says, "So let us come boldly to the throne of our gracious God. There we will receive His mercy, and we will find grace to help us when we need it most" (NLT).

God is waiting for you—don't miss meeting with Him.

MARCH 20

Rooted and Established in Love

In Ephesians 3:17 Paul prays that believers might be "rooted and established in love." It should be a source of encouragement to us that God desires and makes it possible for us be rooted and established in love. Do you ever feel the need for deeper roots? A stronger foundation? God desires it for you even more than you do yourself. And whatever God desires for us, He makes possible. That's one of the great things about God. He not only calls us to spiritual maturity, but He also supplies the grace and the power for such growth. What God calls us to do He enables us to do.

Paul says that this rooting and establishing is *in love.* You see, love is the soil into which we are to be rooted. Love is the platform upon which we are to be established. Where is this love to be found? You guessed it—in Christ. Everything always centers in Jesus. If you feel the need for deeper roots, you're saying you need to go deeper in Christ. If you feel the need for a firmer footing in your spiritual life, be sure that Christ is your only foundation.

Be honest now; look back over the last seven days. Have you lived like a person whose foundation is Jesus? I mean, does it sound too simple to say everything focuses on Him? Is your life complicated these days? I find the closer I get to Jesus, the simpler my life becomes. The farther I get from Him, the more complicated everything seems.

Let's keep our focus on Jesus and become more rooted and established in love.

MARCH 21

Finding Balance in Life

Ephesians 4:1 says, "I urge you to live a life worthy of the calling you have received." Here Paul is getting right down to where we live.

Paul said, "Live a life worthy of the calling." *Worthy* literally means "that which balances the scale." It means that which is an equivalent to. In your mind I want you to picture an old-time scale, the kind in which they would put metal pieces on the one side that would represent one-fourth pound, one-half pound, or a pound; and then on the other side of the scale they would put the item that was to be weighed. The weights on the one side would be balanced by the item to be purchased on the other side.

What are we trying to be worthy of in our lives? What scale is trying to be balanced? What is it that's on the one side and what's on the other?

The fact is that we are on the one side. Our walk, the way we live, is on one side; on the other is God's calling. The scripture says, "Live a life worthy of the calling." Our *calling* refers to the gospel by which God called us. Certainly the gospel is good, noble, and undefiled. So our daily walk must be of like weight, or equivalent, to the gospel by which we have been called. Living the way God wants you to live is the key to finding balance in all of life. I urge you today, friend, to walk worthy of the calling you have received.

What God calls us to do He enables us to do.

MARCH 22

God's Report Card

From early school days it is a pleasant sound to our ears to hear that we made straight As.

Today Paul calls us to make straight Bs. Listen to Ephesians 4:2: "Be completely humble and gentle, be patient, bearing with one another in love." Paul is saying that the four Bs he wants you to realize are—"Be humble," "Be gentle," "Be patient," and "Be loving."

First, Paul says, "Be humble." Too often we think of how humility is expressed rather that what it is. Humility is expressed not so much in what we say or even in what we do—it is primarily in the way we think. *Humility* could perhaps most accurately be translated in an adjective form as "humble-minded."

Second, Paul says, "Be gentle." This means to be meek. Meekness should never be confused with weakness. Rather, it is power under control.

Third, Paul says, "Be patient." When I first found the Lord, people used to say, "Whatever you do, don't pray for patience, because if you do, you'll get tribulation." However, I found out that it doesn't matter whether you pray for patience or not—you *still* get tribulation. So let patience work in your life. Persevere; hold on—God is doing something good.

And finally Paul says, "Be loving." Be Christ-like. Remember that this is not just something we do at church, but also at work, school, and especially home.

"Be humble," "Be gentle," "Be patient," "Be loving."

When today is over, look at your report card and see if you got straight Bs.

MARCH 23

Keep the Unity

Let me ask you a question: As Christians working together, are we to *create* unity or *maintain* unity? Are we to make unity happen or are we to relax and *let* it happen?

In Ephesians 4:3 we read, "Make every effort to keep the unity of the Spirit through the bond of peace."

Notice the Bible does not say here that we are to *create* unity. No, we are to *keep* or *maintain* this oneness.

Our unity comes from our common allegiance to Christ. Again we see that everything that truly means anything always focuses on Jesus.

Granted, unity is inherent in those who are in Christ. However, the scripture does say that we are to "make every effort to keep" this unity. We do have a responsibility; we do have something to do. Any idea what it is we are to do to maintain this unity? It's what we talked about yesterday in the four straight Bs: "Be humble," "Be gentle," "Be patient," and "Be loving."

Recognize the fact that Satan does not like unity among believers. He does all he can to confuse, disrupt, and disintegrate our oneness in Christ.

So when you sense that unity is being threatened—in any relationship—be sure to maintain the unity by practicing the four Bs: "Be humble," "Be gentle," "Be patient," and "Be loving."

MARCH 24

Pray for Your Pastor

What do you expect your pastor to do?

- Preach?
- Be friendly?
- Have administrative skills?
- Be a spiritual leader?

Just what do you expect from this God-called person? Now answer this: How many minutes per week do you pray for your pastor?

In Ephesians 4:11–12 we read that God has given us pastors to help God's people. The Bible literally says that the Lord has given us shepherds, and *shepherds* has a root meaning translated *protectors*—so a pastor is really a shepherd/protector.

I'm sure you have an idea of what a shepherd means to a flock of sheep. The shepherd guides, rewards, and just generally oversees all they do. The shepherd is the one whose voice they know. When the shepherd calls, they know it's for them.

The Bible uses this *shepherd/protector* word to describe our pastors today. Nobody knows us quite in the way our pastor does. Our pastor prays for us in a different way than anyone else in the world.

I encourage you today to help your pastor as he or she approaches the throne of grace. Pray that God will bless your pastor and give him or her His wisdom.

Pray for your shepherd/protector today.

MARCH 25

Satan's Problems Outweigh His Promises

Satan is the great enemy of the universe. He has never been a friend to any person. Listen to Ephesians 4:19, in which Paul talks about those who have gone Satan's way: "Having lost all sensitivity, they have given themselves over to sensuality, so as to indulge in every kind of impurity, with a continual lust for more."

I'm reminded of the millionaire who was asked, "How much money is enough?" His response: "Just a little more." This is a picture of Satan—he brings no lasting satisfaction. As a matter of fact, the best it will ever get with Satan is the first time. From then on it is downhill.

Paul said some people have lost all sensitivity. Literally, they have *ceased caring.* If you get to the place where you stop caring, shake yourself—you are on dangerous ground. Thank God when you realize that you do care, that you have not and will not give up.

Never forget that with Satan there is no lasting satisfaction, just a continual lust for more. And you know, friend—although we don't talk much about hell, without a doubt one of the great torments of that awful place is unfulfilled desires. Yes, the continual lust for more not only is the trick of Satan now, but it will also permeate the realms of the damned forever.

Whatever you do, my friend in Christ, stay sensitive to evil. In other words, never get used to it. Always abhor what is evil and cleave to that which is good.

Satan's promises are many but his rewards are few, and at the longest they last only a little while.

MARCH 26

God's Classroom

After Paul talks of sinners who have a continual lust for more of the world, he says in Ephesians 4:20–21, "You did not come to know Christ that way. You heard of Him and were taught in Him."

This "coming to know Christ" puts and keeps every Christian in the classroom. Nobody is too old to learn. The adage "You can't teach an old dog new tricks" may be true for dogs, but it surely is not the case for you and me. Christians are always learning about the Lord, and their lives reflect this process of continual education.

It would be wise for you to remember that the Christian life is a dynamic, ever-increasing, ever-growing encounter. We not only are saved by the Lord, but we are also being taught while we are in Him.

I know you've had the experience of reading some area of Scripture that you've read many times before and something came alive to you, something was different—you were taught in the Scriptures something new about your life in Christ.

It's exciting to know that God has things to reveal to you, even though you have known Him for years. As you stay in the Word of God, you are going to discover new insights into the life He has planned for you.

Do you remember how yesterday we thought some about hell and how lusting for more is a part of its punishment?

The opposite is true in heaven. We will have peace and satisfaction but will continue to learn. We will continue to be taught in Him throughout eternity.

Thank God, we not only have heard of Christ and know Him but are also taught in Him.

Being in God's classroom is the place to be.

MARCH 27

What about Anger?

All of us have been angry sometime, and yet we still loved the Lord. We hadn't turned our back on God, and yet we have sometimes been confused about it. Most everyone has found relief in Mark 3:5—the fact that Jesus was angry. But in all honesty, do you think this characterized Jesus's life? No, I don't think so either.

Ephesians 4:26 gives a warning about anger when it says, "In your anger do not sin." Evidently it is possible for anger to become sin. Why would the Bible give such a warning? One reason is that people often do things when they are angry that they would not normally do.

Sometimes anger is necessary. Paul was angry in Acts 13:9–10 when a sorcerer was hindering the work of the Lord. And, of course, I already noted the reference to Jesus's anger in Mark 3:5. We need to have convictions strong enough that when something is wrong we will be stirred to action.

In our day we should be angry about such issues as abortion, pornography, and divorce. To *not* be angry about these evils is not Christian either.

But Paul continues his comment in Ephesians 4:26 by saying, "Do not let the sun go down while you are still angry."

While anger may sometimes be justified, it must be cooled down quickly. Anger should subside the same day it arises. When the sun has gone down, let anger be gone.

MARCH 28

God Cares about What We Say

In Ephesians 4:29 Paul said, "Do not let any unwholesome talk come out of your mouths, but only what is helpful for building others up according to their needs, that it may benefit those who listen."

The Bible has much to say about our conversation. In James 3:2 we read, "If anyone is never at fault in what he says, he is a perfect man."

Most Christians have found themselves in situations in which they wondered just how much to say. Gossip is a deadly enemy—many a reputation has been needlessly destroyed by the gossiping tongue.

The Bible is very graphic in its literal definition of a gossip. Literally he or she is a whisperer—"one who pours poison into the ear of another."

If you wonder if what you are about to say is pleasing to God or not, let Ephesians 4:29 be your guide. Four questions surface from this verse: (1) Is it helpful? (2) Does it build up? (3) Does it meet the listener's need? (4) Does it benefit the listener?

If the answer to these questions is no, then it is better left unsaid.

Here's an experiment for you. The next time you start to say something and you wonder for a moment if you should, then *don't* say it. Later look back and see what you really missed by not saying it.

MARCH 29

Obedience

In Ephesians 6:1 Paul writes, "Children, obey your parents in the Lord."

Obedience is a key word in the New Testament. It is the word from which we get our English word *acoustics,* which has to do with sound. In the Bible when children are admonished to obey their parents, it means they are to listen to them and do what they say.

Paul says to do this "in the Lord." This simply means to do so because you are in the Lord, because you are a Christian.

Tell me, friend: How do you view your parents? It should be a sign to you of how pleased or displeased the Lord is with you. These words are written not just to young children. We are all children, and we are all to revere our parents. Whether they are Christians or not, we are to treat them with respect.

The fifth commandment says, "Honor your father and mother." And this is the only commandment with a promise.

I challenge you to live this week in instant obedience to God. Whatever He says to you, do it immediately. Write that note, send that message, make that call, give that compliment, do that assignment. Obedience is for all us kids.

MARCH 30

Satan's Methods

Ephesians 6:10–11 says, "Be strong in the Lord…stand firm against the schemes of the devil." Paul knew what it meant to be strong in the Lord. You see, the believer is called to fight against the devil's schemes.

The word used for *scheme* here in the Bible is translated "method." Satan is a master of methods to trip up the Christian. You may recall that in Revelation 12:10-11 Satan is called "the accuser." Accusation is one of Satan's most popular methods of hindering believers.

It's interesting to note that we can forget Bible verses easily if we're not careful. Hymns and gospel lyrics can slip from our memory. There's often no problem in forgetting spiritual lessons that we thought we had learned once and for all. For example, how many times have you learned how important prayer is? But to forget sins committed in past years requires supernatural abilities.

The devil does his best to keep our failures before us. An off-color joke that you heard years ago can be remembered completely, punch line and all; or a sexual experience before marriage can be flashed upon the screen of your mind with little effort. Lies told in previous years are like leeches fixing themselves to one's memory.

The devil accuses us of our past sins over and over again. He neglects the biblical truth that our sins are remembered against us no more. Friend, we can overcome the accuser with the blood of the Lamb and by the word of our testimony.

Don't let the accuser get you down today. He is a liar.

MARCH 31

God's Armor

In Ephesians 6:11–17 Paul reflects on the armor that a Roman soldier would wear. At this time he was not chained to a soldier but was under house arrest. He was in his home but could not leave. People he spoke to were familiar with the soldier's armor, and he uses it as an illustration to prepare them (and us) for spiritual warfare in the future.

In 6:11 he writes, "Put on the full armor of God." Notice the equipment has to be put on. There has to be a definite action on the part of the believer carefully dressing for battle. To look at the armor is not enough.

Next he says that we are to put on "the belt of truth" (v. 14). You see, if this belt is too loose, the equipment that is fastened to it will begin to fall and impede movement. So the belt is important. The Christian has to ensure that there is truth, that there is reality, that there is integrity at the base of his or her profession.

Having checked out his belt, the soldier then carefully buckles on the breastplate. The breastplate, of course, protects the heart. Paul sees the breastplate of righteousness as an integral part of the believer's equipment. The apostle was probably saying that the soldier must guard his heart by a consistent life. Living right must be a part of the battle; otherwise, the soldier won't last long in battle.

In verse 15 Paul talks about "feet that are fitted to the gospel of peace" as a foundation for a firm footing, which probably refers to a prepared foundation upon which the soldier can stand. This foundation is the good news that brings peace so that even in the most difficult battle the solider has a firm conviction that he is fighting in the name of Christ for the truth, and this will ultimately bring peace.

Next, in verse 16, Paul talks about "the shield of faith." This piece of equipment was a large heavy piece behind which the soldier could take refuge. Paul makes no apology for telling the Ephesians that it's necessary for them to hide themselves in Christ through complete faith and dependence upon Him.

But a soldier is not equipped for battle without a helmet. "The helmet of salvation" refers to much more than just the time a person found the Lord. It refers to the ongoing deliverance from sin's power that God has promised to those who will trust and obey.

And, of course, the soldier needs finally (v. 17) "the sword of the Spirit, which is the Word of God." There is a great need for believers who will take the time to develop skills in the Word of God: memorizing it and hiding it in their hearts so that they can then use the Bible as a weapon against error and as a means of communicating the truth.

Many of our contemporary methods of engaging the devil in conflict lack spiritual cutting power because they leave out the sword of the Spirit.

Put on the full armor today. There's a battle ahead.

APRIL 1

Cheering for Jesus

The gospel of John says in 12:12–19, "The next day the great crowd that had come to the feast heard that Jesus was on His way to Jerusalem. They took palm branches and went out to meet Him, shouting 'Hosanna, blessed is He who comes in the name of the Lord. Blessed is the King of Israel.'"

Jesus found a young donkey and sat upon it." As the scripture says, "Do not be afraid, Daughter Zion; see, your king is coming, seated on a donkey's colt." John is here referring to Zechariah 9:9, which was written over five hundred years before Christ.

At first His disciples did not understand all this. Only after Jesus was glorified did they realize that these things had been written about Him. The crowd who were with Him had continued to spread the word, that He had called Lazarus from the tomb, raising him from the dead. Many people, because they had heard that He had given the miraculous sign, went out to meet Him. So the Pharisees said to one another, "See? This is getting us nowhere. Look how the whole world has gone after Him."

Mass emotion is a dangerous thing and it's always a doubtful procedure to go with the crowd. Christ's enemies said, "Look—the whole world has gone after Him." And the world here is synonymous with the words "the great crowd." A movement is always suspect when it is popular with the world, because the world does not want the way of the cross. This crowd came because of the sensation brought on by the raising of Lazarus. This miracle had made Jesus—for the moment—a very popular hero.

For the moment, they believed what they wanted to believe, that He was the political Messiah who could lead them to victory. They wanted a victor, not a savior. They wanted freedom from Rome rather than allegiance to God. They were about to celebrate the Passover but did not recognize that God's Passover Lamb, whose blood would be shed for them on Calvary, was standing before them.

Even today many so-called Christians are like that crowd, inconsistent and fickle. They want their religion to be popular, their church large and consumer friendly. They resent the stigma of the cross, the blood, the suffering of Christ. The world has crept into the church. Many people are cheering for Jesus. But how many during a time of testing would be willing to suffer for Him? People have not changed since Christ's earthly ministry. So many had cheered Him on the way to Jerusalem, but so few stood by His cross.

Are you cheering for Christ or serving Christ? Let's not only cheer for Him but serve Him as well.

APRIL 2

Stay Away from Sin

In Matthew 26:36–46 we have the familiar Gethsemane account. Jesus took His disciples to this hallowed place of prayer. It was to be an intensive spiritual warfare for Jesus.

There are two things I want us to notice about Jesus's prayer. First, three times He prays about this cup passing from Him, yet saying that not His will but the Father's must be supreme. Here Jesus prays about the same thing three times. I've heard people say that if you really pray in faith, you need to pray only once. As a matter of fact, they insist that to pray more than once about the same thing is to show a lack of faith. Surely, Jesus here demonstrates that in spiritual battles we may need to pray repeatedly about the same thing.

The second thing to note is the word *cup.* When Jesus prayed that this "cup" might pass, what "cup" would He want the Father to remove from Him? It undoubtedly was not the cross. He surely was not praying, "O Father, I don't want to go to the cross."

Jesus had read the writings of Isaiah while on earth. He knew the passage that foretold His suffering. He knew He was to be pierced for our transgressions. It would thus be unthinkable for Him, knowing the Scriptures, to now pray that He wouldn't have to go to the cross.

Think for a moment—though Jesus had become flesh, He and the Father had still maintained intimate contact with each other. Jesus said in John 5:30, "By myself I can do nothing." He even said in John 14:10, "The words that I speak are not my own —they are my Father's." The Father and Son had never, ever been totally separated. But now with Jesus becoming our sin offering, God the Father could not have oneness with a sin offering. That's why Jesus said in Matthew 27:46, "My God, My God, why have you forsaken Me?" Sin caused Jesus and Jehovah God to be separated, and that had never happened before.

Think of it: that's how bad sin is. It caused the Father and the Son to be placed in a situation they had never experienced before. Whatever you do, friend—stay away from sin.

APRIL 3

He Knows Where You Are

In Isaiah 40:25–31 we read these words:

> "To whom will you compare me, or who is my equal? says the Holy One. Lift your eyes and look to the heavens. Who created all these? He who brings out the starry host one by one, and calls them each by name, because of His great power and mighty strength, not one of them is missing. Why do you say, "My way is hidden from the Lord, my cause is disregarded by my God." Do you not know, have you not heard, the Lord is the Everlasting God, the Creator of the ends of the earth? He will not grow tired or weary and His understanding no one can fathom. He gives strength to the weary, He increases the power of the weak. Even youths grow tired and weary, and young men stumble and fall. But those who hope in the Lord will renew their strength. They will soar on wings like eagles they will run and not grow weary. They will walk and not faint."

Do you ever feel like the people of Israel in verse 27? "My way is hidden from the Lord, my cause is disregarded by my God." Do you ever feel God has forgotten you and does not know where you are?

Only when we accept that God is guiding every step of our way will we have peace and blessing. If you yield your life to God, so that He can do His will through you, then you can cease to worry about the outcome of your situation. Only those who continually wait upon the Lord will soar on wings like eagles.

Waiting upon the Lord is one of the great secrets of the victorious Christian life. When you yield your life to God, expect Him to take control and your strength to be made new. Then you will move into a new experience of living because you have a new source, Christ Himself.

Remember from Philippians 4:13, "I can do all things through Christ who gives me strength."

Whatever it is you're facing today, He knows where you are. He sees what is happening, and He is ready to supply your need. Trust Him.

APRIL 4

Prayer Is to Be Our Natural Default System

"Behold I stand at the door and knock. If anyone hears my voice and opens the door, I will come in" (Revelation 3:20 KJV).

Do you ever feel as if God has taken a vacation and didn't let you know? Do you ever feel you stand and shout into an empty sky from which there is no reply?

This passage sounds as if God is as accessible as our quickest petition. But in reality, many times we sense an absence of God's presence. We desire to be aware of His touch and yet sometimes feel we have become numb in the attempt.

One thing needs to be kept in mind: our relationship with God in prayer is just that—a relationship. God is not a robot we pull out of the closet when we wish to talk to Him. Our effectiveness in prayer, our consciousness of His presence in our times of intercession, is born out of an ongoing, dynamic relationship.

In Mark 9:14–29 Jesus healed a boy who had an evil spirit. The disciples were somewhat distraught because they had been unable to help. They were probably confused and embarrassed about the entire situation. So when Jesus was alone they asked Him, "Why couldn't we drive out the evil spirit?" Jesus explained, "This kind can come out only by prayer and fasting."

Though the word *fasting* is not in all early manuscripts, Jesus assumed His followers would fast (Matthew 6:16—"When you fast..."). In the Mark passage more is meant than just skipping a meal and praying. The thrust of it is that there is something about a regular prayer life that has clout with God that a hit-and-miss prayer life just doesn't have.

The more you keep the relationship alive through continuous praying, the nearer God is to spontaneous praying. In 1 Thessalonians 5:17 we read, "Pray without ceasing" (NKJV). The Greek word for *without ceasing* does not mean non-stop but actually means "constantly recurring." In other words, prayer is to become the general attitude of your heart. It is as if prayer is the natural default setting in our minds as we live out our Christian lives.

APRIL 5

Keeping Your Spiritual Fervor

In Romans 12:9–11, at the heart of Paul's admonitions to the Romans, he writes, "Keep your spiritual fervor." The Greek is literally saying here that we are to keep our spiritual temperature at the boiling point. Sounds good, but how do we do that?

Paul tells us in this passage that we must be sincere. That means we must be real, without any hypocrisy.

Second, he says to "hate evil." Yes, there is a hatred that Christians are to have, and it is against evil.

Next Paul says to "cling to what is good." The Greek here suggests being "glued to the good." It is as if we place in concrete our deep desire to serve God.

He continues by saying, "Be devoted to each other." Paul is telling us to treat each other as loving family members would treat each other. It is a sad thing when family members are kinder to people at work or school than they are to those in their own homes.

Then he says, "Never be lacking in zeal," which means to reject laziness. Don't let the pattern of your life be one that wastes time, because to waste time is to waste life.

In this passage we have Paul's outline for keeping our spiritual temperature at the boiling point.

Be sincere. Hate evil. Cling to the good. Be devoted to each other, and never be lacking in zeal. If you do these things you will keep your spiritual fervor.

APRIL 6

God Is Our Father

In Isaiah 64:8 we read, "O Lord, you are our Father, we are the clay, you are the potter, we are all the work of your hand."

One of the great problems of our modern civilization is juvenile delinquency, shown by a tremendous upsurge in teenage restlessness and rebellion. Research by social workers and others has shown that a major cause of delinquency is a broken home, the absence of a father, and a lack of security. Where there is no sense of connectedness and support, there is a very real possibility of frustration and unhappiness. This is true of the rich as well as the poor.

In a similar way, one of our problems in modern Christian fellowship is a "spiritual delinquency" that can impact all people regardless of their age. This, in like manner, springs from a broken spiritual relationship and an inadequate appreciation for the Fatherhood of God.

Many look upon God as a spiritual rich uncle who provides us with things—instead of as a father who cares, disciplines, and guides us. When we can see ourselves in community with believers and truly see God as our Father, then our spiritual delinquency can be cured. Our Father God is deeply concerned about each of us personally. He comforts, He disciplines, He chastises, but He is our Father.

Second Corinthians 1:3 says, "Blessed be the God and Father of our Lord Jesus Christ, the Father of mercies and God of all comfort" (ESV). Jesus has a Father! In 2 Corinthians 6:18 we read, "I will be a Father to you, and you will be my sons and daughters, says the Lord Almighty." We have the same Father. Jehovah God is Jesus's Father—and our Father as well.

APRIL 7

God in You

In Matthew 1, after seventeen verses dealing with Jesus's genealogy, we have the familiar account of His birth.

In Matthew 1:23 we read of one of His names, *Emmanuel,* "God with us." What a tremendous thought not only for Mary and Joseph but also for all those who came in contact with the Christ! At that moment, as never before, the God of all creation had broken into the human arena of life.

Sometimes I wonder if the people of Jesus's day realized how fortunate they were. Never before had God been with man to the extent that Jesus was. History records the fact that many took little notice of Him at all, especially as the God who was with them.

What about us today? How much attention do we give to the fact that God is with us? As a matter of fact, in John 14:17 Jesus said He would send His Holy Spirit not only to be *with* us but also to be *in* us.

Today, Christian friend, think of it: God is not only with you at home, work, or school—but literally He is *in* you right now! Let's thank Him that He is not only *Emmanuel* (with us) but also the *Holy Spirit* (in us).

APRIL 8

There Is Always a Way Out of Temptation

Did you ever burn your finger on a stove? Ever run a splinter under your fingernail? Ever smash your thumb with a hammer? Perhaps you find yourself cringing even now, just a little, as my words remind you of that painful experience.

The Bible says in Hebrews 2:18, "Because He Himself suffered when He was tempted, He is able to help those who are being tempted." But the verb tense used in Greek for the word *suffered* means that through the temptation Christ suffered in the flesh, though it occurred in the past, its effect is permanent. Christ will never forget the suffering brought into His own life through the temptations of Satan. He identifies with every temptation or test we will ever face—because He has been there.

Just as you remember the pains you experienced in the past, so also Christ remembers His agony and temptations. He remembers the hurts, the sense of abandonment, and the sheer isolation that often accompanies times of testing.

This brings tremendous consolation to my heart when I realize that Christ knows what I am going through. He has not only been there Himself, but He has come out victorious. He knows the way through the darkest, loneliest, and emptiest hour of life.

Remember, friend—when you hurt, He hurts. You are not alone in your pain. Jesus knows the way out and wants to show you. In 1 Corinthians 10:13 we read,

> No temptation [regardless of its source] has overtaken or enticed you that is not common to human experience...but God is faithful [to His word], and He will not let you be tempted beyond your ability [to resist], but along with the temptation He [has in the past and is now and] will [always] provide the way out as well, so that you will be able to endure it [without yielding, and will overcome temptation with joy]. [AMP]

Now that's a mouthful! Read it again and believe it.

APRIL 9

Victory over Temptation

In Matthew 4:1–11 we have the record of one of Jesus's greatest encounters with Satan. We are immediately drawn to the fact that Jesus quoted scripture in resisting temptation. That is an excellent pattern of defense for us to adopt as well.

Perhaps as you look back at Jesus's temptations you are prone to wonder if He ever faced the problems we face today. Could Jesus know anything about the temptations of drugs, unfaithfulness, immorality, materialism, or peer pressure? When did Jesus face any of these temptations? Notice what it says about Jesus in Hebrews 4:15, "He was tempted in *every way* just as we are" (emphasis added).

It does not say "He was tempted with the exact temptations as we are"—but in *every way.* How many ways are there in which we can be tempted?

First John 2:16 speaks of three ways when it says, "Everything in the world—the cravings of a sinful man, the lust of his eyes, and the boasting of what he has and does—comes not from the Father but from the world."

All temptations center in one of three things: feeling, fame, or fortune.

The NKJV says, "For all that is in the world—the lust of the flesh, the lust of the eyes, and the pride of life—is not of the Father but is of the world."

All temptations involve either "the lust of the flesh" (pleasure), "the lust of the eyes" (position), or "the pride of life" (possessions).

Jesus was tempted in all these ways but came out victorious. So can you.

APRIL 10

Focus on Him

In John 14:27 Jesus said to His followers, "Peace I leave with you, my peace I give you."

How would you honestly rate the peace level of your life on a scale from one to ten? One is the bottom and ten is the top. One is no peace and all, and ten is peace that passes understanding. Where would you appear on the peace scale?

Do you know anything about the peace that Jesus left with His followers?

Let me ask you another question: What are you thinking about these days? Are you thinking about yourself and your inadequacies, or are you thinking about Christ and His adequacy? Are you thinking more about your problems or more about the problem-solver? Proverbs 23:7 says, "As he thinks in his heart, so is he" (NKJV).

If a medical doctor gave you a prescription for pain that would bring you great relief, you would no doubt take the medicine. Well, I have a prescription for you today. It has the potential of bringing you great relief. It focuses on Isaiah 26:3: "You will keep in perfect peace those whose minds are steadfast, because they trust in you."

"You will keep in perfect peace all who trust in you, all whose thoughts are fixed on you!" (NLT). Here's my prescription for you: Say this passage three times a day for seven days. Do what it says. Keep your mind steadfast—that means to force your thoughts in God's direction. Focus on Him. The result will not be simply peace—but *perfect* peace. Try it!

APRIL 11

Christ All around Me

Titus 2:14 says that Jesus "gave himself for us, that he might redeem us from all iniquity, and purify unto himself a peculiar people" (KJV).

Today the word *peculiar* does not carry a positive connotation. What is this verse saying?

Peculiar is two words in the Greek, one that means "around," as a circle, and the other that means "to be." You can picture the meaning by seeing a dot surrounded by a circle. As the circle is around that dot, so God is around each one of His saints. As the NIV translates it, "We are a people that are His very own."

Here is how the Amplified Bible says it: "Who...gave Himself [to be crucified] on our behalf to redeem us and purchase our freedom from all wickedness, and to purify for Himself a chosen and very special people to be His own possession."

Think of it, friend—God has put Himself around you. You might call it a wall of protection. You are His possession.

Today I challenge you to walk in the confidence that God is not only *in* you but also *around* you. You are never really alone. I remember Bob Benson many years ago explaining what it means when people cross themselves. You have seen people make that sign over their chests. Bob explained it as "Christ above me, Christ below me, Christ to the left of me, Christ to the right of me." In other words, Christ encircles me as His child.

APRIL 12

Satan Doesn't Give Up

In Luke 4:13 we read that when the devil had finished tempting Jesus "he left Jesus until an opportune time." The NLT says, "When the devil had finished tempting Jesus, he left him until the next opportunity came."

The devil did not leave forever. Oh, no—he simply decided to wait for a more favorable time when Jesus would be more susceptible to temptation. The Greek literally reads that Satan "stood off from" Jesus. He kept watching, waiting, and preparing for the best time to try again. Satan never ceased his tempting activity with Jesus—and if Satan never gave up on trying to get Jesus to fall, mark it down: he is not going to give up on you either.

If Satan lessens his activities in your life, it is only that he might stand off from you and wait for another time to launch his attack. In 2 Corinthians 2:11 Paul admonishes us not to allow Satan to outwit us, for we are not unaware of his schemes.

We must never allow ourselves to think we are so strong that we could never be tempted to really turn against Christ.

First Peter 5:8 says, "Be self-controlled and alert. Your enemy, the devil prowls around like a roaring lion looking for someone to devour." Satan is very patient at times. He will wait an entire lifetime to get you.

APRIL 13

Is Jesus at Home in Me?

In Ephesians 3:17 Paul prays "that Christ may dwell in your hearts through faith."

The word *dwell* is made from two Greek words, one meaning "to live in a home" and the other "to settle down." Paul is praying that the Lord might be allowed to settle down in our hearts and be at home.

I'll never forget a young mother who came forward in a service, met God at an altar of prayer, and went home a different person. The next night she came back and said, "Last night when I went home, it was like I went home for the very first time."

Allowing Christ to settle down, to dwell in our hearts, makes every place we dwell different. I guess one way to describe the Christian life is "feeling at home in the presence of Jesus." And yet in this passage the thought is turned around—it's Jesus feeling at home in us.

Ask yourself: Is Jesus at home in me? If so, praise the Lord. If not, why not?

APRIL 14

Delivered from the Penalty, Power, and Presence of Sin

In 1 Thessalonians 4:13–18 we read,

> Brothers and sisters, we do not want you to be uninformed about those who sleep in death, so that you do not grieve like the rest of mankind, who have no hope. We believe that Jesus died and rose again, and so we believe that God will bring with Jesus those who have fallen asleep in Him. According to the Lord's word, we tell you that we who are still alive, who are left until the coming of the Lord, will certainly not precede those who have fallen asleep. For the Lord Himself will come down from heaven, with a loud command, with the voice of the archangel and with the trumpet call of God, and the dead in Christ will rise first. After that, we who are still alive and are left will be caught up together with them in the clouds to meet the Lord in the air. And so we will be with the Lord forever. Therefore encourage one another with these words.

Paul wants to be sure that those who have been redeemed by the blood of Jesus are not ignorant of that which is to come. In 4:15 he indicates that he speaks with authority, for he speaks "according to the Lord's own word" and gives a clear picture of the second coming of Christ in verses 15–17. It is the "Lord Himself" who is the one who will "descend from heaven with a loud shout and cry," but we don't know exactly when this will happen. It is a great comfort for us to live with this wonderful promise of His return. Our response to Paul's words is pictured in 5:6–8: "So then, let us not be like others, who are asleep, but let us be alert and self-controlled. And since we belong to the day, let us be self-controlled, putting on faith and love as a breastplate, and the hope of salvation as a helmet."

Our redemption has a threefold aim. First, Christ died to redeem us from the *penalty* of sin. Then He lives in our hearts to deliver us from the *power* of sin. And in today's passage we learn that He is coming to take us from the *presence* of sin. The Lord's complete work deals with the penalty of sin, the power of sin, and the presence of sin.

This is a completion of salvation. Verse 8 tells us how to prepare for His return: "We belong to the day, so be self-controlled, put on faith and love as a breastplate and the hope of salvation as a helmet." This encouragement is where we bring strength and power to one another. What an exciting, blessed future lies ahead of every follower of Christ!

APRIL 15

Equipped to Minister

If I were to ask you to give me the name of three ministers you know, who would you name? Answer this question before reading on.

Often when people think about those who perform a ministry, they think about a pastor, a missionary, or an evangelist instead of a lay person. Did your list include any lay people?

In Ephesians 4:11–12 we read that it was Christ who gave "some to be apostles, some to be prophets, some to be evangelists, and some to be pastors and teachers, to prepare God's people for works of service."

Today there are no apostles or prophets in the strictest New Testament sense—but we do have evangelists, pastors, and teachers—and note that these people are to "prepare God's people." That means to equip God's people for "works of service," for ministry.

Think of it: in your church the pastor is not the only minister, but every Christian is to be a minister as well. Do you know what your ministry is? When did you last ask God what your ministry is to be? It might be different now than it was at one time.

If you have no idea of what your ministry is to be, do two things. First, be sure to do daily what you believe Christ would have you do. Second, listen—I mean really listen—as your pastor preaches. Listen as the Word is taught. Listen as an evangelist opens the Word to you or a missionary comes to speak. The Bible says these people are to help equip the Christians for works of ministry.

APRIL 16

What to Do about Worry

In Philippians 4:6 we read, "Do not be anxious about anything." The word *anxious* means "full of care." It is a synonym for the word *worry.* The force of the word in the Greek is a strong rebuke to the Philippians. In essence Paul was saying that in your past life you have been worrying, but stop—you're Christians now.

The same Greek word is found in Matthew 6:25, where we read "Do not worry about your life." The suggestion here is that some people have fallen into a habit of worry. So Paul is saying, "Stop worrying about even one thing."

Since we are not obeying God's Word when we worry, we actually commit sin when we do so. We're not trusting God when we worry. We don't receive answers to prayer when we worry, because we're not trusting.

This command not to worry is based on the Word of God. In 1 Peter 5:7 we read, "Cast all your anxiety on Him because He cares for you." The word *cast* in the Greek signifies a definite act of the will in committing our worries to Christ. It is a choice we make. The result is that we are through worrying about the matter and have chosen to let God assume the responsibility for our welfare.

The last part of the scripture says, "He cares for you." That is, your best interest is His concern. You see, when the Lord brought you into His family, He assumed responsibility for your future. Your job is to keep Christ first in your life—and let Him take care of the details!

APRIL 17

Walking in the Light

First John is the epistle of fellowship. It is a family letter written to the children of God. In 1 John 1:7 we have the familiar words "If we walk in the light, as He is in the light, we have fellowship with one another." "Walking in the light" is the conscious and continued endeavor to live in accordance with God's Word.

Fellowship is the result of walking in the light. The word *fellowship* is from a Greek word meaning "to have in common with." One basis of human fellowship is a common interest. An artist and a pilot have no occupational fellowship—their interests are very different. An artist can have great fellowship with another artist and a pilot with another pilot—because their interests are similar.

If a person is to have fellowship with God, there must be a common interest. It's what the Bible calls a "hungering and thirsting for righteousness."

The person who loves what Jesus loves and hates with Jesus hates has fellowship with Him. The person who loves what Jesus hates does not have fellowship with Him.

I challenge you today to be alert. Pray, think on these words, walk in all the light—walk in *all* the light He has given you. Then and only then can you have real fellowship with the Lord and His people.

APRIL 18

Do You Love Jesus?

In John 21:15–17 we have an interesting conversation recorded:

> Jesus said to Simon Peter, "Simon, son of John, do you truly love me?" "Yes, Lord," he said, "you know that I love you." Jesus said, "Feed my lambs." Again Jesus said: "Simon, son of John, do you truly love me?" He answered, "Yes, Lord, you know that I love you." Jesus said: "Take care of my sheep." The third time He said to him, "Simon, son of John, do you love me?" Peter was hurt because Jesus asked him the third time, "Do you love me?" He said, "Lord, you know all things, you know that I love you."

In this passage are two different words that are translated *love.* The first is *agapao*—this is God-like love. It seeks the highest good of the person to whom it is directed. The second is *phileo,* dealing more in the friendship area. You could almost substitute the word *like* for *love* when this word is used.

At first reading the conversation between Jesus and Peter seems unnecessarily repetitive. But the Greek gives the entire conversation a new meaning. The first two times Jesus asks Peter if he loves Him, He uses the word *agapao,* and both times Peter replies, "I *phileo* you."

Jesus was calling Simon to move up from friendship love to God-like love. If Jesus asked you, "Do you *agapao* me?" what would your honest answer be?

How much does your life say you love Jesus?

APRIL 19

God's Calling Is God's Enabling

In Philippians 2:12–13 we read, "My dear friends, as you have always obeyed—not only in my presence, but now much more in my absence—continue to work out your salvation with fear and trembling, for it is God who works in you to will and to act in order to fulfill his good purpose."

The English translation here is good if we understand the words *work out* are like working out a problem in mathematics, that is, carrying it to its ultimate goal or conclusion. This is what the Greek is saying here.

When Paul was with the Philippians, his teaching instructed them, his example inspired them, his encouragement urged them on in their growth in grace. Now in his absence, they were on their own initiative. Thus Paul sets before them their human responsibility for growth in grace. Their growth in Christ-likeness is the salvation of which Paul is speaking. The Philippians are exhorted to live out their growth in grace to its ultimate goal.

The challenge spoken of in verse 12 is made possible for us in verse 13, namely not only being willing to do God's good pleasure but also doing it. That is the Christian's responsibility from the human standpoint. But the believer is not left without resources with which to do both. For God the Holy Spirit indwelling the believer produces in him or her both the willingness and the power to do His will. In verse 12 we have human responsibility, and in verse 13 divine enablement.

You see, God never asks you to do something that He doesn't give you the power to do. God's calling is also God's enabling.

APRIL 20

God's Supply of Grace

In Romans 5:20 we read, "Where sin increased, grace increased all the more."

The first word translated *increased* is from a different Greek word than the second word *increased.* They both mean "to exist in abundance," but the second one carries with it the added thrust of an abundance that is far more than enough.

You could translate the verse, "Where sin existed in abundance, grace was in superabundance, and then some more and on top of that."

There is enough grace available to give every Christian constant victory over sin, and then some more. There is enough grace to cope with all the sorrows, heartaches, difficulties, temptations, testings, and trials of human existence—and more grace added to that.

God's salvation reminds me of a sign on many large trucks today: "Oversize Load." God's salvation is an "oversize" salvation. It is shockproof, strain-proof, all sufficient, more than enough.

It is equal to every emergency—for it flows from the heart of an infinite God. Regardless of how much grace you need today, God has a super-abundant supply.

APRIL 21

A Life Verse

Do you have a life verse? You might wonder, "What's a life verse?" It's a passage of Scripture that God makes come alive in a special way—for you. God often "breathes" on a scripture and makes it come alive for me. But a life verse, though it does come alive, has the added dimension of a directive for the rest of your life.

When I was a young believer, God "breathed" on 2 Corinthians 4:16–18 for me. I memorized it in the King James Version:

> For which cause we faint not. But though our outward man perish, yet the inward man is being renewed day by day. For our light affliction, which is but for a moment, works for us a far more exceeding and eternal weight of glory. While we do not look at the things that are seen, but at the things that are not seen. For the things that are seen are temporary but the things that are not seen are eternal.

Hundreds of times this passage has reminded me that regardless of what comes my way, God has plans for me that stretch into eternity itself. The key is to not focus on what we see but to look ahead to what is unseen. I have never literally seen Jesus but I know He is real. I have never seen heaven and yet I find myself homesick for a place I have never been. Through the Word and the leadership of the Holy Spirit, *this* world takes on less and less significance and *that* world becomes more real all the time.

This passage became the foundation for my philosophy of life: "This life is very short, and that life (eternity) is very long. And since I will spend that life in relation to the choices I make in this life, I have made up my mind to do in this life what counts in that life. If it doesn't count there then it doesn't count here."

All of the Bible is God's inspired Word, but when He "breathes" on a passage it becomes precious to you. If you don't have a life verse yet, ask God to give you one. He will use it to bless and direct you the rest of your life.

APRIL 22

Jesus Goes with Us

In John 14:16 Jesus said, "I will ask the Father and He will give you another counselor to be with you forever" (HCSB).

The word *counselor* is from a Greek word that literally in the verb form means "to call alongside." During the time when Jesus walked the earth, this word was used to describe a lawyer in the Greek courts who was called "alongside" to defend an accused person.

Here in John we're not dealing with the law, for a Christian is not under law but under grace. The word here merely means "one called in to help another."

Sometimes it is translated "comforter," which is a good translation when rightly understood as someone who is our "advocate." To comfort in the sense of counseling someone is just one of many ministries of the Holy Spirit to the believer. His many-sided work can be summed up in the phrase "one called in to stand by and give aid."

The scripture says, "The Father...will send you another counselor." The word *another* is significant. There are two words in Greek that mean "another"—one referring to another of a different kind, and the other meaning "another of the same kind." The Holy Spirit is a divine helper of the same kind as Jesus. The Holy Spirit desires to come to the aid of Christians today, just as Jesus did in the flesh while He lived on earth.

The Holy Spirit is indeed the Spirit of Jesus. In John 14:18 Jesus spoke of the Spirit's coming as His own coming: "I will not leave you as orphans; I will come to you."

Remember, friend: Jesus has sent His Holy Spirit to walk along with you today. Think of it: today Jesus is going to go where you go.

APRIL 23

Witnessing

Jesus told his followers in Acts 1:8 that they would "receive power after the Holy Spirit came upon them" and they would "be witnesses in Jerusalem, Judea, Samaria, and the ends of the earth."

In Jesus's words we find an outline for spreading the good news. He said to these early disciples, "You will be witnesses in Jerusalem [their hometown], Judea [their home territory], Samaria [the land of their enemies], and finally the earth"—and that's everywhere.

The Master's plan for witnessing is the same today. He still calls all Spirit-filled Christians to witness for Him. Let me ask you a question: Are you witnessing for the Lord? I mean, are you setting out on purpose to influence others for Christ?

You might say, "Where should I begin?" Do what Jesus said. Start in your hometown—at school, at work, in your neighborhood. Make evangelism your lifestyle.

Next, do what you can to influence your country for good and for God. Be a living example of patriotism and citizenship.

Then be open to witness to those who are hard to love—your enemies. Pray about being a witness to that person who has given you a bad time. Look for a God-given opportunity to tell him or her of the difference Christ has made in your life.

Finally, Jesus expanded the witnessing horizon to include the ends of the earth. Think of it: when you are faithful where you are, God multiplies your efforts and virtually changes the world.

By the way, witnessing is not necessarily preaching. A verbal witness can be anything from "Isn't this a beautiful day God's given us?" to a personal testimony of His presence in your life.

APRIL 24

The Holy Spirit Helps Us Pray

In Romans 8:26 we read, "The Spirit helps us in our weakness. We do not know what we ought to pray for, but the Spirit Himself intercedes for us with groans that words cannot express."

The Holy Spirit, Paul says, will help us in our weakness. The Greek word translated *help* literally means "to lend a hand together with." The Holy Spirit lends a hand together with us as we are praying.

Note: the Holy Spirit not only helps us bear our weaknesses, but He also helps us in the midst of our weaknesses to do something meaningful. The weaknesses spoken of here deal with two things: the issue of prayer itself and how we should pray, or the manner of prayer.

This scripture indicates that we do not know what to pray for. That is, we may not know the exact details of every prayer situation. We know general subjects for prayer such as for the salvation of the lost, believers to be filled with the Holy Spirit, and our own daily needs—these we know very well.

But being specific in our praying involves knowledge of God's will in particular situations. It is at this point that the Holy Spirit comes to our aid.

Oh, it's wonderful to know what God's will is in a given situation—you can pray with great confidence. But rest assured in those things that are not so clear to you. Keep on praying—the Holy Spirit is with you interceding as you pray.

Here's a challenge for the day: ask the Holy Spirit who or what God would have you pray about today. He might surprise you.

APRIL 25

Looking for the Good

Yesterday we talked of Romans 8:26 and how the Holy Spirit helps us. That is, He lends a helping hand to our prayer life. That verse continues by saying that "The Spirit intercedes for us." The word *intercede* comes from a very picturesque Greek word. It is a word depicting a rescue by one who happens to come upon someone who is in trouble and after seeing this person, pleads on his or her behalf.

It's a reminder of the Good Samaritan, who found the man who had been beaten and robbed and nearly killed. You will remember the Samaritan took the injured man to a place of rest and safety, explained the situation, and made provisions to pay his bill.

As we journey through life we may feel the need for safety and rest as well. We may feel alone and forgotten—but that's always the devil's doing. He tells us there are no more "good Samaritans," that emptiness and loneliness are your way of life. But don't believe it.

The Holy Spirit is the one who passes by your way. He understands your situation. He will provide the needed rescue. He will plead your cause and pay the bill.

When Jesus said He would never leave us—He really meant it. Where have you seen Jesus lately? Keep your eyes open. Every good thing comes from Him. Look for something good and you will see Him.

APRIL 26

God Gives Us His Best

In 2 Timothy 2:15 we read, "Do your best to present yourself to God as one approved, a workman who does not need to be ashamed and who correctly handles the word of truth." The Greek word translated "do your best" can also be translated "make haste," "be eager," "give diligence," "be persistent."

Although Paul is talking directly to Timothy, he is exhorting every believer to be God-like in character and dedicated service.

The Christian life is a matter of reckoning ourselves dead to sin and alive to God, of presenting our lives as instruments to be used by the hand of God. It is a life of dependence upon God, of allowing the Holy Spirit to produce in and through us a Christ-like life. The Scriptures indicate that there is an inner rest to the people of God. But in 1 Timothy we also see another side to the Christian life. It is a rest in one aspect, but it is a battle in another.

Paul writes in 1 Timothy 6:12, "Fight the good fight of faith." There must be an eager, active, intense determination to live a life pleasing to God even when our faith is challenged. We must not only yield to the Holy Spirit's fullness, trusting in Him to produce in us God-like character, but we must also definitely choose to do the things God would have us do.

Today, friend, you can count on God to do His best. Be sure you do *your* best.

APRIL 27

The Holy Spirit and Your Human Spirit

In Galatians 5:13–16 we read these words:

> You, my brothers, were called to be free. But do not use your freedom to indulge your sinful nature; rather, serve one another in love. The entire law is summed up in a single command: "Love your neighbor as yourself." If you keep on biting and devouring each other, watch out or you will be destroyed by each other. So I say, live by the Spirit.

In the New Testament the word *live* is often interchangeable with the word *walk,* just as it is here. Paul is telling these Galatians to walk in the Spirit.

We know that the Holy Spirit is the third person of the Trinity, and often when we see the word *spirit,* that is who we think of. But *spirit* can also refer to a person. We sometimes say that a certain person "has a good spirit." By that we are actually referring to a *human* spirit.

Here in Galatians "the Spirit" refers neither to the human spirit nor the divine Spirit as separate from each other, but to the divine Spirit as He indwells the human spirit.

When Paul says, "Live or walk by the Spirit," he is referring to the pattern of our lives. We are to make it a habit to walk with the Spirit. We are to allow our human spirits to be so directed by the Holy Spirit that it becomes the natural, normal thing to depend on God.

As you find yourself thinking about God and His will for your life, realize that this is your human spirit becoming more sensitized to the Spirit of God. Realize that you are allowing the God who made you to have the natural, normal influence in your life that He intended at creation.

APRIL 28

God Is Cutting a Path Ahead of You

Paul is imprisoned in Rome writing to his beloved Philippians. He is assuring them that the circumstances in which he finds himself are contributing to, rather than hindering, the advance of the gospel. He says in Philippians 1:12 that "what has happened to me has served to advance the gospel."

The word *advance* is from a Greek word thought to have been used in the first century. It referred to a group of woodcutters preceding the progress of an army, cutting the road through the forest so that they might advance unhindered.

Paul says his circumstances are divine woodcutters, cutting away the opposition so that the gospel might be advanced. What were the circumstances? His liberty was gone—he was chained to a Roman soldier night and day. God had built a fence around the apostle. He had put limitations about him. He had placed handicaps upon him.

However, Paul said these handicaps were God's woodcutters making a road for the advancement of the gospel. The gospel was now being proclaimed from the pulpit of the Roman Empire. The praetorian guard of ten thousand handpicked Roman soldiers were the ones hearing it from the soldiers chained to Paul. The jealous people in Rome were announcing Christ more energetically—out of envy, of course, but yet they were announcing Him. The friendly brethren, out of love for Paul, were more zealous in their preaching. Without doubt, Paul was underscoring the fact that God works in all things for good. Even his incarceration, even this limitation to his preaching schedule, God worked in it for good.

Whatever you're facing today, my friend, keep your testimony clear and strong. God is cutting a path ahead of you so you can carry out your desire to spread the good news.

Can you see the path God is cutting for you right now?

APRIL 29

How Will God Grow You Today?

Yesterday we talked about Paul being in prison, and yet the gospel was advanced. The barriers of humanity's making served only to help Paul in the spread of the gospel. So it is in every Christian's life—the things that hedge us in, the things that handicap us, the tests we go through, and the temptations that threaten us are the woodcutters used by God to hew out the path for sharing the gospel.

It may be that our fondest hopes are not realized. It could be that we are in difficult circumstances. Illness may be befall us. Yet if we are in the center of God's will, all these are contributing to the progress of the gospel. They draw us close to the Lord so that the testimony of our lives will count more for God, and thus we become more efficient in proclaiming the good news. Thank God for the handicaps and the testings. They are blessings in disguise.

When we have limitations imposed upon us, we do our best work for the Lord, for then we are most dependent upon Him. Paul said in 2 Corinthians 12:9, "Most gladly therefore, will I glory in my infirmities that the power of Christ may rest upon me."

Every circumstance that God allows is an opportunity for us to grow in faith and witness to a needy world.

APRIL 30

Living by Faith

Today would be a good day to read the faith chapter of the Bible—Hebrews 11. In verse 1 we read, "Now faith is being sure of what we hope for and certain of what we do not see."

In Hebrews 11 we read of Abel, who was a shepherd; of Enoch, who was a mystic; of Sarah, an elderly, childless woman; of Moses, a Jewish leader; and Rahab, the harlot. Quite a different group they were, yet they all had one thing in common: their faith was such that God commented on it.

Concerning Abel, God speaks of His gifts; of Enoch, that he pleased God; of Sarah, who through faith had strength to bring about what seemed humanly impossible; of Abraham, that he was willing to offer of his only son, Isaac, because he believed the promises of God; of Moses, that he esteemed the reproach of Christ greater riches than the treasures of Egypt; of Rahab, that she did not perish in Jericho because she believed the reports she had heard of Jehovah's mighty power.

What a roll call of unwavering faith! How about *you* today? How is *your* faith? Are you able to stand against the powers of Satan or do you trust only on the good days and grumble and doubt when trials come your way? How are you doing now? Maybe your job is providing more money and your health is a little bit better. Are you just as excited about trusting God now as you were when you were going through the tough times?

In 1 John 5:4 we read, "This is the victory that overcomes the world, even our faith." Never forgot it—we do live by faith and not by sight.

Ask yourself: Am I living by faith or am I living by sight?

MAY 1

Good Days Ahead!

In Hebrews 10:35–36 we read, "Do not throw away your confidence; it will be richly rewarded. You need to persevere so that when you have done the will of God, you will receive what he has promised."

The word I want us to focus on today is *persevere.* Here the writer says, "You need to persevere so that when you have done the will of God, you will receive what He has promised."

Persevere literally means "to have patient endurance." This is the attitude that bears all things, not simply with helpless resignation but with blazing hope. It is not the defeated spirit of a person who sits statically enduring what comes, but rather an enthusiastic spirit that bears things because of the knowledge that these things are leading to a goal.

How are you doing today in the area of "patient endurance"? Do you find yourself filled with blazing hope? Or in all honesty, does the blaze sometimes turn into a fizzle?

Note: our scripture says that if we will persevere, we will receive what God has promised. These words also work in reverse order. That is, knowing what God has promised helps us to persevere.

Have you thought lately about what God has promised for you?

In John 14:2 Jesus said He was going to prepare a place for us. Can you imagine what heaven must be like? Think of it. Our earth was made in six days, but Jesus has been preparing a place for us for almost two thousand years. What must be the grandeur, the awesome beauty, the sheer splendor of the place He is preparing!

I feel a "blazing hope" within my spirit, that regardless of what this day holds, our eyes have not seen, our ears have not heard, and our minds have not imagined the things that await us who persevere. Good days are ahead!

MAY 2

A Ministry Mentality

In John 15:16 Jesus said, "You did not choose me, but I chose you and appointed you so that you might go and bear fruit —fruit that will last."

In a strange and yet wonderful way, God has purposely limited Himself in working on earth through men and women. He could have chosen angels to proclaim the gospel message. He could have arranged for all mission work to be done by angels alone. Think of how much easier it would have been in one sense: no missionary boards, no missionary training campaigns, no praying and struggling for blessings—everything would have been just perfect.

But God did not choose to work that way. Instead, He has limited Himself to using ordinary men and women just like you and me, people who are willing to offer themselves in service.

In Isaiah 6:8 we have the voice of the Lord saying, "Whom shall I send? And who will go for Us?" This was the voice of God that Isaiah heard more than twenty-seven hundred years ago. And yet those words are relevant for us today. Let me ask you a question: Are your ears and mind open so that God may speak to you and call you personally into some new form of service?

Maybe God wants you to teach a class, serve in the nursery, go on a mission trip—who knows?—maybe to help and encourage your neighbor. If He did, would you be surprised, shocked, embarrassed, scared, or would you be willing and honored to be used how and where God leads you? Do you have a "ministry mentality"?

Mark it down, friend: God has chosen you to go and bear good fruit. Follow His leadership today.

MAY 3

God Is Preparing You

In John 1:6–9 we read, "There was a man sent from God whose name was John. He came as a witness to testify concerning that light, so that through him all might believe. He himself was not the light; he came only as a witness to the light. The true light that gives light to everyone was coming into the world."

In the business, professional, and scientific worlds, these are the days of the specialist. Such is the competition and complexity of our modern, highly organized society—specialization is the most efficient way of getting the job done. It is interesting to see how God trained many of His servants for special work He had planned for them.

Moses was trained for forty years in the culture of the Egyptian court. Then he was left in solitude, in the desert, for another forty years before God was ready to use him.

David was driven out by Saul and suffered years of hardship and deprivation that he might lean only upon God.

Saul of Tarsus, educated, influential, successful, had to be blinded for three days, then go to a part of Arabia to be alone with God for three years before he could start his great ministry.

And then John the Baptist, here in our scripture, is an excellent example of God's way of specialization. John was trained thirty years to do a job that lasted only several months. This is a quality of preparation that we do not ordinarily and naturally indulge in. It is too expensive; it is too time consuming. But with God things are different.

God wanted a man to prepare the way for the coming of His beloved Son. John the Baptist was that man. For years he lived in desert places, apart from the contamination of the disease-ridden world. He lived a hard life, free from any comforts of the flesh, dedicated only to communion with God. Then for a brief moment his voice was heard preparing the way, preparing the people; then he vanished.

It could be, friend, that God is preparing you—right now—for one of your greatest moments of usefulness. Abraham was seventy-five when God called him. And then at ninety-nine he was presented a special challenge by God.

What has God used in your life to prepare you for your next ministry?

MAY 4

The Family of God

A couple of days ago we talked about the things that Christ has prepared for us. Though that is mind boggling to say the least, today I am even more impressed by what is said in Romans 8:17: "If we are children [that is, God's children, those who are born again], then we are heirs—heirs of God and co-heirs with Christ."

All of us have heard about wills, formal documents that assure the desired distribution of a departed person's estate. They become effective only after the death of the person owning the estate. The writer of the will designates heirs for any or all of his or her possessions. If you and I were co-heirs of an estate valued at one million dollars, it would not mean that I had right to five hundred thousand dollars and you had right to five hundred thousand dollars. No, co-heirship means that you have the same rights to the entire one million dollars as I do. We both have access to one hundred percent of the estate.

Jesus in essence talked of heaven and eternal life as part of His estate or His will. Upon His death and resurrection He set into motion the future realization of all He has prepared.

But note that Romans 8:17 says we are *co-heirs* with Christ. This is not a fifty-fifty situation. Oh, no—Christ has made available to us one hundred percent of all He is heir to. We are in such oneness with Christ that all He has He wants *us* to have. At the moment we are born again, we become family. Think of it: we really are a part of the family of God.

MAY 5

Your Weakness—His Strength

In 1 Timothy 1:18–19 Paul says to this young believer, Timothy, "Fight well, and keep your faith and a clear conscience" (GNT).

Seeking to establish a pattern for the early Christians to follow and to bring them the message of salvation, Paul writes to Timothy that he has given him a charge to "wage the good warfare, holding faith and a good conscience" (RSV).

You see, Timothy and Titus were men set apart by God for a particular task on earth. They were so yielded and committed to God that He could use them in Ephesus and in Crete.

Timothy seems to be someone who was frequently ill (1 Timothy 5:23). Paul often told him to be brave, strong, and to fight a good fight. Some scholars say Timothy did not have a dynamic personality but was shy and retiring. Though he served in a place of leadership, the picture we have of Timothy is of a young man with many challenges and weaknesses, which is encouraging for us today. He resembles so many of us in our weaknesses.

We can take heart and go forward with the assurance that the God who used people like Timothy can use us as well. We can see without a doubt that whatever success there was in Timothy's life was not due to his inherent gifts but rather to a life that was yielded to God. As a result, God gave him strength to overcome his weaknesses.

I'm reminded of 2 Corinthians 12:9, in which God says to Paul, "My grace is sufficient for you, for my power is made perfect in weakness." And Paul responds, "Therefore I will boast all the more gladly about my weaknesses, so that Christ's power may rest on me."

Let God turn your weaknesses into His strength today.

MAY 6

Investing in Eternal Things

In Philippians 4 Paul writes about how the Philippian church had helped him in his time of need.

In verse 14 he writes, "It was good for you to share in my troubles." Then he continues in verse 15: "You Philippians know...when I set out from Macedonia, not one church shared with me in the matter of giving and receiving, except you only."

Paul reaches into the business world when he speaks about giving and receiving. Here he was painting a word picture that would remind his hearers of a ledger with a credit and debit page. It was as if the Philippians kept a ledger in which they recorded the good things received from Paul and also what they figured they owed to Paul. He acknowledged the receipt of their gifts in verse 18 by using a business term meaning "I have received in full."

But note what he says in verse 17: "I am not looking for a gift, but I am looking for what may be credited to your account."

The word *credit* is taken from financial language. It is used, among other things, when referring to the accumulation of interest. The word *account* is used here as we would use the term *bank account.*

The "credit" of which Paul is speaking is the reward accumulating for the Philippian Christians in the bank of heaven.

I'm not sure what's happening with your earthly bank account today, but I know everything you do in Jesus's name is going to pay dividends in the next world. Be sure to invest in what has eternal dividends.

MAY 7

God Has Something to Say to All People

In 1 Timothy 2:1–6 Paul wrote,

> I urge, then, first of all, that petitions, prayers, intercession and thanksgiving be made for all people—for kings and all those in authority, that we may live peaceful and quiet lives in all godliness and holiness. This is good, and pleases God our Savior, who wants all people to be saved and to come to a knowledge of the truth. For there is one God and one mediator between God and mankind, the man Christ Jesus, who gave himself as a ransom for all people.

Why Christ came is clearly set forth in these six verses. The little word *all* appears six times and seems to tie the entire message together.

Look at verse 1, in which Paul writes, "first of all," which speaks of the priority of the message. There's nothing in the world, in the sight of God, more important than the message of the gospel, which encompasses "prayers for all" and "prayer of every kind for all people." This has always been vital in the work of the gospel. More important than preaching is the power of prayer behind it.

In verse 2 the words *all in authority* speak of prominent people. The Bible teaches in several places that we should pray for all in authority, which is something the Christian church may overlook. It's easy to be critical of those in authority, but the Bible says we must pray for them.

The passage continues by saying, "We should lead peaceful and quiet lives in all godliness and holiness." This speaks of peace, the kind of inner peace so many are missing today.

In verse 4 is the phrase *who wants all people to be saved.* This is a tremendous *all,* for it tells of the desire of the heart of God that no soul should be lost for eternity.

The words in verse 6 *who gave himself a ransom for all* speak of God's perfect plan through Jesus, who gave His blessed life and shed His precious blood as a ransom for every individual. He is perfect. God's plan for salvation is perfect. But people are imperfect and can miss God's plan by not receiving Jesus into their lives.

Verse 1 refers to the four kinds of petitions: *petitions* (asking or begging prayers), *prayers* (simple communication with God), *intercessions* (praying for others), and *thankfulness* (thanking God for all His blessings, even when circumstances at the moment do not seem to be filled with much blessing).

Do your prayers fall into these four categories?

MAY 8

Paul, a Servant of Christ

In Romans 1:1 Paul calls himself "a servant of Christ Jesus." Do you ever think of yourself as a servant? What is a servant anyway?

The New Testament contains six different Greek words that can be translated as "servant." One refers to a person captured in war and then sold as a slave. Another refers to a household servant like a maid or a butler. Another refers to a person who simply helps someone in need.

The word that the Holy Spirit led Paul to use is the same one found in the book of Philemon. Philemon had a servant by the name of Onesimus. By definition, *servant* means "one who is bound to another, one born into slavery, one who is pledged to his master until death." This word is the one Paul found most descriptive of his devotion to Jesus. He saw himself as being bound to Christ. Nothing could force him to reject Jesus.

Paul was born into this servant role at the time of his conversion. And further, he saw it as a commitment unto death. To be a servant to someone who was a heartless taskmaster, with all the misery and cruelty that it would consist of, is one thing. But to be a servant of Jesus, with all the implications of fellowship with one's master and the high privilege of serving the Lord of Glory, is quite another.

Jesus, who was Himself the greatest of all servants, is also the greatest of all to serve. Serve Him today with all your heart, soul, mind, and strength.

MAY 9

Concentrate on Your Personal Development

In 1 Timothy 4:15-16 we read, "Be diligent in these matters, give yourself wholly to them, so that everyone may see your progress. Watch your life and doctrine closely. Persevere in them, because if you do you will save both yourself and your hearers."

Paul often viewed the Christian life as a battle to win or a race to run. Whichever picture he used, he always taught that success was based upon discipline.

Timothy was young, but not too young to be disciplined in his godly walk. He must live so that no one could look down on him for his youth. Rather, he must be an example in word, his manner of life, his chastity, his spirit, in truth, and in purity. He must meditate upon these things and give himself wholly to them. There could be no looking back, no slacking off. His eyes must always be fixed on the goal ahead.

In verse 16 Paul gives a note of challenge and warning: "Watch your life and doctrine closely. Persevere in them." The Amplified Bible says, "Concentrate on your personal development." One of the signs of a well-disciplined athlete is his or her persistence and focus on the goal. It is the determination to keep on keeping on when others give up.

This power of continuing, or what you might call "stickability," is the real key to all success. You can always find believers who had enough enthusiasm to start a project such as personal Bible reading or personal prayer for those in need. And yet at times their determination seemed to fade.

Enthusiasm is easily aroused, but that's not enough. There has to be a sense of utter daily "yieldedness" to Christ, to His indwelling Spirit, and an awareness of 1 Corinthians 6:19—"You are not your own, but you are bought with a price."

I am not the one who "calls the shots" in my life—I am owned by another. My challenge is to concentrate on my personal development.

The fact that you are reading this book indicates your desire for personal growth in Christ.

MAY 10

Fellowship Forever

It is a wonderful thing to feel that you belong, that you are a part of something, to sense that you really have a friend, someone who understands and loves you.

In 1 John 1:3-7 listen to the apostle's words:

> We proclaim to you what we have seen and heard, so that you also may have *fellowship* with us. And our *fellowship* is with the Father, and with His Son, Jesus Christ. We write this to make our joy complete. This is the message we have heard from Him and declare to you: God is Light, in Him there is no darkness at all. If we claim to have *fellowship* with Him yet walk in darkness, we lie and do not live by the truth. But if we walk in the light, as He is in the Light, we have *fellowship* with one another, and the blood of Jesus, His Son, purifies us from all sin. (emphasis added)

Four times in these five verses John uses the word *fellowship,* which suggests unity, a oneness. The key idea is that of partnership.

Here is a sense of belonging that transcends any other fellowship known to humanity. One person has defined *fellowship* as two *fellows* in the same *ship.* It is two or more people united under one purpose.

Christians have a heavenly source that creates their oneness. We are able to have fellowship with each other because we have fellowship with Christ.

Remember today wherever you are: you are a part of an earthly yet eternal fellowship.

MAY 11

The Fight of Faith

In 1 Timothy 6:12 Paul says to his young convert, "Fight the good fight of the faith." The Greek word for *fight* here was a term used in athletics. It meant not only to fight but to *keep on* fighting. It's a word from which we get our English word *agonize,* applied not only to athletes but to soldiers as well. It describes a person straining and giving his or her best to win the prize or win the battle. It means to contend for victory to strive as in a contest, straining every nerve in an attempt to reach the goal. Does that ever describe your life?

The early Christians were well acquainted with athletic terms. For the Greeks, athletic games were well known in the large cities of the Roman Empire. The Greek stadium was a very familiar sight to these early followers of Christ.

The biblical writers used common words to illustrate in a vivid way the purpose and the activity that should characterize Christian living and service. We are not to be surprised when the life of a believer encounters challenges of all kinds.

In the twenty-first century our national football games give us a good example of the physical struggle exemplified in ancient competition. We are all aware of the fact that football players do not start playing football the first day of the season. But for weeks in advance of the first kickoff, they are running, throwing, blocking, working hard in preparation for the first game.

Paul is trying to make the point that if we Christians would live our lives with the same intensity of an athlete, we could have a tremendous influence in our world for God.

Near the end of his life Paul wrote, "I have fought a good fight" (2 Timothy 4:7). My prayer is that we can all say the same at the end of our own lives. Remember: it is always too soon to quit.

MAY 12

You Are God's Treasured Possession

In 1 Timothy 6:1–2 Paul writes,

> All who are under the yoke of slavery should consider their masters worthy of full respect, so that God's name and our teaching may not be slandered. Those who have believing masters should not show them disrespect just because they are fellow believers. Instead, they should serve them even better because their masters are dear to them as fellow believers and are devoted to the welfare of their slaves. These are the things you are to teach and insist on.

In the days when Paul wrote those words, conditions were very different from what they are today. Many of the early Christians were slaves and a few of them were wealthy masters, rich in land and servants, probably more than even in money. Class distinction was far more prominent. And this difference would cause obvious difficulties among members of the church whom Timothy was left to guide at Ephesus.

Servants were to honor their masters, and masters were to treat their servants with respect and decency. Paul stresses the fact that riches are not the answer to our needs, but "godliness with contentment is great gain" (1 Timothy 6:6).

This "great gain" is twofold, first to God and then to the one who is practicing godliness. The Jews believed that ownership of riches and possessions was a sign of divine blessing, and a person with them was received with great respect. But Paul wrote in 1 Corinthians 1:26, "Brothers and sisters, think of what you were when you were called. Not many of you were wise by human standards; not many were influential; not many were of noble birth."

Today our attitude toward possessions seems to be focused on what we can do with them. In the early church the emphasis was not on the riches of people but rather on the riches of God. Rich men were not sought after but took their place with the rest of the people. It was the lives of the members and not so much their possessions that mattered most.

Friend, your life is more important than what you have. It's what you are that really counts. You are "his treasured possession" (Deuteronomy 14:2).

MAY 13

Suffering with Him

In 2 Timothy 1:7 we read, "God did not give us a spirit of timidity, but the spirit of power, of love, and of self-discipline."

In this passage Paul impresses on Timothy the need to be an unashamed witness and stresses the fact that there should be an absence of fear.

This does not mean there are no fearful circumstances and conditions, but that God has not given us the spirit of timidity or fear. Fear there may be, but God did not put it there—He gave us the spirit of power and love and self-discipline. Satan is the father of lies, and he is the author of fears. So if you have fears, recognize where they came from. A fearful Christian is a joyless Christian—and a joyless Christian is a useless Christian with no testimony or witness that exalts Jesus.

Paul uses the word *ashamed* three times in this chapter, the most famous use in verse 12, in which he writes, "I am not ashamed, for I know whom I have believed."

Paul was not afraid to confess his Lord. In verse 8 he admonished Timothy to "not be ashamed of our Lord, nor me His prisoner."

Timothy was likely a timid soul and Paul was always urging him on, seeking to strengthen him. He calls on him to join him in suffering for the gospel.

The word for *suffering* here literally means "suffering evil with." It means going beside and suffering also. This is what Moses did. It is what Paul calls Timothy to do. And it is what Christ calls you and me to do, to be prepared to stand alongside Him and to share the evil attacks, to share the pressure for His sake.

As Jesus said in Luke 9:23, "If anyone wishes to follow Me [as My disciple], he must deny himself [set aside selfish interests], and take up his cross daily [expressing a willingness to endure whatever may come] and follow Me [believing in Me, conforming to My example in living and, if need be, suffering or perhaps dying because of faith in Me]" (AMP).

"If we endure we will also reign with Him" (2 Timothy 2:12). Hold steady.

MAY 14

God Hears What You Say

Do you consider yourself a "religious" person? The word *religious* in the New Testament denotes the scrupulous observance of what you say and do in relationship to the God you serve.

Do you continuously screen your activities by asking, "Is this pleasing to God?"

Notice the words of James 1:26: "If anyone considers himself religious and yet does not keep a tight rein on his tongue, he deceives himself and his religion is worthless."

Here James is saying a Christian is to put a bridle on his or her own mouth. The believer is to show self-discipline in all actions, especially in what he or she says.

Do you remember the last time you started to say something but stopped? You thought about it and decided to be quiet. That's a picture of what James is talking about.

Christians are not only anxious to do to others what they would have done to them, but also to say about others what they would have said about them.

Today I encourage you not to deceive yourself, not to make your religion worthless. Watch what you say—God is listening!

MAY 15

Payday Someday

In Romans 6:23 we read, "The wages of sin is death, but the gift of God is eternal life through Christ Jesus our Lord."

Supposed I said I wanted you to work for me and you could do anything you wanted—no restrictions—but when payday came, you would have to give me your life. That's right—you would have to die. That doesn't sound very good, does it?

Well, that's what the Bible says Satan does. The word *wages* here refers to a soldier's pay. It was a meager amount, just enough to keep him going. That's what Satan does—he gives just enough pleasure, just enough profit to keep you going in his direction. But when payday really comes, he offers *eternal death.* Not a very good deal, huh?

Paul shares the good news, that there is an alternative, a better way, for "the gift of God is eternal life through Christ Jesus our Lord." God has made a payday also for that person who chooses to do God's will. It is the promise of blessing in this life and in the world to come—*eternal life.*

You would think everyone would serve God, because everyone wants eternal life. But the sad fact is that many are deceived by the devil. That's one of his greatest talents—he's a deceiver.

Satan's promises are many, his rewards are few, and at the longest they are short lived.

Jesus's promises are numerous, His rewards are many, and at the shortest they are *long* lived.

Remember, friend: payday is coming someday—for both the sinner and the Christian.

MAY 16

God's Word Is God's Will

In 2 Timothy 3:14–15 we read, "Continue in what you have learned and have become convinced of, because you know those from whom you learned it, and how from infancy you have known the Holy Scriptures, which are able to make you wise for salvation through faith in Christ Jesus."

Paul had earlier called on Timothy to be an approved workman for the way he handled the Word of God (2 Timothy 2:15) so that he could strengthen and build up others in the faith.

Now beginning in verse 14, Paul seems to reverse the whole procedure. Timothy was to work with the Scriptures, but they, in turn, were to work on him. Timothy must continue in the things he had learned and been convinced of. *Convinced* here literally means "made steady." All the things he had learned had served among other things to make him steady and effective in God's work.

In verse 15 Paul tells how Timothy had known the Holy Scriptures from childhood. He had learned his first lessons from his mother, Eunice, and his grandmother Lois. At the time Paul wrote, Timothy represented Paul. Important as that might be, he would never reach the place at which he could dispense with the study of Scripture. Paul knew this was essential to Timothy's success as a man of God. How much more is the Word of God necessary for us today!

Verse 16 says, "All Scripture is God-breathed," given by the inspiration of God. Friend, do you believe that? Do you believe the Scriptures are inspired by God? I trust you do. Scripture is profitable for doctrine, reproof, correction, and instruction in righteousness. We cannot base our Christian behavior on the pattern of a man or a church. Scripture alone is the authority by which we should measure our lives and conduct.

You see, friend, you are not really serious about God's will until you are serious about God's Word. God's Word is God's will.

MAY 17

Faithful to the Word

In 2 Timothy 4:1–5 Paul writes,

> I give you this charge: Preach the Word, be prepared in season and out of season, correct, rebuke, and encourage, with great patience, and careful instruction. For the time will come when men will not put up with sound doctrine. Instead, to suit their own desires, they will gather around them a great number of teachers to say what their itching ears want to hear. They will turn their ears away from the truth, and turn aside to myths. But you, keep your head in all situations, endure hardships, do the work of an evangelist, discharge all the duties of your ministry.

In verse 1 Paul puts a solemn charge upon Timothy, almost as if he is entrusting Timothy with the responsibility of carrying on his own life's work. In verse 2 he says, "Preach the Word in season and out of season." That is, he must always be alert, ready to reprove, rebuke, and exhort. But notice it must be with patience and careful instruction.

In verses 3–4 we find that even though we preach the truth, some people turn away and accept myths. How many people have itching ears, always ready to listen to anything, to believe anything other than the Word of God? The phrase *having itching ears* literally means "having the hearing tickled." The ear-tickler designs the message to communicate what the audience wants to hear.

History tells us that Paul was beheaded as a criminal, in the eyes of the world a useless end to a fruitful life. But Paul apparently thought otherwise. For in verse 6 he wrote, "I am now ready to be offered." He had lived his life for Christ and his death was a natural continuation of his living as anything else. He wrote, "To me to live is Christ, and to die is gain." His death was going to magnify Christ just as his life had done.

You see, Paul had made up his mind that he was going to serve God regardless of the cost. Ask yourself: Am I willing to serve God regardless of the cost? I pray, friend that you have made the same decision Paul did.

MAY 18

Jesus's Parade

In 2 Corinthians 2:14 we read these words of Paul: "Thanks be to God who always leads us in triumphal procession in Christ."

The words *triumphal procession* would instantly bring to Paul's readers and hearers the mental image of a parade, that of a military hero returning to his hometown after a successful conflict. It would consist of the city officials followed by trumpeters, next the spoils taken from the enemy, followed by white oxen intended for later sacrifice. Next, the conquered king and his people marched in the processional. Toward the end would appear the officials of the victorious army and musicians dancing and playing. Finally would be the general himself, in whose honor the entire pageant was taking place.

Here Paul pictures victorious Christians as soldiers marching ahead of the victorious general. The symbolism is very clear: Jesus Christ is the general we are marching with. We have pledged our undying support to His cause. And that cause is to win as many as possible, as fast as possible, to the purposes of God.

Romans 8:37 says, "We are more than conquerors." Think of it. The best an earthly conqueror could have ends in death. But we have a parade that will march right through the grandstands of eternity. I don't want to miss that parade!

MAY 19

The Holy Spirit in You

In 1 Corinthians 2:15 we read, "The spiritual man makes judgments about all things." But in Matthew 7:1 we read, "Do not judge, or you too will be judged."

Sometimes scripture seems to be contradictory—but what at first appears to be in conflict can turn out to be complimentary.

How can these two verses be harmonized? When Jesus in Matthew said, "Do not judge," the Greek reveals more than the word *judge* communicates. Here it has to do with the spirit of a person. In Matthew, Jesus is saying not to have a sharp, unjust, critical spirit.

Paul, on the other hand, was encouraging the Corinthians at times to make judgments. He wanted them to examine, to evaluate, to call to account, to discern. And this was made possible by the Spirit of Christ within the believers. For Paul is saying the spiritual person is able to consider and appraise all things because they are not only inspired to understand what they see but are also furnished with a moral standard—the Word of God, by which all things may be measured The Word enables us to see what God sees.

It is a wise Christian who guards his or her spirit when making judgments. Be sure today that no one can fault the spirit with which you do anything. Let His Holy Spirit control your human spirit.

MAY 20

Simple Faith

I remember being in Bedford, Indiana, home of Bedford stone, a native stone shipped hundreds of miles to customers all over the country. I watched as bulldozers pushed the rock scraps into a waiting disposal area. I saw hundreds of massive boulders bigger than semi-trailers stacked like wooden blocks. It looked like a range of manmade mountains.

Hundreds of hours and scores of bulldozers, cranes, and other machinery had been used to assemble the quarried rock. Can you imagine the looks on the faces of those workers if I had simply said, "Bedford stones, move five hundred feet to the left"? Why, those workers would have fainted in disbelief!

In Matthew 17 Jesus told the disciples they did not have the power they could have because of their little faith. In verse 20 He said, "Truly I tell you, if you have faith as small as a mustard seed, you can say to this mountain, 'Move from here to there,' and it will move. Nothing will be impossible for you."

Sometimes we as Christians pull out the "heavy machinery" of our own making to move boulders that are in the way. We try to figure out why "So and So" did what he or she did. We wonder how a certain relationship could ever be mended. We may talk to our friends and even pray about these challenges. And all the time Christ has given us the key to moving obstacles: *simple faith.* What obstacle have you been working on lately? What machinery have you been working with? Have you tried faith yet?

Don't be fretful about the faith you don't have. Simply act on the faith you *do* have!

MAY 21

Saying vs Doing

In Titus 1:10–11 Paul wrote, "There are many rebellious people, mere talkers and deceivers. . . . They must be silenced, because they are ruining whole households by teaching this they ought not to teach."

Paul speaks out very forcibly as he writes thoughts to Titus. In this entire epistle of forty-six verses, the phrase *good work* appears five times. Obviously Paul thought the people of Crete needed special admonition. Crete was a small island well separated from the mainland. There was evidently great corruption even among professing Christians, especially among those who had come over from Judaism.

Paul is amazingly honest in describing their corruption. One of Crete's own prophets has said it: "Cretans are always liars, evil brutes, lazy gluttons."

In verse 13 he adds, "This testimony is true. Therefore, rebuke them sharply, so that they will be sound in the faith"

These people had a belief. They professed to know God. But their behavior did not correspond with their profession. By their works they denied Him. Paul's answer to this deficiency was to present the gospel in all its fullness and obligations to all those who believed.

Could we be guilty of the same offenses? Have we received Christ as Savior for our sins, yet carry on in the same way as before? Does our behavior show other people that we have been with Jesus and have learned of Him? Our manner of life is far more convincing to people than even our preaching from the pulpit.

What you do speaks louder than your words.

MAY 22

God Is Speaking. Are You Listening?

Matthew 2:1–2 says, "Jesus was born in Bethlehem of Judea during the time of King Herod. Magi from the east came to Jerusalem and asked 'Where is the one who has been born King of the Jews?'"

One of the remarkable things of the story of the wise men is that when they inquired where the King was to be born, the authorities were able to say immediately that it was in Bethlehem. The chief priests and scribes knew all this, but they did nothing about it. It was left to Gentile strangers from afar to welcome the Christ child, who was God's gift for Israel.

The educated Jews knew from scriptures that God's special man would be born of a virgin in Bethlehem and that He would be despised and rejected. They knew of the prophecy regarding Judas and the thirty pieces of silver.

But the tragedy is that although they knew all these things and were proud of their knowledge, it made no difference in their daily lives. It was merely head knowledge. It had never touched their hearts. They did not relate God's truths to situations in which they were living and to the Christ whom they were rejecting.

Do you see the Word of God relating to you right now, right where you live, where you work? The Word of God is as contemporary as tomorrow's news. Don't miss what God is saying to you.

Ask yourself: What is God saying to me these days?

He's speaking—are you listening?

MAY 23

Jesus at Birth: King, Priest, and Savior

In Matthew 2:11 we read, "On coming to the house, they [the wise men] saw the child with his mother Mary, and they bowed down and worshiped him. Then they opened their treasures and presented him with gifts of gold, frankincense and myrrh."

Gold was viewed as the most precious metal during the day of Christ's birth. It stood for all that was glorious and majestic. The wise men's first gift recognized Jesus's right to rule. How incongruous it must have seemed to them in this humble surrounding to try to create an atmosphere of a palace! Our service for Christ and His church may often seem lowly and unspectacular—but it is more valuable than gold to Christ if our hearts are surrendered to Him.

The second gift was frankincense, which suggested the office of a priest, who with His incense was the mediator between humanity and God. God was holy and humanity was sinful. Therefore humanity needed one appointed by God to act as an intermediary. Jesus is our great priest—our "go-between." He came to open up the way to God for all people.

How strange it is to realize that one of the gifts Christ received, as well as the last gift He received, was myrrh! Thirty-three years later, in John 19:39, Nicodemus brought a mixture of myrrh and aloes to the cross. With Joseph of Arimathea he wrapped the body of our Lord in spices with strips of linen.

In Exodus 30 we have the instructions for making the holy anointing oil. And the principal ingredient was myrrh. This oil was most holy—whatever it touched became holy. Myrrh represented Christ's atoning death, a death that could cleanse away sin and make whoever believed on Him clean and holy in God's sight.

Gold represented His kingship, incense His priesthood, and myrrh His sacrificial death as our Savior. Praise God for His complete plan in His Son, Jesus!

I doubt the wise men knew all they were doing when they brought the gifts. But God was working mightily all the time. Do you think God might be doing something in your life you never dreamed of? How exciting!

MAY 24

God Knows Who You Are

In Mark 5:23 a synagogue ruler named Jairus came to Jesus and fell at His feet. He pleaded earnestly with Jesus: "My little daughter is dying. Please come and put Your hands on her so that she will be healed and live."

Jairus, we are told, was a ruler of the synagogue, whose duties included conducting the synagogue worship and selection of those to lead in prayer, read scriptures, and to preach. His only child was dying, and in desperation he came to Jesus. Nicodemus came by night, but Jairus pushed through the vast crowd in the daytime to reach the one he believed could help him. Jesus agreed and went with him to his home.

On the way to Jairus's home, a woman who had been bleeding for twelve years was healed simply because she touched the garment of Jesus. Jairus must have felt further encouraged, but at that moment he received a message that his child was already dead.

Did he still want Jesus to come to his house, believing He could restore his daughter to life? Or was he simply too upset to care what happened? God knew what the desire of his father heart was. And that measure of faith was rewarded.

We never hear Jairus's name mentioned again, but that miracle must have transformed his household. Often we wonder why God pulls a curtain over the future happenings of such people. Only in heaven will we learn of the work and witness carried on by many whose lives were touched by His hands. Surely they will be included among those we read of in Acts 17.

In Acts 17:6 the jealous Jews said, "These people who have been turning the world upside down have come here also" (NRSV). We know some of the names of those early followers, but many of them are not mentioned by name. Many living for Christ were unknown, not spectacular but faithful. They will also one day hear Jesus's words "Well done, good and faithful servant" (Matthew 25:23).

Undoubtedly, there will be more "faithful servants," whose names we did not know on earth. Be a "faithful servant." God knows your name and He sees what you are doing.

MAY 25

Committed

In John 3:1 we read, "There was a man of the Pharisees named Nicodemus, a member of the Jewish ruling counsel. He came to Jesus at night."

Nicodemus is described as a Pharisee and a ruler of the Jews, that is, he was a member of the Sanhedrin. He came to Jesus by night, perhaps because he feared the scorn of his fellow Pharisees, or perhaps he wanted to have Jesus to himself. Whatever the reason, he obviously was a man in earnest who was attracted by the character and teaching of Jesus.

Nicodemus speaks four times and every time he is asking a question. The first question is not really recorded, but there must have been one because we are told of Jesus's answer in verse 3. Nicodemus was a teacher, a learned man versed in the Scriptures, but he did not understand the things Jesus spoke. To him "You must be born again" was a confusing statement. Jesus knew the thoughts of Nicodemus and that his greatest need was to forget his position, his learning, his preconceived ideas, and to become again like a little child.

We are not told what Nicodemus's decision was at that point, for we hear nothing more of him until John 7, when he protests against the condemnation of Jesus without giving Him a hearing.

The last time we hear of him is after the crucifixion, when he brings a gift of myrrh and aloes for the body of Jesus. It appears that Nicodemus must have been a secret believer. We can only admire his final burst of courage as he was willing to be identified with this man who died on a cross.

He was committed to Christ without understanding everything that was going on. Are *you* committed to Jesus in the face of things you cannot understand?

MAY 26

Believing

In John 20:25 we have these words from Thomas: "Unless I see the nail marks in His hands and put my finger where the nails were, and put my hand into His side, I will not believe."

This account takes place on the second Sunday after the resurrection. Thomas had missed a great experience on Easter Sunday when the other disciples had seen the risen Christ. He had made up his mind what he would believe. He had heard the testimony of the others and heard the words of Jesus, but as with so many of us, he wanted visible proof. Jesus knew the questions that had been in Thomas's mind and even stopped to answer them. What a change this brought about! Thomas met the risen Christ face to face, and all the doubts vanished. In breathless adoration he exclaimed, "My Lord and my God!"

Many of us are challenged by the claims of Jesus but are not changed. A preacher can reach the conscience but not the will. Only God Himself can reach the citadel of a person's will, because this is the last part of us that we ever want to give up.

Are you faced with doubts? Do you say like Thomas, "Unless I can see with my eyes, understand with my mind, I will not believe"? No one can understand God's will and God's plan totally. Faith, my friend, holds out empty hands for God to fill. Believing is a choice.

MAY 27

Grow in Grace and Knowledge

In 2 Peter 3:18 Simon Peter writes, "Grow in the grace and knowledge of our Lord and Savior Jesus Christ."

The primary concern of every Christian is to glorify God and then to know Christ better. If we are not careful, we can begin to put major emphasis upon minor issues. We can focus so much on what we are *not* to do that we lose our primary business of simply imitating Christ.

Sometimes when making decisions we get very concerned about guidance, for we want to know God's will and don't want to waste a moment. But in the process we can be so concerned about guidance that we fail to give primary concern to the Guide—but it is the Guide we need to seek even more than the guidance.

The word *Christian* includes the suffix *-ian.* Webster's dictionary says that the suffixes *-ian* and *-an* refer to someone or something that is *of* or *belongs to* something else.

For example, an American is someone who is associated with, or belongs to, America. A Christian is someone associated directly with Jesus and belongs to Him.

Peter is telling Christians, people who belong to Christ, to grow in grace and knowledge of Him. That is a very encouraging thing to me. To think that Peter's words, written to Christians and directing them to increase in grace and knowledge, are just as possible for twenty-first-century Christians as for those early followers!

Peter's words are my prayer for you and me today: *O God, help us to grow in grace and knowledge of Your Son, Jesus Christ.*

MAY 28

What Is That in Your Hand?

It is a familiar Bible story of how Moses was used by God to deliver his people from Egyptian bondage. Moses was somewhat hesitant to strike out immediately on his challenging assignment. He wondered if the people would accept him, if they would really believe he was commissioned by God.

Read these words from Exodus 4:1–4:

> Moses answered, "What if they do not believe me or listen to me and say, 'The LORD did not appear to you'?" Then the LORD said to him, "What is that in your hand?" "A staff," he replied. The LORD said, "Throw it on the ground." Moses threw it on the ground and it became a snake, and he ran from it. Then the LORD said to him, "Reach out your hand and take it by the tail." So Moses reached out and took hold of the snake and it turned back into a staff in his hand.

There are three things I want you to see in this passage. First, God asked Moses, "What is that in your hand?" Just an ordinary rod—that's all. Second, God said, "Throw it on the ground." Finally, God said, "Pick it up."

God took what Moses had, worked on it, gave it back to him, and then Moses was equipped for whatever was ahead.

Do you hear God asking you, "What is that in your hand?" Give it to Him—He has plans for you.

There's a pattern for us. God asks all of us what He asked Moses in verse 2: "What is that in your hand?" Next God tells us to give Him what we have—and then note: He gives back to us what we give Him because now we use it on God's terms. We give to God and God gives to us and we always get the best end of the deal.

As you go through this day, be sure to listen closely. God may ask you, "What is that in your hand?"

MAY 29

When Jesus Passes By

In Luke 19:1–5 we read this account:

> Jesus entered Jericho and was passing through. A man was there by the name of Zacchaeus; he was a chief tax collector and was wealthy. He wanted to see who Jesus was, but because he was short he could not see over the crowd. So he ran ahead and climbed a sycamore-fig tree to see him, since Jesus was coming that way. When Jesus reached the spot, he looked up and said to him, "Zacchaeus, come down immediately. I must stay at your house today."

Here we have one of the great pluses of life. Notice Zacchaeus had a number of obstacles to overcome to see Jesus. First, there was a big crowd gathered because Jesus was passing by. Next, since Zacchaeus was a chief tax collector, the crowd was not particularly fond of him. Additionally, the entire situation was complicated by the fact that Zacchaeus was a short man.

The great plus, the great surprise of it all, was that Jesus shocked Zacchaeus out of his skull—for the Christ, the Son of God, had seen the "wee little man" named Zacchaeus.

Are you ever tempted to feel that the Christian life is too much of a hassle? In the midst of all your other responsibilities you need to take time to read, pray, go to church—I mean, it's just a lot of effort, isn't it? But wait a minute. After all that Zacchaeus did to see Jesus, fighting the crowd, climbing the tree—the Master's eyes connected with his.

I encourage you today to do the things you know to do. There is a great plus in store for you—because Jesus is about to pass by. Today you too may get to look into His eyes.

MAY 30

God's Training Program

In 1 Corinthians 9:24–25 we read, "Do you not know that in a race all the runners run, but only one gets a prize? Run in such a way as to get the prize. Everyone who competes in the games goes into strict training. They do it to get a crown [a laurel oak leaf], that will not last but we do it to get a crown that will last forever."

This passage is one of the key references in which Paul refers to the Greek games. The word *race* in verse 24 is from a Greek word that comes over into our language in the word *stadium.* Here Paul is using the figure of a race to illustrate the life of a Christian.

The words *strict training* refer to the ten-month preparatory training and practice done before the games ever begin. Much of the athlete's discipline was centered not only on his physical activity but also in the food he would eat.

Paul is saying to us that if an athlete goes through ten months of rigorous training, involving rigid self-denial in order to compete in a contest that may last only a few minutes or a few hours at most, and for a prize, a simple laurel of oak leaves—should not the Christian be willing to subject himself or herself to just as much rigid discipline and self-denial that he or she might serve the Lord Jesus to the fullest and obtain a crown that will last forever?

How are you doing with God's training program?

MAY 31

Forgetting the Past

Yesterday we talked about the Greek athlete and his extensive training with the ultimate goal of getting a crown that would not last. Paul uses the fading oak leaf prize in contrast to the unfading victor's crown, which the Christian will wear someday.

Paul speaks of the Greek runner who speeds down the race course, not uncertainly but straight as an arrow for the goal. Likewise, a Christian should run the race, refusing to allow anyone or anything to turn him or her from the consuming desire that Jesus is preeminent in the Christian's life.

In Philippians 3:13–14, Paul writes, "One thing I do, forgetting what is behind and straining toward what is ahead, I press on toward the goal, to win the prize."

Here we catch a glimpse of Paul's knowledge of racing technique. He uses the illustration of a runner "straining toward what is ahead." That is literally "Pursuing toward the mark for the prize." See him racing down the track— he forgets the things which are behind. Here the Greek is saying "completely forgetting" what is behind.

Paul knew that the moment the Greek runner thought of the men behind him and the sounds of their approaching feet, his own speed would be slackened. So he presses home the lesson that when God's children think of their past failures, the things they should have done but failed to do, or the things they did but should not have done, their onward progress in the Christian life is hindered. When a Christian has made things right with God and his or her fellow man, the proper thing to do is to forget the past and press on to the future.

Is there anything you need to forget about your past?

JUNE 1

What Troubles You Today?

What bothers you? What really gets under your skin?

Years ago there was a young man by the name of David. The nation of Israel was literally being put to shame by one man: Goliath. David could not believe the situation. He was troubled that a godless giant could intimidate the followers of the true God. David was so troubled that he did something about it.

The man Elijah lived during a wicked time in history. Ahab and Jezebel led God's people into misguided worship. Four-hundred fifty prophets of Baal were free to influence thousands. Elijah stood up against the powers of Satan. Yes, Elijah was troubled and did something about it.

Amos was a prophet. He could hardly contain himself as he saw the sins of God's once-holy people. Amos cried out to the people, "Listen to this funeral song that I sing about you, people of Israel" (Amos 5:1). Amos was troubled and he did something about it.

In the New Testament, Paul was called upon to perform a tremendous task. The gospel had primarily been a message for the Jews. But now Paul carried it out to the Gentiles and virtually the entire world. Paul was troubled about the spread of the gospel and he did something about it.

What is it that troubles you today? Is it that your church does not get enough volunteers to care for the children? Is it that very few are interested in prayer? Is it that many are quick to let someone else do the work? Is it that people seem to feel no passion for witnessing? Is it that you do not have a sense of belonging? Is it an uncertain future?

David, Elijah, Amos, and Paul were all troubled men—and they did something about it.

Friends, chances are that whatever troubles *you,* God wants you to do something constructive about it. He has burdened you for a purpose?

JUNE 2

Seeking His Face

In 2 Chronicles 7:14 we read, "If my people which are called by my name will humble themselves and pray and seek my face, and turn from their wicked ways, then will I hear from heaven and will forgive their sin, and will heal their land" (KJV).

This is God speaking a challenge to His own people. But, friend, are we Christians not God's people? Though the words were first spoken to Israel, does that diminish their challenge to us? The Jews certainly are God's people, chosen in Abraham, and they constituted a special divine inheritance in all the nations. But in a far more profound spiritual sense, it is the blood-bought and Spirit-born people of Christ who are God's people.

The Bible says we were chosen before the foundation of the world. We, the body of Christ, are His chosen people. The great need of the hour in which we live is for true believers to seek a fresh awareness of the Holy Spirit, to give themselves to a regular persevering intensive ministry of prayer.

Prayer is the invisible determining power that shapes the course and destinies of people, movements, and even nations. Many professing Christians know all too little about the power of prayer. The prayers of many never break beyond their own personal needs or those of their families. There are comparatively few who know anything about engaging in prayer as the spiritual warfare that is discussed in the book of Ephesians.

The writings of Paul reveal how intense his own personal warfare was. All the men and women who have had great power for Christ on this earth have been men and women who have prayed.

Yes, 2 Chronicles 7:14 says, "If my people will do their part, and seek my face," God says, "I will heal their land" (author's translation).

As we seek His face and draw near to Him, healing will be on the way.

JUNE 3

Christ in You

In Galatians 5:22 we read, "The fruit of the spirit is love, joy, peace, patience, kindness, goodness, faithfulness, gentleness, and self-control."

Now I know you've heard those words many times, but ask yourself a question. In the context of this verse, what is *fruit*?

Often we hear the word *fruit* used in the context of service. We remember that people will be known by the fruit they bear and the works they do. But fruit (here in Galatians 5) is not primarily service related. Fruit is not so much what we do. Look closer at the nine fold cluster: love, joy, peace, patience, kindness, goodness, faithfulness, gentleness, and self-control. Although all of these are expressed through behavior, something far deeper than service is meant in these words. For here we are talking about *character,* or what a person is, not just what a person does. As a matter of fact, we are talking about Christlike character.

And this is a very encouraging thing for two reasons. First, as you see this fruit in your life, it is an inner testimony and an inner witness to the indwelling presence of the living Christ. Christ expressed *through* you is an assurance of Christ living *in* you.

Second, fruit is enlarged through growth. Don't be discouraged if your fruit is not as mature as you would like. Just keep faithful, feed on God's Word, and as a result the character of His Son, Jesus Christ, will shine through you more and more each day.

JUNE 4

Doing Your Best

In Ephesians 2:10 we read of the good works that God has before ordained and that we should walk in them. "For we are God's handiwork, created in Christ Jesus to do good works, which God prepared in advance for us to do."

You see, God has a plan for each life. Now this tremendous truth, when firmly grasped, can have a revolutionary impact upon our thinking and living. Everything that happens to us becomes recognized as a foreseen contribution to the development in the plan of God. It is tragically easy to miss God's envisioned plan for us.

Besides God's original plan for us, there is His permissive plan. Never for a moment must we think that everything that happens to human beings is predetermined by God. God never predetermined sin or disobedience as His will. But sin and suffering belong in this lower level of things that God allows. All that God permits, however, He foresees and can overrule.

You see, God always does have a plan. Our responsibility is to get in on His plan and stay in His plan. The way to get in it and stay in it is complete and continual consecration. When we abide in Christ, our eyes become gradually open to the wonderful unfolding of the plan.

A deep and settled peace possesses us. We rest in what the Bible calls the good and acceptable and perfect will of God. When we are living according to plan, there may be many incidents, but God can work in them all. God makes no mistakes.

Another lesson we need to learn is that if we are to live out His plan, besides consecration to Christ, there must be daily consultation with Christ. He is the master of the plan in all its details. We must practice consulting Him about everything, but especially about those things that seem like frustrations, even contradictions in our lives.

A foreman on an assembly line told a new employee, "Remember: if you have a problem, send for me." Now the new worker did eventually have a problem but decided to work on it without the aid of the foreman. The problem only got worse. During a routine check, the foreman noticed that there had been a problem. He asked the new employee, "Why didn't you send for me?" In response, the worker said, "I'm sorry, but I did my best." The foremen responded, "Remember: doing your best *is* sending for me."

Today I can hear the Lord saying to us, "Remember, friend: doing your best *is* sending for Me."

JUNE 5

His Goal for Your Life

In Hebrews 12:1–2 we read, "Let us run with perseverance the race marked out for us. Let us fix our eyes on Jesus, the pioneer and perfecter of our faith."

Earlier this year we noted that *perseverance* in the New Testament means "patient endurance." It is the spirit of the person who endures hardship gladly because of the assurance that he or she is moving in the direction of eternal reward.

In this passage Jesus is called the "pioneer" of our faith. In Greek writings this word was used for a hero who founded a city, gave it its name, and became its guardian. It was used of someone who was the head of a family. The term also had a distinct military connotation, referring to a commander of an army who went ahead of his soldiers and blazed a trail for them. The idea in this passage is that we should patiently endure whatever comes our way because Jesus has already gone ahead of us. He is blazing a trail. He is making a way when there seems to be no way at all.

In verse 2 Jesus is also called the "perfecter" of our faith. By *perfecter* the Bible means "one who brings a person out to a desired goal."

Friend, it could be that right now it doesn't appear you're gaining any ground on God's goals for you. But continue to patiently endure, confident that the trailblazer, Jesus, is bringing you closer and closer to His goal for your life every single day, even today.

JUNE 6

What Has Your Attention?

Yesterday we talked about Hebrews 12:1–2. We noted that patient endurance is key to our victory, and also that Jesus, the pioneer and perfecter of our faith, is going ahead of us, making a way for us to live victoriously.

Right in the middle of this passage we have these words: "Let us fix our eyes on Jesus." That is the key that unlocks the door to victory.

In the Greek, "fixing our eyes" means looking away from one thing and concentrating on another.

Right now I want you to try something. Look at the palm of your hand. Go ahead—right now look at your palm. Can you see your elbow at the same time? Oh, perhaps with your peripheral vision you can catch a glimpse of it, but you really can't see it very well. Too many times our attention is so fixed on our problem that at best we see Jesus only with our peripheral vision. But spiritual peripheral vision is not going to lead us to victory. We must look away from the potentially defeating situation and look to Jesus.

We've heard the scripture "Where your treasure is, there your heart will be also" (Matthew 6:21). Well, it is equally true that where your attention is, there your strength will be also. If you're constantly looking at the problem ahead of you and your own personal fortitude to deal with it, then your strength is limited to yourself.

But if you change your focus, if you consciously choose to redirect your attention to Christ, then your strength is outside of yourself. You are literally linked up with the infinite resources of God.

Ask yourself: What has my attention in the situation I'm facing? Am I focusing on the problem or on the problem-solver?

JUNE 7

True Joy and Peace

In Romans 15:13 we read, "May the God of hope fill you with all joy and peace as you trust in him, so that you may overflow with hope by the power of the Holy Spirit." Here Paul talks about the joy and peace we have in believing. It is not mere wishful thinking but is a sober truth. We Christian believers are the only people on the face of the earth who have found the secret of real joy and peace. There are many others who think for a time or they feel for a moment that they have found the secret of life. But anything less than Jesus, anything less than New Testament Christianity, causes people to be deluded into thinking they have true joy when in reality it is temporary at best.

You see, in Jude 13 the lost are described as "wandering stars." In Greek this referred to a shooting star that "fell out of the sky" and was quickly engulfed in the darkness. Such is the destiny of those who trust in anything or anyone less than Christ.

Friend, let us rejoice this day that we have found such joy and peace in believing. Why is it better to have this spiritual joy and peace in our hearts than all the material possessions and embellishments that could ever come our way? Because these are treasures that will outlive the grave, outlast the years, and outshine the sunsets.

Let us rejoice. We are not deluded by conceit as that of the Pharisees, who imagined themselves as special objects of God's favor. No, let us rejoice in grateful humility and pure hearts, that to possess Jesus is grace beyond all measure.

Let us this day be prayerful concerning those who have not yet found the joy and the peace that come from believing.

JUNE 8

Keep Your Grip

In 1 Timothy 6:12 Paul says to the younger Timothy, "Take hold of eternal life" (HCSB). "Keep your grip" (PHILLIPS). Never was sounder advice given by an older man to a younger. Paul knew how glamorous this world can be to a young person. Paul would have Timothy set his mind on life eternal. He would have his young friend live for what is true and permanent. He says in effect, don't live your life just for the temporary or for a mirage. No, take hold of the real—that will last forever.

To take hold of eternal life as our text urges is in reality taking hold of Christ Himself, for He is eternal life.

"Taking hold" is a metaphor for faith. We have to take hold of Christ as a person takes hold of a discovered treasure; or as someone dying of thirst would take hold of a canteen of water that rescuers bring; or as a drowning person may take hold of a lifeline. Yes, the Greek here is saying to get a good grip on eternal life. Paul is not saying to Timothy, "Have hope in the future for eternal life." No, he is saying, "Timothy, eternal life begins right now. Take hold of it. Hold on to it right now."

We are to take hold of Christ, but how? We do so by believing His promise in John 3:36: "He that believes in the Son has everlasting life."

JUNE 9

Praying in Jesus's Name

In John 14:14 Jesus said, "You may ask me for anything in my name, and I will do it."

Here we have one of the great promises in God's Word. Note that Jesus said, "You may ask," *not* "You may think about" or "You may desire"—but "You may ask." Our Lord knew the importance of actually *asking.*

Very often, until there is specific asking, our thoughts and desires remain vague and unorganized. Asking brings our generalized thoughts into specific requests. We must be specific in our praying for God to be specific in His answering.

When Jesus said, "We may ask for anything," He gave us about as broad a promise as you could get. Did Jesus really mean what it appears He said? Of course. Jesus always means what He says, but we must meet the conditions. Not only are we to ask, but we are to ask in Jesus's name. What do you think it means to ask in Jesus's name? Do you think it means that before we say, "Amen," to our prayers we should say, "In Jesus's name we pray?" If it does, why didn't Jesus say it at the close of His model prayer (commonly called "The Lord's Prayer")? Jesus meant more than just adding a few words at the end of our requests.

The expression "in my name" is equivalent to "for my sake." Prayers offered in Jesus's name, whether the words "in Jesus's name" are used or not, are prayers in line with Jesus's purposes. Obviously, then, we cannot pray in His name for something that is not in harmony with His will.

The phrase "in my name" is not just a handle by which we turn things our own way. It is the Savior's all-inclusive condition for advancing His purposes in the world. Friend, are your prayers in Jesus's name?

JUNE 10

The Word of God: Your Guide and Your Guard

In 1 Corinthians 15:2 Paul wrote, "Keep in memory what I have preached to you" (KJV). What a world is in that one word *memory*! What rapture it can bring, or what torture!

Aristotle once described memory as "the scribe of the soul." Memory—what a valuable ally it can be to the Christian! How useful a partner that leaps to our rescue in some emergency! It brings a promise or a warning from God's holy Word.

Memory—what a ministry it can have if we use it wisely! That is why the Scriptures repeatedly exhort us to remember. There is much to be said for memorizing the words of Scripture. But we should also remember that the reading of Scripture allows its truths to sink in even when we can't remember all the exact words. Its purifying and fortifying power is beyond all estimation.

"Keep in memory what I have preached," Paul said. What was it he had in mind for the people to remember? Basically it was two things. In 1 Corinthians 15:1 he talks about remembering the gospel that he had preached. He had now been preaching the good news of Jesus for over twenty-five years. He had never veered away from the historical facts he had received from eyewitnesses or from the spiritual truths received by direct witness from God Himself.

In verse 3 he writes, "What I received I passed on to you." He had taught them both the rich spiritual provisions and the high moral challenges of the gospel. He would have them keep all these things in memory and keep on proving their dynamic power in daily living.

Second, why should we keep in memory these things? Paul tells us, "Keep in memory what I have preached to you, by which also you are saved." The master passion of all true believers is to help those who would hear them and see them to be drawn to the saving knowledge of Jesus Christ.

The word translated as *keep* is quite a forceful verb that the RSV well renders as "hold fast." Hold fast the Word. If you hold it, it will hold you. If you hold onto the Word, the Word will hold on to you. Let the Word of God be your guide, and it will be your guard.

JUNE 11

God's Silence Does Not Mean God's Absence

In John 14:1 Jesus said, "Trust in God, trust also in me." In its ultimate meaning, faith is not just believing for the forgiveness of our sins or the answering of our prayers, but also believing in Jesus Himself, because of who He is—even when our problems remain unsolved and our prayers seem unanswered.

In the book of Job we are shown that behind his great trial was a supernatural reason, a divine plan, even though Job did not know it. The point, however, is not merely that Job did not know, but that he was *not supposed* to know. If he *had* known, the very purpose of his trial would have been short circuited. God's silence was necessary for Job to develop properly—and so it is with us. If God were always explaining our trials and showing beforehand the reason for our difficulties, there would be no strengthening of our faith muscles.

The Lord wants us to trust Him regardless, to rest in His faithfulness even when we are puzzled by what He permits. Sometimes the puzzle may not be answered in this life. But trusting in Jesus brings assurance that He is working on a higher purpose.

There may be someone reading this devotional who is in great pain. It could be physical or emotional; it could be a new pain or it could be a lingering, wearying, almost mystifying frustration. Jesus says, "Trust in Me." Remember: Jesus Himself once said, "My God, why...?" Don't feel your desire to ask, "Why?" is displeasing to the Lord. He understands.

Never confuse God's silence with God's absence. He is always around.

JUNE 12

Excited about Jesus

In Acts 1:8 Jesus said, "You will be my witnesses."

The high service Jesus calls us to is that of being witnesses of Him as Savior and Lord. Witnessing is not necessarily preaching. For preaching is the exposition and application of God's written Word, whereas witnessing has to do with what we ourselves, subjectively, have proved and experienced. The indispensable qualification and prime importance of a witness is firsthand experience. It's like the healed man in John 9:25 who said, "One thing I know is that once I was blind, but now I see." It is not cleverness or education or preaching ability that constitutes a witness, but firsthand experience of whatever is being testified to.

In our law courts a witness is not asked what he or she thinks but what he or she actually knows by direct contact with the case under trial.

Friends, if we dare to be true witnesses of Jesus, we must have a firsthand, up-to-date experience with Him. We must be excited about Jesus in us.

You can't sell what you are not sold on yourself. You can't get someone else excited about something you are not excited about.

Answer this question: How excited am I about my relationship with Jesus?

JUNE 13

Jesus Hears What Is Being Said

As noted in an earlier devotional, when our Lord was on His way to heal the daughter of the synagogue ruler named Jairus, He was delayed. But meanwhile, according to Mark 5:35–36, word was received from Jairus's house: "Your daughter is dead. Why bother the teacher anymore?" Ignoring what they said, Jesus told the synagogue ruler, "Don't be afraid; just believe."

The words *ignoring what they said* can also be translated in the Greek as "overhearing what they said." Now there is a captivating idea. Jesus is always overhearing what is said.

As you reflect on that, be assured that those sudden appearances and disappearances during the forty days between His resurrection and ascension were meant to teach us this very thing. Jesus is always present. He is always overhearing, even though invisible.

In John 9 the healed blind man is cast out of the synagogue and verse 35 says, "Jesus heard," or you could say "overheard," that they had cast the man out. Jesus always overhears when one of His children is cast out.

It's interesting to note in Jairus's situation that it was not something Jairus himself said that Jesus overheard, but it was something said to him by others. Jesus overhears not only all we say to others, but also all that others say to us.

Jesus not only overheard that the people said Jairus's daughter was dead—he also overruled what they said. He spoke the word, and death had to flee.

Whatever you face today, remember: Jesus knows, He is overhearing, and when the time is right, He will overrule.

JUNE 14

Studying God's Word

I have hundreds of books in my personal library (not to mention the nearly three thousand on my computer), but there are two I refer to more than any others. The first is the Bible and the second is a dictionary. To be aware of their contents, I must do one basic thing—study them. Reading them is not enough by itself (although essential).

John 5:39 says, "Diligently study the scriptures." The thrust of the message here is that we should search or investigate the Scriptures. No casual or hurried reading is suggested here, but a thorough examination of Scripture truth.

Too many Christians limit their reading to books *about* the Bible or the use of devotional aids (such as this book). However, these are only helps and should never become substitutes for the personal study of God's Word itself.

Paul said to the Corinthian believers in 1 Corinthians 3:1–2, "You are mere infants in Christ. I gave you milk and not solid food."

Could it be that one of the reasons some Christians look to the past for their best days spiritually is because the milk of the Word was so satisfying? But today they cannot mature on infant food—they need to go deeper.

One tool that can help you go deeper is a good study Bible. Ask your pastor to suggest a good one. In Bible times the culture, language, and even geography had influence on the meaning of Scripture. Although commentaries and study notes must not replace your reading of the Word, they can give background information that will add to your own study.

You say, "Hey—that sounds like work; that sounds like personal effort on my part." Yes, that's right. You are not an infant anymore. Diligently study the Scriptures.

JUNE 15

God Will Never Leave You

In Hebrews 13:5–6 we read, "God has said, never will I leave you, never will I forsake you. So we say with confidence, the Lord is my helper I will not be afraid. What can man do to me?"

Note the sequence of these verses. First, "God has said," second, "So we say." That is the proper pattern; that is the ground upon which God directs, and that is the basis of our faith. For faith is more than presumption. Faith is our response to what God has said.

That's one of the reasons Bible study is so important. It helps us know what God has said so we'll know what to say ourselves.

One of the characteristics of doubt is that it turns God's statements into questions. Remember, in the Garden of Eden it was Satan who turned God's statement into a question. He turned what God had said into "Has God said?" Perhaps if Adam and Eve had been more attentive to what God said, they would have recognized Satan for the deceiver he was.

In the Greek our scripture contains at least five negatives. A literal translation is somewhat awkward, but it would go something like "No, not will I leave you nor, no, not will I forsake you."

A more emphatic statement of support could not be given, for the Lord is saying, "I will never, never leave you. I will never, never forsake you."

Friend, stay close to the Word of God—study it—and you will stay close to God as He stays close to you. He promised.

JUNE 16

At the Feet of Jesus

Three times in the gospels we come across a person by the name of Mary of Bethany, and each time she is at the Master's feet.

In Luke 10:38–39 we read, "As Jesus and His disciples were on their way, He came to a village where a woman named Martha opened her home to Him. She had a sister called Mary who sat at the Lord's feet listening to what He said."

Next in John 11:32 we see Mary mourning her brother Lazarus's death. She carries her grief to the feet of Jesus. "She fell at His feet and said, 'Lord, if you had been here, my brother would not have died.'"

The third and last time we see her is in John 12:3, where six days before the Lord's crucifixion she breaks the container of expensive perfume and as verse 3 records it, "She poured it on Jesus' feet and wiped His feet with her hair."

From these three fleeting glimpses of Mary, we see an example from which we have much to learn.

First, she sat at the Lord's feet, listening to what He said. Although I know the entire Bible is inspired, I also know I get a special blessing from simply reading the words of Jesus. Sometimes I take a red-letter New Testament and just focus on the words of Jesus. I love to sit at His feet and learn.

Second, she knew where to take her greatest hurts. Her brother had died and she "fell at the feet of Jesus with a broken heart." Whatever hurts you most today, friend, take it to Jesus, He is ready to listen, ready to help you bear the load.

Finally, she gave to Jesus the best she had. It was expensive perfume she poured on the feet of Jesus. And note: she did it with the best possible attitude, for she wiped His feet with her hair.

Whatever you do today, friend, be sure to spend some time at the feet of Jesus.

JUNE 17

Strong in His Strength

A paradox, says the dictionary, is an assertion seemingly self-contradictory that nevertheless may be true. In 2 Corinthians 12:10 we have such a paradox, for here Paul writes, "When I am weak, then I am strong."

When we are deeply conscious of our weaknesses, then and only then does the strength of Christ rest upon us.

In 1 Corinthians 10:12 we read, "If you think you are standing firm, be careful that you don't fall." Here Paul is cautioning those who indeed were standing, warning them not to become overconfident in themselves.

I've met people who have served the Lord over sixty years and have heard them say that there were times, even after decades of Christian living, that they would be confronted with a new temptation, a new trial. Once again they were reminded of their dependence upon the Lord.

When we are living in entire dependence on Jesus, we are strongest where we are weakest. For at our weakest point the strength of the Lord has its fullest expression; but when we are living the self-sufficient life, we are weakest where we are strongest, for there is where we are most liable to a surprise attack.

Friends, remember: in ourselves we are weak even where we are strong. In Jesus we are strong even where we are weak. Let Him be strong in you today.

JUNE 18

The Preciousness of Jesus

In 1 Peter 2:6–7 we read, "I lay a stone in Zion, a chosen and precious cornerstone; the one who trusts in Him will never be put to shame. Now to you who believe, this stone is precious."

The essential meaning of these verses is that Jesus Himself is precious, more precious to us than anything or anyone else.

It is obvious as you move through this world that He is not precious to everyone. Who is it that He is precious to? The verse says, "to you who believe." The Greek tense would add "to you who are believing right now." The preciousness of Jesus is directly related to our present-day walk.

Sad to say, a person can be so distracted by legitimate endeavors that the preciousness of Jesus is lost.

This verse says, "He is a precious cornerstone." The word *cornerstone* refers to one of two things: either a massive stone placed at the upper corner of a building in order to bind the walls firmly together, or the keystone in the middle of an archway. The thought is the Lord is foundational to our very existence.

How precious is the Lord Jesus to you today? How much pressure does it take to get you to stop sensing His preciousness? The songwriter wrote, "He is so precious to me." Is He precious to *you* today?

JUNE 19

Reflecting Jesus

In 2 Corinthians 4:6 Paul writes, "God who said, 'Let light shine out of darkness,' made His light shine in our hearts to give us the light of the knowledge of the glory of God in the face of Christ."

This verse does not mean that God has shone in our hearts to give this new light to us as an end in itself. What it teaches is that He has shone in our hearts with the purpose of transmitting His light through us to others.

The Amplified Bible reads, "God, who said, 'Let light shine out of darkness,' is the One who has shone in our hearts to give us the Light of the knowledge of the glory and majesty of God [clearly revealed] in the face of Christ."

So then, the intention is that what God shines in us we are to let shine out of us. The receivers of the light are to be reflectors of the light.

Psalm 96:2 says, "Sing unto Jehovah, bless his name; Show forth his salvation from day to day" (ASV).

Note this translation says not only to sing but also to "show forth his salvation." If we cannot shout with a mighty voice, we can shine with a saintly life. If we cannot trumpet the truth in people's ears, we can transmit its light to their eyes.

Just as the sun's rays directly upon your skin will bring a tan, their impact is doubled when you are in the water.

God directly shines on many a needy heart, but by reflecting off believers, His impact is doubled.

JUNE 20

Willing to Be Made Willing

In Acts 15:26 we read of Paul and Barnabas as men "who risked their lives for the name of our Lord Jesus Christ."

If we would know how Barnabas and especially Paul risked their lives, we need only to read the last half of Acts. But the word *risked* may well capture our attention for another reason. More strictly translated from the Greek, these words of Acts 15:26 should read, "Paul and Barnabas, men who have handed over their souls," or "men who have handed themselves over."

The risks they faced in life were incidental compared to the great "handover" of themselves to Almighty God. They were men who had voluntarily handed themselves over. This describes what real consecration to Christ is all about: a complete handing of ourselves over to Him.

The story is told of how F. B. Meyer used to compare consecration as handing over to God a bunch of keys. In his own life he had given Him all his keys—all except one. For some time he struggled. It seemed unfair that God would expect him to relinquish his last key. Yet as long as he withheld it, he did not have the fullness of spiritual joy and peace. One day he cast himself before the Lord with this prayer: "Dear Lord, I am not really willing to yield this key to you, but I am willing to be made willing, by whatever means you choose."

The Lord answered that prayer, and victory was the result.

How about you, friend? Is there some key you're struggling with? Are you will to be made willing to surrender it to God?

JUNE 21

Jesus: Our Rock

Symbolism is used throughout the Scriptures to give us insight into divine truth. One such symbol is a rock. At least six different times Jesus is expressed to us in this form.

Isaiah 32:2 mentions the kingdom of righteousness and how there is a "great rock in a weary land" (KJV).

Jesus is a rock of shelter for the weary. Large rocks meant much to the dwellers in Palestine years ago. They made fortresses for protection. They provided caves for housing and also gave shade from the scorching sun. Psalm 91:1 indicates that there is "rest under the shadow of the almighty." For those who are weary there is a place of rest. More than that, there is a person who gives rest. In Jesus we find the shelter we need and the rest required for spiritual renewal.

Next, in Song of Songs 2:14 we read of a "dove in the clefts of the rock." The dove is the gentlest of all birds. It is not created to battle fierce storms, yet even the dove is protected from the greatest storm by the clefts in the rocks.

Jesus is our cleft in the rock. He is our place of security in an insecure generation. Though revival fires are spreading throughout our country, there is a tide of evil and immorality in epidemic proportions. It would be easy to fall into a maze of confusion. But Jesus is our stabilizer. We can slip into His presence and there sift through the confusion and threat of the day.

Remember, friend: Jesus is a rock of shelter for the weary and a rock of refuge from the storm. He is your Rock. You don't need to be afraid.

JUNE 22

Jesus: Our All in All

Yesterday we talked of Jesus as the rock of shelter for the weary and the rock of refuge from the storm.

Today, in Exodus 17:1–7 we have the rock of Horeb giving water to the thirsty. The children of God, escaping from Egyptian bondage, found themselves in the desert without water. God told Moses to go on ahead to Horeb. There he would find a rock. Moses was to hit the rock and then water would come forth. First Corinthians 10:4 says that the rock in Horeb was Christ. In other words, Jesus was the source of water for the thirsty.

What are you thirsty for today? Come to Jesus. He will satisfy your need.

Next, in Matthew 16:18 Jesus says, "On this rock I will build my church." What rock was He talking about? It's the revealed truth of Peter's confession in Matthew 16:16: "You are the Christ, Son of the living God." The rock of foundation is Christ. We are not building our lives on sand or wood but upon the very creator of the universe— Christ Himself.

Next, we note in Romans 9:33 the Christ is described as the "rock that causes men to stumble." This is the rock of conviction. When Christ deals with the sins of humanity, He becomes an offense to them.

Finally, in Isaiah 26:4 we see the Lord who is the "rock eternal." In Hebrew the words *rock eternal* can be translated "rock of ages." In other words, Christ is the dependable, ever-present Son of God.

How wonderful in these past two devotionals to see Christ as the rock of shelter for the weary, the rock of refuge from the storm, the rock of water for the thirsty, the rock of foundation for the believer, the rock of conviction for the world, and finally the rock of ages—the Christ of eternity. Jesus is truly our all in all.

JUNE 23

Lost Sheep

Luke 15:4 says, "Suppose one of you has a hundred sheep and loses one of them. Does he not leave the ninety-nine in the open country and go after the lost sheep until he finds it?"

By this illustration of shepherd and sheep, Jesus was dealing with the Pharisees, showing how He had come to seek all who were lost. The Pharisees were upset that He would spend time with those they considered undesirable. But Jesus was trying to illustrate His concern for *human* lost sheep, as a shepherd would express his concern for a lost animal.

The difference of attitude between the Pharisees and Jesus was that they stood for a *form* of *religion*, whereas Jesus had come to show the *facts* of *salvation*. Religion by itself never saved any person's soul. Not even Christianity, considered as a system, can save a single soul.

What people need is not merely religion but redemption, not a new ethic but a new life, not just a new system but a Savior.

It's interesting to note that the shepherd in Luke 15 had ninety-nine sheep safe in the fold. If he had had only four or five to start with, you could see that one lost sheep would have been a great loss. But when you still have ninety-nine, losing one seems to be no big deal. Yet in this chapter the shepherd immediately takes out after the one lost sheep because he loves all the sheep.

There are millions of Christians all over the world. Isn't it humbling to realize that God was not satisfied with the millions? He wanted one more—He wanted you.

JUNE 24

You Matter to Jesus

First Peter 5:7 notes the importance of "Casting all your care upon Him, for He cares for you" (NKJV).

There are two kinds of care in this text: (1) anxious care, "Casting all your care upon Him," and (2) affectionate care, "He cares for you." On the one hand we have our anxious care and on the other our Savior's never-fail, affectionate care.

The first part of verse 7 reads, "Casting all your care upon Him." The word *casting* in the Greek signifies a once-for-all casting. There is, of course, a sense in which we cannot cast upon Him all the anxieties of days yet to come, for we do not know what a day may bring. But we can pledge to the Lord that regardless of what does come, we're going to keep on casting and keep on leaving with Him the things that could bring anxiety into our lives.

Oh, I know we can't hand over our cares to Jesus in the sense of exemption from them, but we can transfer the *weight* of them to Him so that if we must still carry them, He will carry us.

The Weymouth New Testament translation renders verse 7, "Throw the whole weight of your anxiety upon Him." This verse closes by saying, "For He cares for you." In essence the Greek here is saying, "It really matters to Him about you."

I'm not sure how God keeps us all straight in His mind; I guess that's part of being God. But today cast all your anxiety on Him, whether you're going to work, church, school, or just staying home. Remember: His thoughts are on you, and you really matter to Him.

JUNE 25

The Second Coming

How do you feel about the second coming? Do you think about it at all? Does it have any influence on your daily living? If you knew that Jesus were coming in seven days, how would it impact your priorities this week?

James 5:7–8 says, "Be patient…brothers, until the Lord's coming. See how the farmer waits for the land to yield its valuable crop and how patient he is for the fall and spring rains. You too, be patient and stand firm, because the Lord's coming is near."

The fall rains normally begin in Palestine in late October or early November. They are anxiously awaited because they are necessary to germinate the dormant seed. In April and May the spring rains are responsible for the maturing of the crop. Without these rains even a heavy winter rain cannot make up for what is lost in the fall and spring.

Some things, as important to the farmer as they are, are obviously out of his control. He is dependent upon seasons and sunshine to bring life to his crops.

However, there is much the farmer *can* do. He can prepare the soil, obtain good seed, cultivate the crop, and, of course, eventually take in the harvest.

There are many things about the second coming we have no control over. The events of that great hour are going to be orchestrated by God Himself. However, there is much we *can* do. Keeping our souls warm before the Lord is *our* responsibility. Influencing our loved ones to be ready is *our* responsibility. Witnessing to the lost is *our* responsibility.

There's no question that God is taking care and will take care of His responsibilities. How are you doing with *yours*?

JUNE 26

Dependence

When you go back in your mind to those who lived in Bible times, do they seem real to you? Or should I say, do they seem like normal, physical, human beings to you? Were Adam and Eve real, or were they the superhuman people of the race? Were Moses, David, Isaiah, John the Baptist, Peter, and Paul really people just like us?

James 5:17–18 talks about one such man. His name was Elijah. Note the scripture: "Elijah was a man just like us. He prayed earnestly that it would not rain, and it did not rain on the land for three and a half years. Again he prayed, and the heavens gave rain, and the earth produced its crops."

The thrust of the Greek here indicates that Elijah was no superhuman power. He had the same feelings, circumstances, and experiences of many others. The Greek underscores the fact that Elijah's power did not lie in some supernatural greatness but rather in his humanity and his dependence upon the Father.

Why is it we feel so dwarfed by these spiritual giants? Why were they able to depend on God for so much more than most people?

I guess the answer to that is wrapped up in the fact that the key to the power in their lives was *their total dependence upon God.*

Paul said in Philippians 4:13, "I can do all this through him who gives me strength."

David said in Psalm 23:1, "The Lord is my shepherd, I shall lack nothing."

Jesus Himself while walking on this earth said in John 5:30, "By myself I can do nothing." And in John 14:10 He said, "It is the Father, living in me, who is doing his work."

The common denominator of them all is *dependence.*

How about you today, friend? How dependent are you upon the Lord? Have you gotten to the place where "by yourself you can do nothing"? Good. Now you're ready to do all things!

JUNE 27

Respond to Jesus's Call Right Now

In Matthew 13:12 we read words that deal with the kingdom of Heaven: "Whoever has will be given more, and they will have an abundance. Whoever does not have, even what they have will be taken from them."

Here our Lord gives a scriptural principle we should consider carefully. This verse works two ways. In one way it brings multiplied blessings: "Whoever has will be given more." In another way it brings terrible loss: "Whoever does not have, even what they have will be taken from them." We need to think upon these words seriously because they will impact us all one way or another.

At first reading this verse seems too severe and too final, yet in the nature of things it is an unalterable fact.

The context of this passage finds the disciples asking Jesus why He speaks to the people in parables. Jesus said in Matthew 13:13, "I speak to them in parables because seeing they do not see, and hearing they do not hear."

Jesus's unresponsive listeners were hearing the simple teachings about the kingdom without being obedient. By their own attitude they were not only adding to their personal guilt but at the same time destroying their capability to respond.

Some time ago I injured my right shoulder. For six weeks I had to keep that arm idle, supported by a sling. When I removed the sling, my arm was very weak. Doctors indicated that the failure to use an arm contributes to the inability to use it.

The same is true spiritually. Idle, unresponsive living brings its own judgment. What we will not use we will eventually lose. That is a fundamental principle of life.

Respond to God's Word immediately so that your spiritual arms will not grow weak and incapable of a quick response. Respond to Jesus's call right now.

JUNE 28

Is It Time to Dig Out?

Yesterday we talked about the fact that what we fail to use we often lose. Today we continue that thought with one of the most vivid scriptural injunctions of the entire Bible.

In Matthew 25:14–30 we have the story commonly referred to as the parable of the talents. A talent is a measure of money worth over one thousand dollars. The servant with over five thousand dollars put the money to work and doubled it. The servant with over two thousand dollars put the money to work and likewise doubled his portion. But the servant given one thousand dollars feared his master and failed to invest the money. He dug a hole and hid it in the ground.

Upon the master's return, he checked to see how the servants had done. The two who put the money to work were praised, but the fearful one was condemned. As a matter of fact, the one thousand dollars he did have was taken from him and given to the servant with over ten thousand dollars.

Here is a vivid warning. What we will not use we lose.

Some Christians are always *going to* start praying more regularly and for longer periods of time, but they keep putting it off and finally the capacity for praying at all leaves them. Others are always *planning to* spend more time in serious Bible study, but there's always some reason *not* to start today. As a result, they miss many opportunities for going deeper spiritually.

All of this points to the fact that we are responsible to respond to the opportunities that are ours. God wants us to be stewards who use our talents—not gravediggers who bury them.

How about you? Do you have talents that have been buried in the grave of feelings of inferiority? They should never have been buried, for they were buried alive and have died underground. Some are buried but are still alive. What about digging them out and using them again? It's not too late.

JUNE 29

God Is Right on Time. He's Never Late

Three times Paul had prayed that his thorn in the flesh be removed, but in 2 Corinthians 12:9 the Lord said, "My grace is sufficient for you, for my power is made perfect in weakness."

Few scriptures have brought more comfort to Christians than this one. The Lord said, "My grace is sufficient for you." How much better this sufficient grace was than even the granting of Paul's request. Had Paul's thorn been removed, what losers we all would have been! Paul learned dependence and as a result gave us an example that gives us courage when our thorns are not removed.

No one but the divine Christ could say, "My grace is sufficient." Think how meager those words would be from anyone but the divine one. For wrapped up in those words we have omnipotence, omnipresence, and all that God possesses. Think of it, friend—God's perfect knowledge of all human needs and God's perpetual presence everywhere are a part of His sufficient grace.

When God says *sufficient,* He *means* sufficient. His supply has exact correspondence with our need. Never too much, never too little, always just right. Never too soon, never too late, always on time.

Grace for tomorrow's needs will not come today. Grace for today will not come tomorrow.

Whatever you need today—anticipate God's grace at exactly the right time.

JUNE 30

Praise Him

Let's suppose that today when you woke up, you looked outside and noticed you had two flat tires. Or suppose the washing machine decided to throw a bearing and spot your newly washed clothes with oil.

Now be honest. Would 1 Thessalonians 5:18 come to your mind? It reads, "Give thanks in all circumstances, for this is God's will." Do you think "all circumstances" really means *all* circumstances? Yes, it does! We continually say we walk by faith and not by sight. We say we do not go on feelings but on the facts of God's Word. Tell me: When would we have a better time to witness to this fact than in the midst of nitty-gritty daily frustrations?

Ephesians 5:20 says we are to give thanks to God "for everything." If you thought giving thanks *in* everything sounds hard, what do you think about giving thanks *for* everything?

Why would the Bible say such a thing? Doesn't this just add guilt to an already difficult situation? No, exactly the opposite is true.

I challenge you to try something today. Instead of complaining about the difficult things that come your way, why not thank God in and for the situations He has allowed in your life? There is something about praising God that releases His power in our lives.

Praise has always been the conscious decision that opens the door to God's presence. And isn't that what we really need in life's difficult times—the presence of our loving God?

Try praise today and see what happens.

JULY 1

God Doesn't Change

In Malachi 3:6 we read, "I am the Lord, I do not change."

We live in a time of great change. Science, medicine, cultures, and nations have undergone significant changes, and many more are in store for us. As we continue into the twenty-first century, numerous things will change that we never imagined. However, throughout all time the words of Malachi are certain to remain: "I am the Lord, I do not change."

When we become disheartened by the storms on the horizon, it is well to recognize that God is still sovereign. He is in command of this universe. He does not change in His holiness or judgment. His love, His mercy, His grace, and His sufficiency remain the same. He is the same God whose creation of the heavens and the earth we read about in Genesis. And the last book of the Old Testament reminds us that He is still the same.

The psalmist reminds us of another great certainty. In a time when textbooks are rewritten and soon become obsolete, when some theories are disproved and others proved, we have God's Word—the unchangeable, powerful Word of God.

Psalm 119:89 says, "Forever, O Lord, Your Word is settled in heaven" (NASB). Daily the Scriptures are being confirmed to us in the field of archaeology and even more dramatically in people's lives.

In Isaiah 40:8 we read, "The grass withers, the flower fades, but the word of our God stands forever" (NASB). The fact remains that until the heart of a person has changed, his or her ways cannot be changed. From Adam on, every person has needed forgiveness from his or her sins and God's life and power to quicken the person and give them strength in which to live. God's purpose for the world will always be under His control. His plan will culminate in the time when we will reign with Him forever.

May this knowledge of our unchangeable God and His immutable ways draw us closer to Him day by day, confident that "He who began a good work in you will carry it on to completion until the day of Christ Jesus" (Philippians 1:6).

JULY 2

Sharing Jesus

Jesus spoke to His disciples about remaining in Him. The result of this brings great glory to God. In John 15:8 He said, "This is to my Father's glory, that you bear much fruit, showing yourselves to be my disciples."

In this fifteenth chapter of John are four verses all speaking of this union with Christ or the discipleship involved in following Him. In verse 5 we are "branches," in verse 15 we are "friends," in verse 20 we are "servants," and in verse 27 we are "witnesses."

Do you catch the significance in these four verses? We are branches, so we live in Him. We are friends, so we have joy in Him. We are servants, so we do what He commands. We are witnesses, so we speak for Him. We are called branches, friends, servants, and witnesses. So you see, He is our life, He is our joy, He is our Lord, and He is our theme.

If we are sincere and thoughtful readers of God's Word, we will find ourselves confronted by a great truth. We will find our hearts both blessed and challenged at the same time.

With these four aspects before us, let us ask ourselves four questions. First, am I vitally united to Christ as one of the branches, growing in Him and part of His program? Second, am I living closely and daily in fellowship with Him, taking time every day to know the reality of His presence? Third, am I faithfully serving Him, even though incurring the world's hostility, serving Jesus regardless of what people may say at work, at home, or in my neighborhood, with my focus upon Jesus? And finally, am I daily giving witness for Him, as opportunity allows, to the power of the Holy Spirit?

As branches, friends, servants, and witnesses, it seems that we should regularly be telling others about Him. Ask yourself this question: When was the last time I told anyone about Jesus?

Look for an opportunity today to share Jesus—my guess is that you will find one.

JULY 3

Jesus: The True Vine

In John 15:5 Jesus said, "I am the vine, and you are the branches."

With this metaphor of vine and branches before us, we would do well to ask, Am I really, vitally, savingly united to Christ as one of the spiritual branches in the living vine?

It is important to appreciate the force of the first sentence in this chapter. For when our Lord said, "I am the true vine" (John 15:1), He was giving us a pattern for the rest of the verses.

The emphasis was on the adjective *true* and with good reason. In the Old Testament the nation of Israel is spoken of again and again as the vine that Jehovah planted and nourished. But the covenant nation had failed to realize God's plan or His "vine" ideal for them. That vine was blighted by their sinful living. Their spiritual fervor was gone.

It was not enough to be a branch of that vine—there was no saving or regenerating power whatever in simply being a member of the nation of Israel. For you see, Christ was the true Israel, He was the true vine, and He is the true vine today. Wrapped up in Him are all the ideals, longings, and blessings God has planned for us.

Even to this day, Christendom is not the true vine, the Roman Catholic Church is not the true vine, Protestantism is not the true vine. A person may be an ardent Episcopalian, a sincere Presbyterian, or a "good Baptist," and yet not be in *Christ,* the true vine. There must be a personal, individual, heart-to-heart union with the living Savior.

Ask yourself: Am I in the true vine? If I am, then am I daily abiding in Him? Am I bearing fruit for Him? In my character and acts of service, am I bearing the fruit that testifies that I am in the vine?

Think about it, friend: Jesus Christ, the true vine, calls us to be branches in His vineyard. What kind of a branch are you?

JULY 4

At Home in the Presence of Jesus

Today we continue looking at John 15:5, in which Jesus said, "I am the vine and you are the branches." In this metaphor of vine and branches, our Lord shows us that there are three prerequisites of fruit bearing.

First, there must be pruning or cleansing. In verse 2 Jesus said, "Every branch that bears fruit, He prunes it, so that it may bring forth more fruit."

Second, there must be abiding. In verse 4 Jesus said, "The branch cannot bear fruit of itself unless it abides in the vine, so neither can you unless you abide in Me" (NASB).

Third, there must be obeying. In verse 10 He said, "If you keep my commandments, you shall abide in my love." Yes, there must be this cleansing, abiding, and obeying.

How are we cleansed? Jesus tells us in verse 3: "Now you are cleansed, or pruned through the Word which I have spoken to you." That word is now to us the Holy Scripture, and as we read it, learn it, and respond to it, it has a cleansing, purifying power and is working this very moment.

How do we abide? To abide is to allow nothing in life that breaks our communion with Christ. We must not leave any sin unconfessed, unjudged, unforgiven. By a prayerful faith we draw close to Him, and His strength and His wisdom flow through us. Abiding is "being at home in the presence of Jesus."

How do I yield to the required obedience? To those of us who are already His, our Lord's one, all-inclusive requirement is in verse 12: "This is my commandment, that you love one another as I have loved you" (ESV). When we love one another as He did, with the love that seeks only their truest good, even to the point of our own personal self-sacrifice, we fulfill the law of Christ. We are cleansed, we abide, and as the Bible says, there is much fruit.

JULY 5

Jesus Will Never Drive You Away

In John 6:37 Jesus says, "Whoever comes to me, I will never drive away."

Various rules and steps have been proposed for seeking after salvation, for the fullness of the Spirit, for guidance, and for other experiences of the Christian life.

Sometimes this leads to great confusion. You see, no two people's experiences are exactly alike. We tend to make a norm, though, out of our own experiences and assume others will see things as we do. But coming to Jesus is a very personal matter. It is not a dry business procedure.

A person does not fall in love by reading books on how to fall in love. Usually he or she meets someone, associates with that person, and gets to know the person. And sometimes they fall in love.

Likewise there are indeed certain conditions that must be met in a personal knowledge of Christ. It is more like falling in love than a cold business deal or decision.

There is a sense of need—a drawing near, a fellowship that deepens with the years. The expressions and manifestations vary with different types of temperaments. Don't try to imitate a made-to-order experience handed down from someone else. Jesus invites you to come as you are and know Him for yourself.

Friend, bring whatever need you have to Jesus today, and be confident that He who loves you wants to grow His love in your heart. He will never drive anyone away—ever.

JULY 6

Do What You Know to Do

In James 4:17 we read, "Anyone...who knows the good that he ought to do, and does not do it, sins.

Historians describe the degeneration of Christianity under the Greek scholars of the tenth century. They were the ones who handled the literature and spoke the language of spiritual people, and yet knew nothing of their own personal spiritual dedication.

The historian says they held in their lifeless hands the riches of their fathers, but they did not inherit the Spirit who had created and imparted that sacred heritage to their predecessors.

The historian was saying that there were many who knew what to say but did not have the presence of the living Christ in their own lives. The Pharisees of Jesus's day handled the things of God, they read the Scriptures, they faithfully kept the letter of the law, and they were painstakingly separated from sinners. But the Bible says Publicans and harlots went into the kingdom before them.

To have grown up in a Christian home and in church, early being able to speak the language of the church, familiar with its subjects and observing its practices, yet never a believer, produces a type of sinner often harder to awaken than the most ignorant heathen person. Truth that is long heard yet not acted upon brings a terrible self-deception.

I encourage you, friend, to do what you know to do. Follow the truth you already know, and do the things God has already revealed to you. Remember: God has no grandchildren. You either know Him straight on, personally yourself, or you do not know Him at all. I say it again: do what you know to do. God will take care of the rest.

JULY 7

Make an Angel Rejoice

In Like 15:10 Jesus said, "There is rejoicing in the presence of the angels over one sinner that repents."

These words are woven into the wonderful fabric of our Lord's threefold parable of the lost sheep, the lost coin, and the lost son.

This verse is one of the best-known and best-loved passages in the entire Bible. It is challenging to reflect on what is implied here concerning these unfallen angels.

To begin with, these words clearly indicate that there are such beings as angels. But to speak about angels where you work or live today is to invite sarcastic ridicule. When the sacred truths of Christianity are thus made fun of, it is easy for the younger Christians to be bluffed into doubting them.

But here in Luke 15, it is the infallible Son of God Himself who tells us about this joy among the angels over repenting sinners, and He prefaces His words with the weighty "I tell you".

But further the words imply that the angels observe us. How can they rejoice over us when they see us turning to God if they cannot see us? Surely it is artificial to suppose that they are completely screened off and can know about us only when God deigns to tell them. That idea is out of keeping with the general tenor of Scripture.

For instance, do we not read in Hebrews 1:14 that the angels are ministering spirits sent forth to minister to the heirs of salvation? But how can they so minister to us if they cannot even see us?

Again, our Lord's words imply that the angels feel concern for us. If they had joy at our conversion, they obviously had feelings about us before our conversion. Living as they do in the spiritual and eternal realm, they know far more vividly than we do what it means for a soul to be lost and for a soul to be saved.

They see in a sharper and a clearer way than we do the tragedy of human sin. They see the utter bitterness of Satan's rebellion; they see the tremendous issues at stake. In each human life they see the transcendent marvel of the gospel.

Yes, the angels are intensely concerned. That is why we read in 1 Peter 1:12, "Which things the angels desire to look into." They have a desire to see what is going on in our lives.

Once more, our text implies that at the conversion of sinners, the angels respond with an extraordinary joy. It surely must be extraordinary if it can bring added bliss to them in their already-perfect state. Perhaps the most amazing thing of all is that this special joy of angels is over one sinner who repents. Just one!

What must have been their joy at Pentecost? What must be their joys in times of revival at your church? Mark it well: this joy of the angels is over one sinner, one drunkard, one addict, one impure evildoer. When one person repents, the angels rejoice.

Friend, how do you plan on causing angels to rejoice today?

JULY 8

God Will Forgive Our Forgetting

In Jonah 3:1–2 we read, "Then the word of the Lord came to Jonah a second time: 'Go to the great city of Nineveh and proclaim to it the message I give you.'"

Jonah, a runaway prophet, paid his fare and boarded a ship that would take him away from the responsibility God had given him. He must have been more than eager for the anchor to be hoisted and the vessel to sail in the opposite direction from the capital city where he had been called to minister.

He knew God was a God of mercy and used that fact to justify his own sin. For he said he fled to Tarshish because "I knew that you are a gracious and compassionate God, slow to anger and abounding in love, a God who relents from sending calamity" (Jonah 4:2).

How it must have grieved the heart of God when Jonah willfully sinned in the confidence that he could be forgiven! And how it must grieve God's heart today when people sin again and again, just banking on God's forgiveness!

What a presumption on God's mercy Jonah made! It must have been a rude awakening when he later realized how deliberate his sin was and how it displeased God. Oh, the grace that led him to repentance, and oh, the grace that granted him a second chance!

It has been pointed out that after Jonah's disobedience, he was less competent to fulfill God's assignment. His powers had been impaired by his disobedience. Disobedience brings the moth and the rust to our spiritual lives. When we recognize this, it should bring us to our knees to plead with God to make us faithful and adequate for the job we are given to do.

We need to be alert, looking for every opportunity to serve, not missing any call the Lord has for us.

Christ told His disciples to remember Him. And we are also told to remember Christ as well.

My heart is heavy when I think of how often I forget. It becomes even heavier when I realize that He always remembers. At any time I may call on Him. He is there. Christ does not forget to listen and show me the way.

Dear friend, take hope in the fact that God will forgive our forgetting. May the knowledge He gives us not make us complacent but rather compel us to be faithful and obedient. Never harbor the thought that we could catch the first ship to Tarshish to do our own thing.

I challenge you today to move instantly in the direction of obedience.

JULY 9

Let's Bring Joy to Heaven

The day before yesterday we looked at Luke 15:10. Let's look at it again: "There is rejoicing in the presence of the angels over one sinner that repents."

It may sound rather starling yet it is true that we can augment the joy of heaven. Those unfallen angels are there amid the pure ecstasies and the shadowless raptures of the glory land, yet somehow all that joy is increased when sinners on earth are converted to Christ.

Oh, what soul-winners we should prayerfully endeavor to be, for if the winning of a soul to Jesus means such joy to the angels, what joy it must be to our Lord Jesus Himself!

Further, we should feel as the angels do about impenitent sinners. The angels evidently grieve over them. Do *we*? How unconcerned some of us seem! How little we persevere for their conversion! How seldom we pull up our courage to warn them of the wrath to come, or try to draw them to the Savior with the cords of love.

I find no hint in the Bible that angels get excited over battles that are won among countries, or the amassing of wealth. Political debates mean nothing to them. Huge commercial ventures and scientific discoveries mean little or nothing at all, but the thermometer of their pure joy immediately rises when souls are won to the Savior.

Every soul is a world in itself, with immeasurable possibilities for good or evil, in time and in eternity. When a soul falls away from God, demons no doubt rejoice in darkness, but when a soul is saved through union with God's dear Son, heaven sounds its trumpets in joyful fanfare. What must be the jubilation in heaven when one is born again?

Finally, with the thought that you and I can bring joy to the heavenly host, let's determine to do so. Today let's determine to bring joy to heaven!

JULY 10

How Much of God Do You Want?

Ezekiel 47:1–12 tells about waters that issued from under the threshold of the temple. Whatever these waters were, or whatever they referred to, either in the historical past or the prophetical future, one thing is certain: they are a remarkable parable of spiritual possibilities opened for you and me.

Again and again in the holy Scriptures water is used as an emblem of the Holy Spirit, so these waters in Ezekiel 47 may well speak to us of His gracious outflowing toward the Lord's people.

It is interesting to note that these waters were just a trickle, then fifteen feet farther they were to the ankles, a little farther they came to the knees, a little farther to the thighs, and a little farther it was enough to swim in—and it all came from just a trickle. Yes, the trickle had become a river.

This was a special river—a river of God. Some authors relate this to the work of the Holy Spirit in our lives.

Young Christian, do not think that you must wait for years before the Holy Spirit can be to you as waters to swim in. You may swim as deep and as far as you want to go. God is ready to take you to some of the deeper truths of spiritual living.

Older Christian, if you have been a believer for years and you feel you have water only to the ankles, I guarantee you that the fullness is for you just down the stream a little ways. In other words, friend, the deeper you and I make the channels through our hearts and lives, the more deeply the Holy Spirit will flow through us. How do we deepen those channels? Through prayer, obedience, and the Word.

I am convinced that we have just as much of God in our lives as we really want. How much of God do *you* want, friend? Just a trickle—or do you want to swim in His presence?

JULY 11

Get into the Deeper Water

Today we continue with Ezekiel 47:1–12. All of us who love the Savior want to live the kind of Christian life that allows us to swim in the fullness of His presence. We long to experience the deeper depths of the Holy Spirit within us. We cannot be satisfied with waters merely to the ankles or even to the thighs. No, it is the waters you can swim in that we long to be a part of.

Some people seem always to be in the shallows. Why? In many cases it is because we confuse "claiming" with "yielding." We think blessings from God will come from our praying, our begging, and our claiming, whereas the truth is that when once we are really yielded to the Holy Spirit, for His total possession, then there is no need for all our asking, praying, begging, or claiming.

You and I cannot force these waters; we need to let them have their way through us. There is no hesitation on the part of the Holy Spirit. He is anxious to bring us into His presence. The heavenly waters have flowed to us and even do to this moment. This water shed of spiritual power has flowed since Pentecost.

This deeper and fuller experience in our lives is not to be confused with either natural or spiritual maturity. No, for as maturity comes only from experience, this filling of the Holy Spirit is wholly a matter of yielding to Him.

There are many older believers who find an entire yielding more difficult than young believers do. They have evaded or postponed, or they have become so set in their ways that any further work by the Spirit is not on their radar screen. I'm concerned that we can fall into a "spiritual default" mode and not realize we are missing what God has for us.

Whether you are a younger or older believer, the fresh flowing, the ever-deepening, heart-gladdening, life-transforming, river is there for us all.

Oh, that we might go to the depths and find those waters to swim in, which not only fill our hearts but also flow through us to the renewing of others. It's time to get out of the wading pool and into the deep end!

JULY 12

Crackers and Cheese

Romans 8:32 says, "He who did not spare his own Son, but gave him up for us all—how will he not also, along with him, graciously give us all things?"

I had the privilege of speaking to a group of young people on a cruise ship. The ship handled nearly nineteen hundred people those seven days upon the Caribbean waters. It would have been foolish for some people to have sat in one section of the ship and just eat cheese and crackers, thinking their tickets gave them simply a place to sleep. No, when you pay for that ticket, you pay for meals and all.

You see, salvation includes more than just pardon from sin and deliverance from hell. It is more than a ticket to heaven. It includes all that we'll need on our journey.

Sin has been dealt with in the Son, but Jesus is not only our Savior—He is our sustenance, our daily supply. We are not to exist on our own crackers and cheese. No, all things are yours, according to the Bible.

Indeed, the supreme thing is that God spared not His own Son but delivered Him up for us all. That is the message of Calvary, that God has freely given us all things in the gift of His Son. Our assurance, our sanctification, our peace, our joy, our wisdom, all we need for body, mind, soul, and spirit, all we need to do God's will, is available to us. A new body at the resurrection, eternal life in heaven—all of this is included in the ticket. What a ticket, paid for by God's own Son!

Hey, friend—throw away the crackers and cheese. You have a right to sit in the main dining room.

JULY 13

Faith in Faith or Faith in Him?

In Matthew 9:29 Jesus said, "It shall be done to you according to your faith" (NASB).

Do you ever wonder if you have a right to that kind of faith? Do you ever wonder if you experience the faith that Jesus talked about? One has said, "If you have any faith at all, you may be sure it is the right kind." Don't waste time taking your faith apart. Don't expect saving faith to be some strange, different kind. You believe in Christ with faith, like the faith you use when you trust someone or something else.

It is the object that makes the difference. If you have any uncertainty about the matter, come to a definite decision; trust Christ now for whatever you may face in your life. It may help you to put down the time and the place concerning a specific commitment about some area of your life.

You must have confidence in the decision and consider it settled, but don't confuse *faith in your faith* with *faith in the Savior.* Let me say it again: don't confuse *faith in your faith* with *faith in the Savior.* You see, faith has no value of its own. It has value only as it connects us with Jesus.

It's a trick of Satan to get us occupied with examining our faith instead of resting in the Faithful One. Go to Him just as you are and He will meet you—but the good news is that He doesn't leave us the way we are.

JULY 14

He Will Fill Your Mouth

In Ezekiel 29:21 the Lord says, "The day will come when I will cause the ancient glory of Israel to revive, and then, Ezekiel, your words will be respected. Then they will know that I am the Lord."

At certain times Ezekiel had been silent, but now the Lord gave him the opportunity and the liberty to proclaim his message. God opened the mouth of His servant to comfort the people and to give praise to God and make Him known.

With our wonderful opportunity to share the riches available in Christ, some of us still keep our mouths closed. What a tragedy, that we remain silent while the doors are wide open! A word in season could bring eternal life to someone who hears us. Ours is the glorious opportunity to shed light in darkness.

For those who are afraid to speak—the Lord has promised to guide your thoughts, to supply the words that would bear fruit. Thus, we do not share the good news alone but in the presence and in the power of the Spirit of God. He brings to mind the words to be used and graciously assists us. We will be enriched as we experience the reality of His leadership.

When by faith we speak the words of Christ to those who have been on our hearts, it is a glorious experience. We may draw assurance from a background of prayer and Christian concern and the knowledge that His Word does not return void. For He says Psalm 81:8–10 "Listen to me, O my people, while I give you stern warnings. O Israel, if you would only listen to me!...For it was I, the Lord your God, who rescued you from the land of Egypt. Open your mouth wide, and I will fill it."

I challenged you today, friend: open your mouth wide and witness for Christ. He has promised to fill it.

JULY 15

You Are a Fellow Worker

In Philippians 2:25 Paul describes Epaphroditus as "my brother, my fellow worker, and fellow soldier, who is also your messenger whom you sent to take care of my needs."

Paul first describes Epaphroditus as "my brother," by which he means the two of them are brothers in Christ. They have both been born again from the Holy Spirit, both possess the same new spiritual life and nature, both are members in the family of the redeemed, both are children of God in Christ, and both have the same indwelling Savior. Can you think of a fellowship more powerful or more meaningful?

Paul continues by describing Epaphroditus as a "fellow worker." There are too many believers who are not workers. Zeal without knowledge is bad, but knowledge without zeal is even worse. Without workers the cause of Christ would drag to a full stop.

Lazy visionaries are of little or no value to the kingdom at all. You see, we must witness as well as worship. We must work as well as wish. Mind you, spiritual work must be done by spiritual people, people who are in vital union with Christ, people filled with the Holy Spirit. Such a worker was Epaphroditus. You see, he was also a *fellow* worker. He could work well with others, and others could work well with him, and that is a most commendable quality.

Have you ever heard it said of a person that he or she is a fine Christian but nobody can work with him or her? This is a paradox of terms. Such porcupine individualists can be a real hindrance to the cause of Jesus Christ. One mark of those who know Him is that they are *fellow* workers.

But Paul has another description of Epaphroditus, as a "fellow soldier." And this connection is quite a study. Note the following:

First, in verse 25 he is a "messenger"—like a dispatch rider, not regarding his own life.

Second, he has the willingness to be an ordinary private in the army, a minister to others, as verse 25 notes.

Third, verse 26 speaks of his love for them.

Fourth, the same verse speaks of his illness.

Finally, in verse 30, his willingness to hazard his own life in service is noted.

Indeed, Epaphroditus is a good example for us all. May God help you, and God help me, to be more like this brother, this fellow worker, this fellow soldier of the Cross.

JULY 16

Make Your Reservation

For many years my wife, Joy, and I traveled to churches across America and foreign countries in special services. Often it was necessary for someone to call ahead and make reservations at a hotel. Many times driving in the wee hours of the morning, we would pull into a hotel, check in at the front desk, and find that since we had made reservations, there was indeed a room available for us.

I have seen times when others could not find a room because their name was not in the book. They had not made a reservation.

Jesus said in John 14:2, "I go to prepare a place for you." It is as if Jesus has made a reservation for us. Oh, we cannot walk up to the gate of heaven after death and obtain a dwelling place merely by asking for it. No, our abiding place up there is secured in advance while we are down here on earth. Jesus has gone to prepare a place, but there are places only for those who make reservations.

Let me ask you a question, friend: Is your name in the Book? Have you made a reservation? Many will come in that day and make various claims, and He will say, "Depart, I never knew you." The dying thief made a reservation: "Remember me," he said.

Reservations are made, not on the basis of what we deserve but on the basis of who we believe in and who we have given our lives to.

Friend, have you made a reservation? How about your son, how about your daughter, how about your spouse? How about your friends? Do they have reservations for that heavenly hotel?

JULY 17

He Is with You

In Psalm 91:15 we read, "I will be with him in trouble." This comes as something of a surprise, for up to this point in the psalm there has not been a hint that trouble could ever swoop down upon the godly man envisioned in this psalm. He seems to live a charmed life.

The chapter talks about angels who are given special charge over him, and in verse 10, "No harm will overtake you, no disaster will come near your tent." Even if there is a lion or a cobra, He tramples them underfoot. Glance through the verses again and see that providence has all the smiles and no frowns for him. So it seems—until we reach this fifteenth verse. Then we are gently jolted from our easy misunderstanding. God loves us too much and too wisely to leave us continually amid enchanted dreams and flowery beds of ease.

Always remember: trouble is permitted on purpose. All of us find days of blessing and good times. But from time to time, loss and sorrow says, "Walk with me for a while." And hesitantly we walk on, one step at a time.

Yet trouble not only is permitted on purpose, but it also can bring a deeper understanding with it. It offers to give God's timeliest opportunity to prove His power in the time of pressure. God says in Isaiah 43:2, "When you pass through the waters, I will be with you; and when you pass through the rivers, they will not sweep over you. When you walk through the fire, you will not be burned; the flames will not set you ablaze."

It was when Shadrach, Meshach, and Abednego were flung into the furnace that suddenly they realized their most thrilling moment, the presence of Almighty God. It is when the seas roar and the mountains shake with a swelling thereof that our heavenly keeper shows Himself a very present help in trouble.

It is the fourth watch of the night as the storm lashes most fiercely that He tramples the billows and scatters the night and comes to us with the words of John 16:33: "Be of good cheer; I have overcome the world" (KJV).

How many married couples happy in each other's love will tell you that although they were truly one in heart on their wedding day, they never knew how deeply they loved, or how much they meant to each other, until they had to go through trouble together.

How many of the choicest saints whose hearts have found the joy of His presence will tell with gratitude that it was when they were in trouble that they made their richest discovery of all that Christ could be to them?

Dear Christian, let it be your endeavor neither to cause trouble nor to fear it. Remember: Jesus said, "I will be with him in trouble." And He is with you right now.

JULY 18

Jesus Is More than Enough

In 2 Corinthians 9:8 we read, "God is able to make all grace abound to you, so that always having all sufficiency in everything, you may have an abundance for every good deed" (NASB).

There is a pressure about life today. People in business tell us about the strain in modern commercial life. And all too often the strain tells on them. In the professional world things are ramped up to a high point of tension. Home life is filled with nerve-wearing problems, such as the anxiety of parents for children who have been brought up amid unprecedented social conditions and godless psychological theories. They refuse many of the healthy restraints that beneficially condition family and social life in the younger days of their lives.

Much of the pressure of today is the product of uncertainty. There is uncertainty about the big things, such as international issues, and the repercussions from these filter down to the individual worker and his or her entire household.

Uncertainty engenders anxiety. Below the surface of many lives today is a state of chronic suspense, arising from a sustaining chain of uncertainties. Life itself becomes anxious, anxiety breeds fretfulness, and fretfulness brings tension, strain, and pressure.

Paul has a good expression for it in 2 Corinthians 1:8: "We are pressed out of measure" (KJV). To the Christian these days are both exacting and challenging. The true Christian life has never been easy. Crises of outward persecution often call for a spectacular depth of character and commitment. But day after day of inward pressure tends to wear one down, both nervously as well as spiritually.

A non-Christian may become impatient or sour or sullen, and nothing would be thought of it except the nuisance of the moment. But the spirit and temper of the Christian when under pressure always reflects upon the Christian faith.

Does our Christian joy, peace, and patience survive under the strains of day-by-day living? Or, does it merely struggle against them? Dare I ask, could someone be thriving in the midst of pressure?

The prince of evil makes Christian people his main target these days. He tries to wear out our patience, disturb our peace, and smother our joy. He seeks to make us give in to the pressures of the day in which we live. His scheme is to occupy our minds with cares and to swerve our gaze away from Christ, that we might be "pressed out of measure."

Now take that word *pressed* with its prefixes. You could say "depressed," "suppressed," "repressed," or even "oppressed." All these are states into which Satan would like to bring us through pressure. But over against all of this is the all-sufficiency of our triune God, the Father above us, the Son beside us, and the Spirit within us.

Be assured today that God is able to "make all grace abound toward you so that you always, having all sufficiency, in all things, may abound to every good work." I challenge you today to find your sufficiency in Christ. He's more than enough for what you are facing today.

JULY 19

God Really Knows You

God says in Jeremiah 1:15, "Before I formed you in the womb I knew you, before you were born I set you apart; I appointed you as a prophet to the nations." These words were spoken to Jeremiah and he was led to record them for our good, for us who live these centuries later.

These words may well find our attention captivated. For they certainly speak to us as they originally did to Jeremiah. If in reading the words again we listen inwardly, we can hear God saying to each of us, "Before I formed you, I knew you. Before you came forth, I set you apart, and I ordained you."

Reflect for a moment on the divine knowledge God has of us. God knows us better than the outer world knows us, better than our closest friends know us, better than we know ourselves. He knows us! He knows every breath, every heartbeat—every thought, word, and act—throughout our entire lives.

As the wondering psalmist says in Psalm 139:2, "You know when I sit and when I rise; you perceive my thoughts from afar." In a word, God knows us *absolutely*: "Before I formed you," He said, "I knew you." How foolish, therefore, to think of concealing anything from God! Have you ever tried to hide anything from God?

Listen to another of His words to us through Jeremiah 23:23–24: "'Am I only a God nearby,' says Jehovah, 'who can hide in secret places so that I cannot see them?' declares the LORD. 'Do not I fill heaven and earth?' declares the LORD." How foolish it is to reject God's verdict upon us!

See what God says to Jeremiah about the human heart in 17:9: "The heart is deceitful above all things and beyond cure. Who can understand it?" That is true of the best people as well as the worst. And the best know it as well as the worst. It is not because God originally willed this to happen, but rather because humanity has fallen in Adam. Humanity needs saving, not only from the guilt of their transgressions but also from stony and wicked hearts.

That is why God says in Ezekiel 36:26, "I will give you a new heart and put a new spirit in you; I will remove from you your heart of stone and give you a heart of flesh."

I thank God today for the new heart He has given to me and to all who will follow Him.

Friend, He formed you, He knew you, and He knows you right now. Mark it down: a God who knows you that well determines to be with you until the end—even into eternity.

JULY 20

He Can Make You Strong Even in Your Weakness

The writer of Hebrews in 11:34 speaks of champions of the faith who "out of weakness were made strong" (NKJV).

The eleventh chapter of Hebrews has been called "the Westminster Abbey of the Bible." Here are the heroes and heroines of Old Testament times. Here are men and women of faith who wrought exploits in the name of the Lord.

Here are the monuments and the epitaphs of illustrious worthies who were great in the sight of the Lord. As we read the account of what they did, we are captivated and challenged. Yet at the same time a subtle suspicion sticks obstinately in our minds, that they were different from us therefore we could not ever be expected to act as they did; they were specialists, whereas we are just plain, average, ordinary people.

Then we suddenly come across this revealing little clause in verse 34: "out of weakness were made strong" (NKJV). Now this gives new insight into the whole story. Here is comfort and hope. Out of weakness *we also* can be made strong. Those men and women of long ago were real flesh-and-blood heroes and heroines, men and women of like passions as ourselves. We must look at them again.

If they were indeed weak humans as we are, then could we, through Him, become like them? Yes, we may, but how? In all those Old Testament worthies we see triumph, a triumph that can be ours as well. The key to all of this is *faith.* Out of weakness they were made strong by believing, and so can we.

Is the writer thinking especially of Job and Hezekiah when he says, "out of weakness were made strong"? Or do the words cover a wide field, like Moses, Gideon, Jeremiah, and others? Is not this the story of every human soul who has risen to a life of victorious godliness? Is it not the story of every Christian worker blessed in the service for Christ and of every righteous cause that has won its way to victory? Yes, "out of weakness were made strong" applies to all of us.

Are you a fearful person? Do you have poor health, or is your complaint that you are not made of hero stuff? Then let these heroes file before you one by one, all under the same banner that reads, "out of weakness were made strong."

Friend, today out of your weakness God desires to make you strong. Believe Him and allow Him to do what only He can do.

JULY 21

Are You Listening?

After Jesus gives the parable of the sower in Luke 8, He gives us a warning in verse 18: "Consider carefully," He says, "how you listen."

This is not the only place in which our Lord refers to the way people listen to the preaching of the truth. Again and again He punctuates His teachings with words like "He that has ears to hear, let him hear." Jesus evidently realized with much concern that His biggest problem was not the subject of His preaching but rather the way people heard it.

In the parable of the sower, Jesus likens His hearers to different kinds of soil. He shows how the seed sown is largely at the mercy of the soil. This matter of the way people hear is still the Bible preacher's nagging concern. Often his or her most disheartening problem is the way people listen to what is said.

This same problem has been a heartbreak for apostles and prophets down through history. When God sent Ezekiel, He said in verse 7 of chapter 3, "But the house of Israel will not listen to you." Then why in the world send him in the first place? Because the people must be given a chance to hear. God wants you, He wants me, He wants us all to have a fair chance, a chance to hear and respond to His Word.

In Acts 7 we read of Stephen's address to the Jewish supreme council. Those Jewish leaders heard only too clearly what Stephen said. And had they responded, the entire course of history would have been affected. But in another sense, they did not really hear at all. Verse 57 says, "They put their hands over their ears and began shouting. They rushed at him" (NLT).

The problem that day was not in the preacher, but it was in the hearers. When they "put their hands over their ears," they were symbolically acting out what they had already done in their own hearts.

No people are so deaf as those who refuse to hear. Friend, there is no question that God is speaking these days through His Word, through prayer, through preachers, through many other ways. The real question is this: Are you careful about how you listen? Listen today, friend—God is speaking.

He Answers before We Even Ask

Second Peter 1:3 says, "His divine power has given us everything we need for life and godliness."

A daughter who was writing home to her mother asked her to send some money for the Christmas holidays. The daughter said, "You will never know how many debts I have incurred. I have not even started to buy presents yet." Her letter included the added impact of a P.S.: "Send today as much as you can." It was signed, "Love, Judy."

The mother replied with a rather unusual note. "It is not possible for us to send the money that you need today. We are really sorry. Have a wonderful Christmas. Love, Mother."

Mother's letter also contained a P.S. It simply read, "Turn the page." On the other side of the letter was a note that read, "I cannot send the money today, because I sent it yesterday." Now there was great relief in Judy's young heart. The needed resources were already on the way, sent even before she had asked. This was real provision from one who really loved her.

At times we Christians find ourselves in this type of dialogue with the one who forever loves us, our heavenly Father. Sometimes we pray, we plead, we beg, that He will send the things we need. And the answer comes back as somewhat of a disappointment in the form of "No" or "Wait." Sometimes our hurt feelings resemble Judy's toward her mother—until we turn that sacred page and experience great relief of heart and mind.

Second Peter 1:3 says, "His divine power has given us everything we need for life and godliness." You see, sometimes we've been asking for blessings that are actually already ours in Christ.

May we live such confident lives that we demonstrate that Jesus is our only source so that others will see our inner security and want Jesus too.

In Isaiah 65:24 God says, "I will answer them before they even call to me. While they are still talking about their needs, I will go ahead and answer their prayers."

He knows what we need before we do.

JULY 23

Having The "Blesser" Is Better than Any Blessing

In Colossians 1:17 Paul writes, "In Him [Christ] all things hold together."

The supreme experience in life is to get past all lesser experiences and get to Jesus Himself. Many people stop short of the giver because they are forever seeking this or that special gift. Many saints can testify to years of being occupied with this doctrine or that, this blessing or that, but coming one day into a larger place of resting in the Lord Jesus Himself. As a result, they found in Christ their reward, in Christ the focus of their entire lives.

Anything short of focusing in on Jesus is temporary, immature, and incomplete. You see, we are completed with Jesus, not in any experience or favorite doctrine. Here is the experience that excels all experiences, because knowing Jesus includes everything that is of great value.

The whole is greater than any of the parts. You see, getting through to God is not some strange emotional experience, although it may indeed move your emotions, but simply arriving at the blessed point at which we rest in the "blesser" and not in the lesser blessing. Then, whatever we may lose, we have Him, and in Him we have everything. All things are ours. We are Christ's, and Christ's is God's

Yes, Paul hit the nail on the head: in Jesus all things hold together. I challenge you today, friend: keep your focus on Jesus and watch as all things hold together in Him.

JULY 24

He Comes, He Sees, He Conquers

In Like 4:38–39 we read, "Jesus left the synagogue and went to the home of Simon. Now Simon's mother-in-law was suffering from a high fever, and they asked Jesus to help her. So He bent over her and rebuked the fever and it left her. She got up at once and began to wait on them."

Jesus went into Peter's house. It is an interesting circumstance that Peter's home was there at that time. John 1:44 tells us that he lived in Bethsaida. But here we find his home in Capernaum. There had been a move. Why? Jesus had now come to live in Capernaum, according to Matthew 4, and at some point Peter apparently decided to move there himself.

Whether the move had to do with the heat and humidity or there was an epidemic, we do not know. But in their moving something had happened. They had not been there very long until Simon's mother-in-law was stricken with a high fever.

Affliction comes even to those who follow Christ. But the blessing is that He is always with us, even in our afflictions. The more fully we follow Him, the more immediate is His help. Peter and his wife asked Jesus to help, to heal this afflicted loved one, and at once Jesus came.

Not only did Jesus come to them, but He also saw. You see, Luke was a doctor. He is the one who tells us that it was a "high fever." This patient's condition was serious. Her loved ones were very anxious. Jesus took in the situation at once. He saw with eyes such as no other physician could ever see.

Not only did Jesus come and see, but He also conquered. The Bible says the fever left her. This was no slow, uncertain reducing of a fever. The cure was immediate and complete. The Bible says, "She got up and began to wait on them."

Luke adds a vivid touch when he writes, "Jesus rebuked the fever" as though there were an evil intelligence behind it. If that were the case, then both disease and demon fled at the omnipotent touch of the hand of Jesus.

All of this illustrates what happens or is meant to happen when Jesus comes into a human heart. He comes, He sees, He conquers. The big question for you and me, friend, for each of us, is this: has Jesus really come, has He really seen, has He really conquered my heart and life? Am I allowing Jesus to do in my heart, in my home, what he did in Peter's heart and Peter's home?

JULY 25

The Winds and the Waves Know His Name

One day a fierce storm arose on the Sea of Galilee. In Matthew 8:26 we read, "Jesus got up, He rebuked the winds and the waves, and it was completely calm." Four things outlined in this event speak to us today:

1. The storm came.
2. It was beyond human control.
3. Jesus had complete control to calm the storm.
4. There were tremendous lessons to be learned.

The whole episode is kind of a parable for us. The storm came. Just as the Sea of Galilee was subject to sudden disturbances, so are our hearts. Storms are going to come to our hearts. Sometimes these storms come as storms of persecution, adversity, or temptation.

But there's a deeper truth here. Sometimes storms on the outside are not calmed. God allows them to come. He often does not stop the storms of persecution, adversity, or temptation. But by strict comparison, that long-ago storm on the Sea of Galilee speaks to us of those inward tossings, those inward surgings, that trouble our minds and hearts.

Persecution, adversity, and temptation may be the outward causes, but the storm itself, as represented by the turbulent sea, is an inward, mental, spiritual struggle. After all, if persecution and temptation did not inwardly disturb us, there would be no real temptation at all.

The storm we need Jesus to calm is that which the evil one causes on the inside of our lives. Persecution comes our way. Inwardly there is a storm that breaks, a storm of fear, of panic, of temptation to resentment. Adversity besets us. Inwardly there arises a storm of doubt, discouragement, or a temptation to rebellion perhaps.

Temptation allures us. Inwardly there starts up a storm of wrong desire, of impure motive, of evil passions. Maybe jealousy, bitterness, or bad temper. But many such storms that we ourselves cannot calm—Jesus can calm. They seem to be beyond our control. But Jesus is our control center.

Not only can He save us, but He can fill us with His great Spirit so our inner lives may be kept calm and serene. Swellings of fear and temptations to resentment, doubt, and evil passion will die away as Jesus genuinely controls our hearts.

Years ago a song captured this thought with the words "He gives peace in the midst of the storm."

What storm are you facing today? Trust Him. The winds and the waves still know His name.

JULY 26

At Home with Jesus

In Matthew 9:10 we read, "As Jesus was reclining at the table in the house" (NASB). Often in the Scriptures there is found a world in one word, the picture of an adjective, or the tense of a word, or the turn of a preposition. So it is with the phrase "in the house."

In the Greek it is usually translated as "in the home." It sends to the mind a picture of pleasant places and a feeling of contentment and rest.

Jesus was not in His own house. This scripture says he was at the home of Levi, a Jew who had become a tax collector for the Romans. Jesus was quite at home there, but then, He is somehow at home anywhere. He was kind of a land person—yet he was also at home on the water when He was asleep amid a frantic storm.

Jesus was used to the open places, yet He was at home in the city. He was at home when He was alone but also in the crowds. He was at home when He was with the common people and in the dwellings of the poor, the ones who heard Him gladly, but He was also at home in the residences of the rich. He was at home with groups, willing to serve as well as to lead. He seemed significantly at home even in Caesar's judgment seat, where He stood bruised but dignified before the puzzled and ill-at-ease Pilate. He was at home in popularity and somehow at home in adversity—and I say with great reverence that He somehow seemed at home even on the cross.

He said in John 12:27, "It was for this very reason I came to this hour." Yes, Jesus was always at home, but why? It was because to Him the heavenly Father was everywhere, and everywhere Jesus was, He felt a purpose in being there. It was because He was so sensitive to this that He wept the more freely over human sin and blindness. To Him, sin was not just a breaking of God's laws—it was also the breaking of God's heart. The Father was in everything, and thus even at Gethsemane Jesus could say, "Not my will, but your will be done."

Friend, should we Christians not be like Jesus in the sense of "at homeness"? Should we not be like Jesus in our "at homeness" with people? Jesus was holy, harmless, indefinable, and yet had an impact on sinners. He was the best mixer who ever lived. Should we not be like Jesus in this too? No one would ever find Jesus with a notice on His door that read, "No one at home."

Like Jesus, let us always feel at home in our Father's universe and always be at home to human need around us.

JULY 27

Are You a Server or a Sitter?

In John 13:14 Jesus said, "Now that I, your Lord and Teacher, have washed your feet, you also should wash one another's feet."

Here our Lord steps from magnificence into a menial task. The Bible says in John 13:3, "Jesus knew that the Father had put all things under his power," and yet He began washing the disciples' feet.

In the early days of Communism, one leader wanted to admit all who accepted the theory and the purposes of the movement. But Lenin insisted that only those who were devoted, those who were willing to do the most menial task, were received. His motto was "Fewer but better." He said, "Give me a hundred fanatics rather than a thousand indifferent followers."

I am reminded of Jesus's words in Luke 16:8: "The people of this world are more shrewd in dealing with their own kind than are the people of the light."

Considering how we often have to coax and beg church members to do a few things for our Lord, we can easily see how many people are loaded down with excess baggage. Nominal disciples agree in theory but have never learned our Savior's technique of the towel, the service, the washing of one another's feet.

The average church member would do well to look in his or her concordance and see how many columns it takes to list words like *serve, servant,* and *service.* Those references are many throughout Scripture. Too often we come to church to sit and not to serve.

I challenge you, friend: make up your mind right now, that today you are going to be a server—not a sitter.

JULY 28

Rest

The writer of Hebrews 4:9–11 says, "There remains therefore a rest for the people of God. For he who has entered His rest has himself also ceased from his works as God did from His. Let us therefore be diligent to enter that rest" (NKJV).

We live in a day when the calendar is choked with activities. We barely complete one task before another one urgently presses in on us. We are surrounded by the intricacies and complexities that comprise modern living. The pace is so accelerated that there is very little time for real rest.

The very sound of the word *rest* has a quieting effect upon us. Yet, do we comprehend its meaning in the rush of today? How much do we know of calmness and composure? How much do we know of tranquility of heart and mind?

Jesus said in Matthew 11:28, "Come to me, all you who are weary and burdened, and I will give you rest." This verse illustrates a "given rest." The order is very simple. *Come,* and *I will give.* This is the rest known by believers, a rest from the pressure and guilt of sin.

In Hebrews 4:9 we read, "There remains therefore a rest for the people of God" (NKJV). Now this has been described as a "found rest." It is a rest of spirit that stems from a complete confidence in God. In this rest the Christian finds sufficiency, stability, and serenity.

The psalmist wrote in Psalm 16:9, "Therefore my heart was glad, and my glory rejoices. My flesh also shall rest in hope" (NKJV). He was referring to the threefold being of a person: his or her heart, spirit, and flesh. Our emotions come from the heart. Our fellowship with God comes from the spirit, yet David does not forget that the flesh, our physical being, shall also rest in hope. The hope of one day being resurrected and changed into His glorious image is a tremendous comfort to our souls.

Body, soul, and spirit are included in God's loving care and rest. Friend, accept the rest that is yours in trusting in Christ completely. I challenge you today: whatever you do, rest, relax in Jesus.

JULY 29

Power to Deliver

Mark 5:1–20 talks about Jesus going to the country of the Gerasenes. Mark has a vivid way of telling things. And nowhere more than in this account of the Lord's visit where He meets a man possessed by demons.

We observe first that when Jesus came to those people, He came to do good. Everywhere around the shores of Galilee He had bestowed blessings such as had never been seen before. How? He had healed the sick, cleansed the lepers, and cured those who could not walk. He gave sight to the blind, speech to those who could not speak, and hearing to those who could not hear. Along with such works of grace came His sheer presence—God in their midst.

And so it is always: whenever Jesus comes to a community or an individual, He comes to do good. He comes to make wrongs right, to banish sadness and bring gladness. He comes to heal our souls, to remedy spiritual problems, to cure the ugly sores of the social life, to cleanse the moral leper, to set free the sin-enslaved, and to expel the unclean spirit. He comes to drive away the fervor of unholy passion. He comes to enlighten the inwardly blind. He comes to make weak people strong. He comes to infuse new life and new fragrance, new wholesomeness everywhere.

The pity of Mark 5 is that the Gerasenes were self-blinded to who He was, and the tragedy today is that many people are still blinded as to who Jesus is.

When Jesus came to those Gerasenes, the first thing He did was to crush the power of the devil. He was confronted by a demon-possessed man and immediately set this demon prisoner free.

This is surely the worst case of demon possession ever recorded in history. Not only was the frantic demon too strong to be bound by a chain, but the man was indwelled by a whole legion of demons. (A Roman legion of soldiers was often five thousand.) Jesus was the only one who could remove such a concentrated demonic force, and He is the only one who today can remove the evil spirits that plague our human society.

Behind the evils that curse America are the powers of Satan. Behind the modern drink and drug traffic is Satan. Behind much of the deadly trash that the modern movie and television industry puts out is Satan himself.

We never get far with spiritual endeavors until we recognize at least three things:

First, behind all the world's wickedness is Satan.

Second, only the Lord Jesus can overpower Satan.

Third, the Lord Jesus actually does this whenever He is received. Satan's power is no match for Jesus's power. He still has power to deliver.

JULY 30

Christ and vs. Christ or

In Hebrews 11:24–29 we read about Moses, who esteemed the reproach of Christ as greater riches than the treasures of Egypt. Moses had to choose one of two kinds of wealth: the reproach of Christ or the treasures of Egypt. He esteemed the first to be the greater riches, so as a result he laid up treasure in heaven.

Moses chose that which was imperishable. Hebrews 11:25 says, "He chose to be mistreated with the people of God rather than to enjoy the pleasures of sin for a short time." Moses saw the invisible: "He endured as seeing Him who is invisible" (Hebrews 11:27). And, of course, Moses did the impossible with the intervention of God. We read in Hebrews 11:23, "By faith he passed through the Red Sea."

Moses got off to a good start with his parents. This same account tells us in Hebrews 11:23 that Moses's parents hid him when he was a baby; they were not afraid of the pharaoh's commandment. We read later that Moses himself eventually forsook Egypt, not fearing the wrath of the pharaoh either. Like parents, like son.

If you have children, I challenge you today: there is a good chance your children are going to serve God as you do, or less, so I challenge you to be an example they can follow in close steps to Jesus. Generally speaking, they will read the Bible as you do, or less, they will pray as you do, or less, and they will serve God as you do, or less.

Moses's choice was reproach or riches. It is a matter of whether one wants to *get* rich or *be* rich. You can *be* very rich today with very little money. You can *be* rich in Christ Jesus or perhaps *get* rich "in Egypt," but you cannot be both.

It was never "Christ *and*." No, it has always been "Christ *or*." We cannot serve God and money. Friend, who are you really serving these days?

JULY 31

Don't Be Troubled—Christ Is Still Here

Our last devotional this month takes us to John 14:1–6, in which Jesus said,

> Do not let your hearts be troubled. You believe in God; believe also in me. My Father's house has many rooms; if that were not so, would I have told you that I am going there to prepare a place for you? And if I go and prepare a place for you, I will come back and take you to be with me that you also may be where I am. You know the way to the place where I am going." Thomas said to him, "Lord, we don't know where you are going, so how can we know the way?" Jesus answered, "I am the way and the truth and the life. No one comes to the Father except through me.

Here we find the disciples and Jesus in serious conversation. Christ knew that they were troubled about many things, especially about the fact that He would be leaving them. How true it is that when we focus on our security, we often lose our bearings!

Our world is made up of family and friends, of hope, dreams, and aspirations. And if something happens to shatter that world, it seems to us that an end will come. The world of the disciples was breaking up, but Christ spoke words of comfort. "Do not let your hearts be troubled," He said. He knew the world would pass away but that those who did the will of God would abide forever. Christ wanted to get their eyes off the present and on to the future.

In going away, Jesus was preparing a place for them in a world that would never end. When He asked if they knew the way to where He was going, Thomas said no. But Jesus was not angry with his answer—He took the time to explain carefully: "I am the way," the key to eternal life; "I am the truth," the key to all knowledge; "I am the life," the key to abundant eternal living. He added in John 14:18, "I will not leave you as orphans [comfortless, bereaved, and helpless]; I will come [back] to you" (AMP). This is Christ manifesting Himself physically while on earth, yet telling His disciples that He will dwell by His Spirit in the hearts of believers.

The indwelling of Christ through the person of the Holy Spirit is a glorious reality today. No matter what happens, our hearts should rejoice, our happy faces should reflect the peace, the contentment that a troubled world does not know a thing about.

Friend, someday soon—mark it down—Jesus is coming again for His own. What a blessed hope, what a tremendous challenge! Think of it: Jesus could come before breakfast!

AUGUST 1

Even the Bottom Can Be Good

If you have been around someone for many years, you have observed the person in good days and bad. Imagine that you had grown under the person's spiritual leadership. If you had found him or her to be a continual source of blessing to your life, and then suddenly you were made aware that this person was about to die—but before breathing his or her last, the person would give you a final message, a final blessing—how important do you think their final words would be to you?

In Deuteronomy 33 we have such words from the mouth of Moses. He is pronouncing words of blessing upon God's chosen people. These are words that he intensely desires the people to understand, for he is about to die. In Deuteronomy 33:26–27 he says, "There is no one like God. He rides on the heavens to help you. He rides on the clouds in His majesty, He is the eternal God, your refuge, and underneath are His everlasting arms."

It has been suggested that the Hebrew for *underneath* means more than just being under. The Hebrew literally means "the bottom of the bottom." Moses is telling the people that the God who has been with them in the past will continue to be with them even in the future. And when you feel you are at the very bottom, he is saying, "Remember: God's everlasting arms will be even at the bottom of the bottom."

As we serve Jesus, sometimes we face pressures and feel that we ourselves, even though we have been faithful to God, are at the very bottom. But the one thing I have found is that if you will be faithful to God, even though there may be times you feel you are at the very bottom, if you will trust Him—even the bottom will be good because God will be there.

AUGUST 2

Feed on God's Word

Children are a wonderful blessing to our homes. Even if you have no children, you can well remember the bright face and the innocent ways of a young neighbor or relative. These little people have a big influence on our lives.

However, behavior that is cute and appropriate at three becomes irritating and inappropriate at thirteen. As a matter of fact, if the immature behavior persists, the older person not only ceases to be cute—but appears to be sick.

The writer of Hebrews in 5:11–14 is speaking to the same issue, but in a spiritual sense. The passage says that these people are "slow to learn." In fact, in verse 12 we read, "Though by this time you ought to be teachers, you need someone to teach you the elementary truths of God's Word all over again. You need milk, not solid food. Anyone who lives on milk, being still an infant, is not acquainted with the teaching about righteousness. But solid food is for the mature."

To be sure, milk does have its place. There is nothing quite like a cold glass of milk, (of course, chocolate chip cookies can help too!). But milk is technically a previously digested food.

One of the dangers of reading devotional books or listening to recorded devotional material is that they have gone through the spiritual digestive system of someone else. They cannot give you all the meat you really need. The devotional book you're now reading attempts to get us into the Word of God, but don't allow it to be your only time in the Bible.

Jeremiah 15:16 says, "When I discovered your words, I devoured them. They are my joy and my heart's delight, for I bear your name, O LORD God of Heaven's Armies" (NLT).

I challenge you: don't put it off. Get into the Word of God— today. Take time for a real meal. How about a T-bone from Timothy or a roast from Revelation?

AUGUST 3

How Hungry Are You?

In Hebrews 6:1 we read, "Let us leave the elementary teachings about Christ and go on to maturity."

You may recall that when you see the word *therefore* in the Bible, what was said before it relates to what is said after it. Prior to this verse the writer said, "You need more than milk to grow, you need something you can put your teeth into—you need the solid food of the Word."

When the writer says we are to "leave the elementary teachings," he does not mean we should despise or abandon the elementary truths we have learned. The point is that our beginning spot is not a stopping place. It is the door to progress and the springboard to growing in the Lord. Ask yourself: Am I more like Christ today than I was a year ago? How am I different? What has the Lord taught me in the past six months? When was the last time God told me anything?

The phrase "same old same old" has been around a long time—and basically refers to something boring or monotonous. "It's just the same old thing." Does that phrase describe your walk with Christ? If so, it doesn't have to.

The scripture reads, "Go on to maturity." The thrust of the Greek here is that Christians desiring to grow, taking the time to study God's Word and keeping their surrender complete, will naturally move on to maturity.

The primary emphasis of these words is not on Christian character or even the Christian experience, but on advancing in learning the higher teachings of the Christian faith. If you are a little dissatisfied with your spiritual growth, if you are experiencing the "same old same old," check your spiritual menu. You can't grow if you don't eat! And you won't eat if you're not hungry. *How hungry are you?*

AUGUST 4

Rest in Him

In Hebrews 4:1 we read, "Since the promise of entering His rest still stands, let us be careful that none of you be found to have fallen short of it."

The expression *fallen short* refers to someone in a group marching with others who march faster than he or she does. Since the person cannot keep up, he or she falls behind. Falling behind in a religious sense means not fulfilling the demands of the march—it is a result of spiritual negligence, not spiritual inability.

The Greek here indicates that this is not just a past failure or falling but an abiding, continual, habitual condition. No wonder such people have no rest—they are not at peace with themselves, let alone God or anyone else.

But note that the verse says, "There is a promise of entering His rest that still stands." The rest mentioned here is not just a future rest that God's people will have in heaven, but a real relaxation from the nervous struggle of life.

A Christian has at the very center of his or her being a rest, an assurance, an abiding awareness of the fact that God knows what is going on and that God will take care of them. Rest in Christ today and you will find peace in the midst of great pressure. God is always bigger than what's the matter.

AUGUST 5

God Is Listening

Has there ever been a person you would very much like to meet but never had the chance? I was once in a church on the front row twenty feet from the pulpit when Billy Graham spoke. I was so thrilled to see and hear this man of God. I would have given a lot to talk with him. But after he spoke, he nearly vanished into thin air and I had no opportunity to meet him. He was close to me—yet so very far away.

Religion has often been filled with such feelings of awe and wonder. God is so high above, His ways are not our ways, and His thoughts are not our thoughts, yet Jesus changed all that forever. Hebrews 4:14 says, "We have a great high priest."

Jesus understands us as no one else understands us, even better than we know ourselves. And He has broken the barrier, making a bridge between God and humanity. No longer are we at a distance from God, for Hebrews 4:16 continues: "Let us then approach the throne of grace with confidence, so that we may receive mercy and find grace to help us in our time of need."

Think of it: mercy and grace. We do not deserve either one and yet we are to come to the throne *with confidence.* We do not come wondering if God will hear us or wondering if He will respond. We come with confidence.

When you pray, do you have confidence that God really hears you? Out of the multiplied millions of believers in the world, does He hear when you pray? Jeremiah 33:3 has been called "God's telephone number"—"Call to Me and I will answer you, and I will tell you great and mighty things, which you do not know" (NASB).

Rest assured, friend, that when you have a need, you have instant access to the throne of grace. Never a busy signal, never ignored, but always attended to by God Himself.

Whatever you pray about today, pray with confidence. God is listening.

AUGUST 6

We Have an Inheritance

A while back Joy and I sat down with a lawyer and made out our wills. There is a sense of satisfaction that comes with legally putting all things in order. One of our primary concerns is to be sure our children have a clear right to any inheritance in the future.

I did not think of it much before, but that is what God has done for us. He has left us a will and testament. He has provided for our future in the New Testament. In 1 Peter 1:3–4 Peter wrote, "God has given us a new birth…and an inheritance that can never perish."

The word *inheritance* refers to what God has for the believer, not here on earth but in the next world. Think of it: through inheritance we have a share of heaven itself. It does not matter who you are or where you live—if you know Jesus, you are heir to the best that God has.

The inheritances we have here on earth have no real guarantee. Through sickness, financial reversals, and poor economy, your inheritance may dwindle down to nothing before you pass it on to your heirs. But note that verse 4 says our inheritance "can never perish."

The thrust of the Greek here is that we believers have an inheritance that is being kept for us. And this inheritance is guaranteed, it is imperishable, it is incorruptible, it will not pass away. Titus 2:13 calls the coming of our Lord as the "blessed hope" that is before us. Jesus's second coming and our entrance into eternity with God are indeed the hope of all believers.

AUGUST 7

He Is Our Shield and Guard

It is a wonderful thing to do a job well, to look back at the finished product and enjoy the satisfaction associated with a task completed. Many people, however, are frustrated in their jobs because they never see much progress. They are never done, yet in all honesty, whether mowing the yard, painting the house, sitting at a desk, or driving a truck, most jobs, though completed for a while, need to be done again in a year, a week, or maybe even the next day.

In Simon Peter's first epistle he wrote, "Through faith we are shielded by God's power" (1:5). When something is *shielded,* it is guarded; it is watched over. This word is a military term indicating guarding done by soldiers. And the suggestion is that this is a continuous protection in the unending struggle here on earth.

There's a sense in which our job in serving Jesus is never done. The things we face from day to day may vary, but our commitment must stay complete. I have met people who have served Jesus for seventy years. They tell me that sometimes they face trials and struggles they have never faced in all those years. You see, Satan never gives up on us. He is very patient. Satan will wait a lifetime if that is what he thinks it will take to defeat us. He is constantly seeking whom he may devour. But we have a guard, we have a shield, we have a soldier who continually protects His own.

Today, friend, rest in the confidence that He who never sleeps or slumbers (Psalm 121:4) is watching over you right now!

AUGUST 8

Buckle Up

Are you old enough to remember when cars did not have seat belts? When they eventually became the law of our land, I saw something I had never seen before. Flashing across a bank's advertisement marquee were these words: "Seat belt law in effect." Law enforcement personnel were issuing tickets to motorists who did not wear their seat belts.

In 1 Peter 1:13 Peter writes, "Prepare you minds for action." He was saying—tie up, gather up, tighten your seat belt!

The word *prepare* refers to the oriental habit of gathering up one's loose robes with a girdle or belt when in a hurry or starting a journey. This was because the long, flowing robes would hinder a person's physical activity unless tucked under his or her belt.

Peter said, "Prepare you minds." When he used the word *mind,* he meant more than just their intellectual abilities. He was calling his readers to be alert and ready in their whole spiritual and mental attitudes.

Proverbs 23:7 indicates that what people think in their hearts impacts who they are and what they do. If you can control what you think about, you can go a long way in controlling what you do.

Jesus gives us the ability to have self-control because He is at the center of the self that is surrendered to Him. Today, friend, prepare your mind for action. Buckle up; tighten your seat belt—you're going to have quite a ride!

AUGUST 9

He Has a Plan

Do you have any friends who used to serve Jesus but something happened and these days they don't seem to think about Him much at all?

Paul talked of the need to keep himself disciplined in the things of God, lest after preaching to others he himself should become a castaway.

Ever feel that one day you may be a "castaway"? Paul must have been trying to encourage the believers at in Philippi when he wrote Philippians 1:3–6,

> I thank my God every time I remember you. In all my prayers for all of you, I always pray with joy because of your partnership in the gospel from the first day until now, being confident of this, that He who began a good work in you will carry it on to completion until the day of Christ Jesus.

Paul was telling these Christian that the one who brought them into spiritual life would not only start them in the right direction but would also carry them on until they were finally complete. Do you have some areas in your life that God is working on? Don't resist His leadership but rather say, "Lord, what are You telling me by allowing this in my life?"

Today we have the same promise the Philippians did. God will keep us if we will stay faithful. You see, He has not brought you this far to fail you now. Trust Him to finish what He has started in your life. He has a plan whether you can see it or not. Trust Him.

AUGUST 10

Habits

Do you have any habits? When I ask that question, do you feel it's a positive or negative inquiry?

Oh, I know there are habits that hinder and need to be broken, but habits are a blessing too.

This morning when I put my shirt on, I didn't have to stop and think, *Let's see. Do I button my shirt from the top to the bottom or from the bottom to the top?* When I put my jacket on, I didn't stop and ask, *Do I put my left arm in first and then my right, or do I put my right arm in and then my left?* If I had to ask those questions every morning, I would be two hours just getting ready for the day. I don't consciously think about how I button my shirt or how I put my jacket on. I've done it so much that it's just a habit, a habit that saves me considerable time.

In Philippians 4:8 Paul says, "Whatever is true, whatever is noble, whatever is right, whatever is pure, whatever is lovely, whatever is admirable—if anything is excellent or praiseworthy— think about such things."

Paul understood the influence of a person's thoughts on his or her own life. Right thinking is the first step toward right living. What is right thinking? It's thinking that's devoted to life's godly, higher virtues.

The last four words of that verse are illuminating to my heart and mind, for the Greek indicates that when Paul wrote, "Think about such things," he was saying to get into the habit of thinking about what is true, noble, right, pure, lovely, admirable, and praiseworthy. These words imply concentrated, focused effort. The verb form reminds us that we are to keep on stressing those things that share the qualities Paul lists. How much of your thinking is true, noble, right, pure, lovely, admirable, and praiseworthy? Paul's words are not a suggestion—they're a command.

Like me, I'm sure you've met people you felt were a blessing to be around. They made you a better person just by being with you. How often have they been people who had something solid and positive to say? Mark it down—they have developed the habit Paul talked about in this passage.

Is there any new habit you need to develop?

AUGUST 11

Content in Christ

Are you a contented individual? If a person were to look at your life, he or she would see how you appear—but I'm wondering about you down deep on the inside.

In Philippians 4:11–13 Paul wrote,

> I am not saying I am in need, for I have learned to be content whatever the circumstances. I know what it is to be in need, and I know what it is to have plenty. I have learned the secret of being content in any and every situation, whether well fed or hungry, whether living in plenty or in want. I can do everything through Him who gives me strength.

Paul is quick to let his friends know that he is not complaining. His happiness does not depend on circumstances or things; his joy comes from something deeper, something apart from either poverty or prosperity.

Many scholars believe Paul was raised in a family of luxury. He had not known what it was to be without—but here he says that he *learned,* he was made aware of how he could be content with or without life's possessions.

The Greek here indicates that Paul's contentment was something that came from the inside out. He had an inner sufficiency, with contentment that superseded his circumstances.

What was the key to Paul's contentment? His focus was not on what he was going through—his focus was on who he was going with. Contentment is a by-product of keeping our attention on Christ.

AUGUST 12

We Have a Generous God

I want us to look at three verses today. First, 2 Corinthians 9:6 says, "Whoever sows sparingly will also reap sparingly, and whoever sows generously will also reap generously." Paul is saying that miserly giving results in miserly living.

Second, Luke 6:38 says, "Give and it will be given to you. A good measure pressed down, shaken together, and running over." In the mind of Luke's listeners, the picture here was that of grain poured into a container, pressed down and then shaken so that every little corner was filled. More grain was then poured on until it was overflowing the edges.

Luke was underscoring the fact that we can never really outgive God. I'm finding in my life that when God makes me aware of a need and I respond with the time, effort, and money that are needed, He always gives back to me exactly what I need.

Third, Paul expresses in Galatians 6:9 an important insight into the reaping process: "Let us not become weary in doing good, for at the proper time we will reap a harvest if we do not give up."

The Greek here is drawing attention to the fact that at the appointed time there will be spiritual reaping. So, friend, I encourage you today: keep on giving and doing all the good that God shows you to do, and when the time is right, God will open the harvest to you. You just can't out give God.

AUGUST 13

Learning as Jesus Did

How does God teach you things? Do you just read something and all of a sudden you know it's for you? Do you observe the way God works in others' lives and assume that's how He will work in yours?

How about blessings? Does God teach you through the good things He brings your way? How about suffering? Is that how God teaches you?

In Hebrews 5:8 we read about Jesus: "Although He was a son, He learned obedience from what He suffered."

Scholars indicate that Jesus's lessons in obedience came from the way He responded to His sufferings in the flesh. Because Christ was determined to trust in the Father, even His enemies were used by God to teach Jesus what the Father wanted Him to learn. Think of it: if Jesus had responded with bitterness and unforgiveness, He would have forfeited not only His Savior role, but He also would have missed many of the lessons the Father had for Him.

How have you been doing with your sufferings lately? Have you been complaining or learning from the things you have faced? Like Jesus, let's choose to learn through what we suffer.

AUGUST 14

In What Direction Are You Going?

Do you remember the day you first met Jesus? Remember how life seemed to take on new meaning? If you have been a Christian for a while, it will be a little harder to remember—but try really hard. Try to remember the first day the peace of Christ flooded your life. Now move on down in time. Months and years perhaps have passed since that time. Can you still sense the peace of Christ? Do you still feel you're moving in the right direction at the right speed?

Paul was concerned about Christians in Galatia, for some of them had started well but were not doing so well now. In Galatians 5:7 he wrote, "You were running a good race. Who cut in on you and kept you from obeying the truth?"

The Greek here suggests that there was an obstruction, some kind of distraction for these Christians in their course of following the truth. The picture is that of a runner who has allowed his or her progress to be blocked or who is still running but is on the wrong track. I guess you could say he or she was sidetracked.

Isn't that one of our great temptations today? Oh, you probably won't go out and commit some grievous sin, but have you had a tendency to be sidetracked? Are you still in love with Jesus? Some things are wrong not because they are wrong in themselves but because they lead in the wrong direction.

If you have been off track, wouldn't this be a good day to start back in the right direction?

AUGUST 15

With God We Can Face Anything

In 2 Timothy 1:12 Paul wrote, "I know whom I have believed, and am convinced that He is able to guard what I have entrusted to Him."

Paul was saying, "I'm not talking about committing myself to just anyone—but I *am* saying I know the one to whom I am giving my allegiance." Paul personally knows this Christ to whom he has pledged his trust and to whom he will continue to give his life.

The apostle knows that the Lord will guard, protect, keep watch over what he has entrusted to Him. The word *entrusted* is a legal term representing something that one person places on trust in another's keeping. Since Paul had entrusted everything to God, he was able to relax in the confidence that God would do what is right. Are you relaxed in your walk with God?

I wonder if some of our stress does not stem from the fact that we have not *entrusted* to God everything. Oh, I know in our heads and with our mouths we can easily commit everything to God—but what about in our hearts? Have you really given Him your family, your future, your finances. You say, "Of course." Does God know how to handle them? "Well, sure." Okay, then today let us move in the confidence that what we have entrusted to Him—He *really* can handle. As a matter of fact, He can help us face anything that might come our way—anything.

AUGUST 16

Watch Your Words

In the ancient world, useless talking was considered to be caused from a sickness of the soul and demonstrated itself either in the quantity of the words spoken or the quality of the words spoken.

That's what Paul had in mind when he wrote to Timothy in 2 Timothy 2:16: "Avoid godless chatter, because those who indulge in it will become more and more ungodly."

We've often heard it said you are what you eat. However, in a very real sense, you are what you *say.* If you want to find out what people are like, all you have to do is listen and see how they talk about others—they don't have to say one thing about themselves. But you'll know volumes about them by the manner in which they discuss *others.*

Paul says, "Avoid godless chatter"—because it will just make you more ungodly. Have you ever noticed that if you listen to godless chatter, your temptation is to do the same? The opposite is true too. If you will set a pattern of positive, God-filled speech, you'll influence others to do the same.

Your decision today is not if you will talk or not, but if it will be godless or godly talk! What you say says something about who you are. Watch your words.

AUGUST 17

Your Example Has Influence

In 2 Timothy 2:24 Paul wrote, "The Lord's servant must not quarrel; instead, he must be kind to everyone, able to teach, not resentful."

Literally Paul was saying that as servants of the Lord, we should not *fight.* The word was generally used of armed soldiers, or those who engage in hand-to-hand struggle. More directly, it refers to wrangling, quarreling, or disputing—the picture is that of people who wage a war of words.

Does it sound too harsh? I mean, is there such a thing as a "war of words"? Let me ask you this: have you ever been injured by what someone said? Did you feel as if you had been in a war? On the other hand, have *you* ever hurt someone else by what you said? Did you bring some verbal combat into his or her life?

Paul says we are to be kind, to be examples, thus able to teach others. Do you see yourself as an example of Christian conduct? It does not matter whether you see yourself that way or not—you are. The question is this: what kind of example, what kind of teacher are you? Determine today that if everybody did what you do when it comes to Christian conduct, this world would be a better place to live in. Live as if people were being influenced by your example—because they are.

AUGUST 18

Staying Spiritually Sensitive

In 2 Timothy 2:26 Paul says there are some who need to "come to their senses and escape from the trap of the devil, who has taken them captive to do his will."

It is as if Paul was saying that these people are drunk, that they need to sober up, to return to sobriety. The concept of returning to their senses implies some previous dulling of their spiritual life by evil influences, just as in getting drunk. The devil's method is to numb the conscience, confuse the senses, and paralyze the will.

Friend, let's be honest. Do you know of things right now in your life that would never have been allowed the first six months of your Christian walk? Are you doing things now that you would have questioned others for doing back then?

You see, the devil tries to desensitize us to what is right and what is wrong.

Why not be smart? If there are things Satan has lulled you into, almost made you numb to, that you sometimes wonder about, face it: you're becoming spiritually numb. The circulation in your spiritual arm is cut off. No wonder you find yourself spiritually asleep. Shake yourself; come to your senses. Anything that causes you to be less sensitive spiritually—that thing for you must be avoided.

AUGUST 19

Choosing Friends

Write down or at least think about who your three best friends are. Now think about the kinds of persons they are: Are they kind, do they spend time in the Word of God, do they talk of God and His influence in their lives? What are their basic goals for life? Now go look in the mirror. You're probably looking at someone just like the people you described. We tend to become like those we are around.

When Paul talked about the people in 2 Timothy 3:2–5, he said they were "lovers of themselves, lovers of money, boastful, proud, abusive, disobedient to their parents, ungrateful, unholy, without love, unforgiving, slanderous, without self-control, brutal, not lovers of the good...conceited, lovers of pleasure rather than lovers of God, having a form of godliness but denying its power. Have nothing to do with them."

Paul is thinking here about the way people will be in the last days. However, all days have these problems in varying degrees.

There are people in every generation who have these characteristics, but Paul goes on to say in verse 5, "Have nothing to do with them." The warning here in the Greek is a very strong one. Paul is saying, "Stay away from these people as far as being their best friend. These people can kill your spirit. Avoid these relationships at all costs."

Choose your friends wisely—chances are you will be like them.

AUGUST 20

True Freedom

Paul continues his warning in 2 Timothy 3:7, where he speaks of those who are "always learning, but never able to acknowledge the truth."

The Greek here refers to those who desired to listen to other people's advice but their minds had become so undisciplined and warped that they had become incapable of obtaining the truth.

There are some people who seem always to be on an intellectual binge. They are always searching, questioning, investigating but never committing to anything. There are many people who would rather be confused than be committed. It's because real commitment costs you something. It's not wrong for us to ask questions, it's not wrong for us to want to know—but we need to be sure we are filling our minds with the Word of God so we can come to a knowledge of the truth, so we can know what to be committed to.

The Bible says in John 8:32, "You will know the truth and the truth will set you free." Note—when we first read this verse we tend to say, "It is truth that sets us free." However, it is not truth that makes you free—but it is the truth you *know* that makes you free. You could have ten Bibles in your house and not be free. It is what you *know in your heart* that makes you free. It is the truth you personally experience and accept that brings freedom. Today—spend time in God's Word, and the knowledge of the truth will keep you free.

AUGUST 21

No Fishing

In James 1:13–15 we read the phrase "when tempted." *Tempted* is the word used when referring to temptation to sin. God does not bring things our way to lead us to fall into sin. It is contrary to His very nature. He does allow things in our lives that will develop character. Note the passage does not say *if* tempted but *when* tempted. If you have not been tempted today, be alert. You will be sometime—and probably today.

However, the obvious fact is that temptation gives us the occasion either to develop character or to be defeated.

James indicated that our temptation comes from our own strong desire—not sinful or evil desire, but strong desire. We are thus moved toward an object, and it is at that very point where we resist or give in to temptation.

If we give in, James says we have become *enticed.* This word applied to a hunter or especially to a fisherman who would lure his prey from its retreat and attract it with bait. James was saying that in like manner the first effect of temptation is to draw a person out of his or her present state and next, to get the person to take the bait.

Today be on the alert. Satan loves to fish and he will cast his lure in your direction. When he does, just show him the "No Fishing" sign.

AUGUST 22

Get God's Word on It

James advises us "to get rid of all moral filth and the evil that is so prevalent, and humbly accept the word planted in you, which can save you" (James 1:21).

The word *planted* here carries with it a real picture of how God's word impacts our lives. It is the word for an implanting not done at birth but later in life. It is used when describing something that is put within a person and then becomes part of his or her very nature. It is what the Holy Spirit does as we read, meditate, and pray the Scriptures.

The Bible is unlike any book ever written. It so relates to our lives that it becomes part of our lives. James said that this implanted word can "save you."

Are you allowing the Word of God to direct you in any decisions? How about that house you wanted to buy, or that job you were considering, or that text you were thinking about sending? What did God's Word say about those things? Did you talk to Him about them at all?

Friend, be careful not to short circuit God's plan in guiding you as His child. If His Word is ever going to guide and protect you, it will have to be *implanted, memorized, meditated upon.* Get into God's Word today, and God's Word will get into you.

AUGUST 23

Watch What You Say

Do you consider yourself religious? In James 1:26 we read, "If anyone considers himself religious and yet does not keep a tight rein on his tongue, he deceives himself and his religion is worthless."

In James the word *religious* means "pious," denoting the meticulous observance of ritual and regulation. It could be sincerely or hypocritically performed and in both cases it would appear to be devout. The word carries the connotation of strict observance. However, James said that regardless of how religious you consider yourself, how many rituals you keep, or how many spiritual things you do—if you do not control you tongue, your religion is worthless.

James said, "Put a tight rein on your tongue." The picture is that of a person putting a bridle in his or her own mouth.

If you were to be graded on a scale from A to F, where A is superior and F is failing, how would your religion be graded in relation to your tongue?

A good principle for life in the area of talking is this: if you would not write it down and sign your name to it, you probably should not say it.

AUGUST 24

Do You Love Everyone?

Do you ever find it hard to love someone? Is there anyone you are tempted not to like? You may say, "Oh, yes! ____ is hard to love; he [she] just rubs me the wrong way." Does the Lord really mean for us to love everyone? How can we love those who are hard to love?

In 1 Peter 1:22 we read, "Now that you have purified yourselves by obeying the truth so that you have sincere love for your brothers, love one another deeply, with all your hearts." Now there's a handle. There's something we can do with those hard to love.

First, Peter says to purify yourselves and second to obey the truth. As a result, you will develop a deep love for the person. In other words, the way to purification is through obedience to the truth. What does the truth say? It says, "Love one another." If I act out the truth or am obedient to the truth, the purifying will happen. I will be free of me and filled with Him and will have love for others. Obedience leads to purification, which results in love.

You may not feel it right now, but start doing and acting out the way you wish you felt. As you act out your love in what you do and say, you will feel sincere love for your new friend. Today—buy that person a card, take him or her to dinner, phone him or her, and then stand back and watch the love flow in and through a vessel who obeyed the truth—and that is you.

AUGUST 25

Seeing by Faith

In Hebrews 11:1 we read, "Faith is being sure of what we hope for and certain of what we do not see." Ever wonder how to build up your faith? Nearly every day we see people building their bodies. Sit-ups, push-ups, jogging, and aerobics are only a few of the ways. How about your faith muscle—has it gone flabby, or is it growing stronger?

Muscles grow stronger and firmer the more they are used. And just the opposite is true: the less you use them, the less strength there is until finally they begin to experience atrophy. They do not do what they are supposed to do. They do not perform the function for which they were created.

When we first begin exercising a muscle we don't often use, it becomes sore. There is pain sometimes accompanied by stiffness. But the more we use the muscle, the pain and stiffness seem to go away and we sense strength in the muscle.

How are your faith muscles? Are you exercising your faith so it will develop and grow? Are you becoming stronger in what used to be a weak area? Are you flexing your faith muscle to believe for something hoped for or for something you do not see? If we fail to exercise and believe, there will be no new growth or new strength for the next test. Exercise your faith by praising God for what He is doing even though you cannot see it. Exercise your faith by refusing negative thoughts. Exercise your faith by programming the screen of your mind to see the answer to prayer by faith before seeing it with your eyes.

AUGUST 26

What Has Your Attention?

In Colossians 3:2 Paul wrote, "Set you minds on things above, not earthly things." In verse 12 he continued: "Clothe yourselves with compassion, kindness, humility, gentleness, and patience." And then in verse 14 he writes, "Put on love, which binds them all together in perfect unity."

God promises to take care of us, but He does not promise to take all of the stress out of our lives.

Paul said, "Set your minds on things above." He is telling us to deliberately set our minds on God and not on the things around us. I have heard people say they "lose heart"—as if somehow it just kind of happened. You don't just lose heart—you *choose* to lose heart. No one can make you give up. Control what you think about and you have won a major battle. To "set your mind" on something is to consciously make it your central focus.

Paul challenges us to be compassionate, kind, humble, gentle, and patient—and then he says to be loving, for love is the chord that brings all the other virtues together. All of these help to create a positive spirit, and a positive spirit is contagious.

I challenge you today to keep your mind on the things that Jesus would think about. Someone else will learn from you what he or she can do as well.

AUGUST 27

Keep Pressing On

In Philippians 3:13–15 Paul is talking about goal-setting. He writes,

> Brothers, I do not consider myself yet to have taken hold of it, but one thing I do, forgetting what is behind and straining toward what is ahead. I press on toward the goal to win the prize for which God has called me heavenward in Christ Jesus. All of us who are mature should take such a view of things.

The scripture here is talking about an athlete or a runner. This runner has made a decision—to strain and extend his or her body toward the goal. Paul says, "I have discovered something. I have been a loser in life and I have been a winner. I have decided I am going to do whatever it takes to continue to be a winner for Jesus by doing His will. In this race I refuse to lose." What about you, friend? Will you go for God's goal in life? If so, you need a plan.

Two things I want you to do:

1. Count the cost.

There is no gain without strain. Lots of denial and discipline are a part of the journey. Oh, there are some gifts and graces, but great Christians are grown, not born. It is a daily walk and a daily journey toward the goal. It takes training, skill, repetition, and experience. We would not ask an apprentice carpenter to come and build a multimillion-dollar church. He or she would have to begin with smaller projects, doing his or her best and would expend effort on smaller projects first. Strong Christians go for the goal; they respond to training and discipline and grow in their journey. They press to achieve. See—there is no success unless we press to the goal. It is immature to think we can be dynamic Christians without paying the price, the cost of discipline, effort, and goal-setting. If I am going to be anything for God, somewhere along the line I have to decide to spend a minimum amount of time reading the Bible, praying, and listening to His voice every day. If you are going to be for God what you can, you will never achieve it without counting the cost, standing still, establishing some objective, and then running in that direction.

2. Make God's goal your goal.

Have you ever asked yourself, "What am I running for?" What is your goal in life? Are your goals work-related, are they God-related, are they family-and-friend-related? What is it that you think about most of the time? Our work-related goals should be God's goals. Our work should be one of the avenues by which we bring glory to God. If the job we now have is God's will, we should be bringing glory to Him through our work. The way we work is a witness to how we esteem Jesus Christ. Are we a gossip, are we negative, are we critical? If your neighbors or friends needed someone to pray for them, would they call upon you? Today, bring meaning *to* your work instead of looking for meaning *in* your work. Yes, like Paul, we press toward the goal.

AUGUST 28

Keep Growing

Peter advised believers, "Grow in the grace and knowledge of our Lord and Savior Jesus Christ" (2 Peter 3:18).

Growth here refers to the advance that is made in a healthy Christian life. In the Bible the words *health* and *wholeness* are often interchangeable. *Wholeness* in the New Testament is often presented in the present progressive tense. We are whole and at the same time advancing in our wholeness.

If we are obeying God, we are as whole now as we are capable of being, but there is also a continuing wholeness developing.

Let me illustrate. Picture in your mind a tree in winter. The tree is barren of fruit and foliage. It is dull and appears lifeless, but it is doing all it is capable of—considering the temperature and the environment. Is it the whole tree? Is every part there? Yes! But when spring comes, another season in the tree's life, it will leaf out, blossom, and be in full color. Ask yourself: What season am I in right now?

Most likely, if we would measure the tree we would discover that there had been growth. The tree was whole and at the same time was growing in wholeness and toward wholeness. What a picture of the growth of a Christian! We are whole now, we are growing in this wholeness, and we are growing toward the wholeness we will know.

AUGUST 29

Take It for Jesus

In 2 Timothy 3:12 we read, "Everyone who wants to live a godly life in Christ Jesus will be persecuted."

To live a godly life in the Greek means to live for God fearlessly. It denotes living in the right attitude toward God and can also refer to living a life of loyalty.

Do you find that as you live a godly life, as you live loyal to the things of God, that you are persecuted? Or perhaps you say, "I'm never persecuted." Does that mean you're not living a godly life?

To be persecuted means to be followed after, tracked, trailed. Has that ever happened to you? Oh, I know you probably have never had persecution in the worst sense of the word. Yet we face subtle persecutions, such as by the person at work who knows how hard you're trying in some new area and yet does all he or she can to hinder you.

What about a person at church who seems to be gifted at saying the wrong thing at the wrong time? How about people in your own household who should be the most concerned about your spiritual progress but often hurt more than they help? Yes, perhaps your godly life is existing in the midst of pressures you never thought of as persecutions. Perhaps what you are facing today is not right, it should not have happened, and you should not have to take it—can you take it for Jesus?

Our hurts can actually help us if we let them draw us closer to our Lord.

AUGUST 30

God Entrusts Us with His Truth

The book of Jude only has one chapter, and yet hardly any other book in the New Testament is filled with more of a spirit of urgency than this one with its twenty-five verses.

In verse 3 Jude writes, "Dear friends, although I was very eager to write to you about the salvation we share, I felt compelled to write and urge you to contend for the faith that was once for all entrusted to God's holy people."

The word *urge* here means "encourage" or "beseech." It is the word used of speeches of leaders and of soldiers who spur each other on. It is the word used of verbal commands that send fearful and hesitant soldiers courageously into battle.

We are to "contend for the faith." This means we are to be involved in the struggle, and we are to exercise great effort. The word *contend* was used of athletic contests and the struggle and effort of athletes in their games.

Jude said this faith that you are contending for has been entrusted to "God's holy people." In other words, the news of Jesus, the truth of the gospel, is *entrusted* to us. That means just as those before us who have passed the truth to us, so must we pass the truth on to others—today. Do your part to contend for faith. And make sure what you have is worth passing on.

AUGUST 31

Build Yourself Up

In Jude verse 20 we read, "Build yourselves up in your most holy faith and pray in the Holy Spirit."

We have a responsibility to keep ourselves encouraged. Do not depend on the Sunday morning sermon to be your greatest source of spiritual encouragement. Oh, sure—the Word of God preached is a blessing and does give direction. However, our personal excitement about the things of God is primarily our own responsibility.

Jude's reference to "your most holy faith" in verse 20 refers back to verse 3 and the faith that was "once delivered" for all the saints. The writer continues in verse 20 by saying, "Pray in the Holy Spirit."

The Christian must not only study the Scriptures if he or she is to grow in the faith and be of use to others, but he or she must also "pray in the Spirit," for the battle against false teaching is won not so much by argument as by prayers.

In Ephesians 6 we are instructed that our real battles are not with physical surroundings or individuals—but against the forces of evil in spiritual realms.

I challenge you today: pray, build yourself up as you read, meditate, and memorize the Word. When you do, you can pray in the Holy Spirit's power.

SEPTEMBER 1

God Is Coming Your Way

In Hebrews 13:5 we read, "Keep your lives free from the love of money and be content with what you have, because God has said, 'Never will I leave you; never will I forsake you.'"

The word *leave* is not from the usual Greek word but from a word that means "to uphold" or "to sustain." In the Greek there are two negatives before the word *leave*, making it a very strong negative statement. The promise more literally reads, "I will not, I will not cease to uphold or sustain you." This verse assures us of the sustaining presence of God as we go through trials and testings.

The word *forsake* in this promise is a combination of three words in the Greek. The first simply has the idea of forsaking someone. The second suggests rejection, defeat, and helplessness. The third refers to some place or circumstance in which a person may find himself or herself helpless, or forsaken. The meaning of the word here in Hebrews is that of forsaking someone in a state of defeat or helplessness in the midst of hostile circumstances.

In the Greek three negatives appear before the word *forsake,* causing it to be read, "I will not, I will not, I will not forsake you." Not only does this scripture promise God's sustaining power, but it also promises God Himself, present with us through everything. In simplest terms God says, "I will never let you down." Go in confidence today, friend, that whatever comes your way, God is coming your way too.

SEPTEMBER 2

Loving Him with Your Heart, Soul, and Mind

I came across a question recently that I would like to ask you. If you picked up a hitchhiker and led him or her to Christ, or met someone on an airplane or bus and had the privilege of helping the person find Christ as his or her Savior, and if in parting company you had only enough time to give the person one piece of advice to encourage a good start in the Christian life, what would it be?

Go ahead—think about it. What would be your advice? Would you tell the person to join a good fellowship of believers? Read and pray daily? Witness to others? Find a good pastor? What would you say? All these answers are good, but in Matthew 22:35–39 we have perhaps the best answer. Here Jesus says the most important commandment is to "Love the Lord your God with all your heart, soul, and mind," and that makes sense. If we really love God with all our heart, soul, and mind, everything else falls into place. Our love for God will draw us to the Word and prayer. Our love for God will draw us to a fellowship of believers. Our love for God will draw us to the things God wants in our lives.

Listen to me, Christian friend—if you are having some honest struggles in doing the things that show your love, why not start today by praying, "Dear God, help me to love You with all my heart, soul, and mind." When you love God with everything—all the other things fall into place.

SEPTEMBER 3

Security in Christ

In John 6:37 Jesus said, "Whoever comes to me, I will never drive away." Here Jesus uses a two negatives: "I will never, no never, drive you away." The words *drive away* are from two Greek words: the word "to throw" and another, which means "out from within." That is, our Lord is speaking of those who have trusted Him and are living for Him. Here the promise is "You will not be thrown out."

A word appears in the Greek New Testament that is not referred to at all in the English translation: *outside.* Literally the promise reads, "Whoever comes to me, I will never, no, I will never throw him or her outside." Here we have reference to the security that all believers have in Christ. Never will He change His mind about us. He receives us now and plans on keeping us all the days of our lives.

One important point to remember is that the security that the believer has is a conditional security. In Colossians 1:22–23 Paul said that God will "present you holy in His sight…if you continue in your faith." Friend, you just keep on being faithful, live in the freedom of the Spirit, continue in the faith, and God has promised to be with you always.

SEPTEMBER 4

Answered Prayer

In John 15:7 Jesus said, "If you remain in me and my words remain in you, ask whatever you wish and it will be given to you." The word *ask* is in the imperative mood, which means it is a command. It is to be understood in the sense of saying, "I command you to ask." The word *remain* implies fellowship with the Lord and dependence upon Him. To those who remain in the Lord, God says, "Ask whatever you wish." It is more than a command—it is a challenge. It is as if God were saying, "You meet the conditions, and I challenge you to ask and then see how faithful and able I am to answer your prayer."

It's interesting to note that the word *ask* is in the middle voice, which means the asking here is for the person who is praying himself or herself. This person is praying that God will do something in their own life, and because the person is remaining in Christ, the person can ask what he or she wishes. Why? Because by the person's prayer, their wish is to glorify God.

Finally Jesus said, "Whatever you wish will be given you." The phrase *will be given* in the Greek means "to become" or "to come into existence." God will (get it now)—if necessary, bring into existence whatever we ask. Literally this verse reads, "If you remain in me and my words remain in you, I command you to ask at once, and ask for yourselves whatever you wish, and it will be given to you." Wow—what a promise!

What prayer could you pray today that would glorify God?

SEPTEMBER 5

A Spring of Water in You

In John 4:13–14 Jesus said, "Everyone who drinks this water will be thirsty again, but whoever drinks the water I give him will never thirst." The words *will never thirst* are from a Greek construction by which Jesus underscored His words with a double negative. Jesus is saying, "If you drink from my water, you will never, no, you will never thirst again."

In the Greek text the Samaritan woman is talking about a well of water, but Jesus is speaking about a *spring* of water. The thought here is that the person who keeps drinking at the wells of this world—lifeless, dull, polluted, stale waters—will thirst again. But the person who takes one drink of the spring of eternal life need never thirst again.

The reason one drink satisfies is that when the thirsty person takes one drink of eternal life, that one drink becomes in him or her a spring of water leaping up into a fountain of eternal life. This spring becomes a river of living water, and this living water is just a symbol of the indwelling Holy Spirit, who constantly ministers the Lord Jesus to the believer.

What a privilege we have today! Think of it: inside you right now is a spring of holy water. Go ahead—take a drink today.

SEPTEMBER 6

If We Live, We Win. If We Die, We Win

Jesus gave the Christian view of death in John 8:51, where He says, "I tell you the truth, if a man keeps my word, he will never see death." Here again we have the "conditional security" we have talked about before. If we keep the Lord's words—that is, if we observe and obey what God says—then we will never see death.

The thrust of the Greek is very strong here. The idea is that the keeper of God's words "shall absolutely not see death." Then the statement is made even stronger by the addition of a word in the Greek that is often translated *forever.* So literally it would read, "If any man will keep my words, he shall absolutely not see death, no, never."

But you may ask, "Is that really true—don't Christians die?" The key to the interpretation of the verse is found in the meaning of the word 'see.' The word 'see' in John 8:51 is used primarily of one who looks at a thing with interest. It occupies his or her attention as the person fixes his or her mind on the issue at hand. Here Jesus says that the person who keeps His word will not see death. It means the person will not fix their gaze on death; it will not occupy this person's attention.

The reason death will not occupy this person's attention is because he or she has fixed their focus on Jesus—the Author of Life. You know, friend, we have a tremendous thing going for us. If we live, we win. If we die, we win. You just can't beat living for Jesus!

SEPTEMBER 7

Visiting for Jesus

Have you visited anyone lately? By our English word *visit* we usually mean "to call on someone" or to pay a visit in the sense of a social call. Consequently, we sometimes attach this meaning to the word when we find it in the Scriptures. But the Greek word of which it is a translation means something more than that.

The word *visit* is the translation of two closely related verbs that mean, first, to look upon in order to help or benefit, to look after, to care for, or to provide for. And second, the verbs mean to look upon or after, to inspect or to examine with our eyes. Although the word *visit* can contain some of these ideas, it does not totally express the Greek idea.

Matthew 25:43 is that familiar statement of Jesus "I was a stranger and you took me not in, naked and you clothed me not, sick and in prison, and you visited me not." What a richer, fuller meaning we see here in the light of the Greek! It was no mere social call that would meet the need of those in prison but rather a visit that meant to look after—to help, to benefit, and even to provide for.

I challenge you today to find someone you can really *visit*. Visit someone today for Jesus.

SEPTEMBER 8

Fight the Good Fight

In 1 Timothy 6:12 we read, "Fight the good fight of faith." The word *fight* was used among the ancient Greeks in connection with athletic events. It meant to contend for victory, to wrestle as in a contest, straining every nerve to the uttermost toward the goal.

The biblical writers seized upon these terms and used them to illustrate in a most vivid manner the intensity of purpose and activity that should characterize both Christian living and Christian service.

Our present-day National Football League is a good example of the struggle for supremacy in the Greek athletic games that were so typical of the first-century stadium contests. The point is that if we Christians would live our Christian lives and serve the Lord with the intensity of purpose and effort that's put forth in a football game, what God-glorifying lives we would live!

This scripture literally says, "Struggle the good struggle." I have no way of knowing exactly what you are facing these days, but I do know, even though I have been a Christian many years, that Satan brings areas of challenge to us that we have not faced before. He knows how to bring new struggles into our lives. He never gives up. I'm finding that when I keep my focus on Jesus, even my struggles can turn out for the good.

SEPTEMBER 9

Water Baptism

Have you been baptized in water? I mean, how important is water baptism anyway? What real purpose does it serve? In Matthew 3:11 John the Baptist said, "I baptize you with water for repentance." After Pentecost it was Simon Peter who said in Acts 2:38, "Repent and be baptized so that your sins may be forgiven."

Do these scriptures indicate that you are not really saved until you are baptized? Let's look at them. The word *for* in Matthew 3:11 and the words *so that* in Acts 2:38 are both from the same word basically meaning "because of." This same usage is found in Matthew 12:41, in which the men of Nineveh repented at, or because of, the preaching of Jonah; and in Romans 4:20, in which Abraham "did not waver through unbelief regarding the promise of God."

In the case of the men of Nineveh, Jonah's preaching was the cause of their repentance. In the case of Abraham, the reason he did not waver was the promise of God. The word *waver* here is from the Greek word that means "to vacillate between two opinions." So we see it as a repentance of those who received John's message, which was the cause of their baptism. Now the same was true of Simon Peter's converts. A more literal translation of John's words would be "I baptize you with water because of repentance" and also Peter's words "Repent and be forgiven." The scriptural meaning of water baptism is as a testimony that a person has been born again.

Friend, if you have not been baptized in water, I urge you to do it. It is a further biblical testimony of the new life you have in Christ. Think of it: even Jesus was baptized.

SEPTEMBER 10

Be Still and Think

Psalm 46:10 has been a continuing source of blessing in my life, especially the first eight words: "Be still and know that I am God."

Is it as hard for you to be still as it is for me? I mean, I like to do things. I like to go places, read books, study the Word, and even fish (let's hear it for fishing!). Sometimes I don't seem to have much time to be still. But I'm finding that this is foolish logic. Divine instruction often comes in our times of stillness and quietness before God. The distractions will diminish as we simply seek His presence and then become more eager for time alone with Him.

A precious saint listened as a scholar friend described his day. He did not believe in wasting time. He meticulously outlined his time for his day. Hour by hour, studying this subject, writing this book, handling this task, and almost breathlessly moving from one assignment to another—this was the pattern of his life. The dear saint listened patiently and waited for a moment when the scholar would pause for a breath. Then she quietly asked, "Friend, when do you think?"

You know, it's easy to be busy, even busy for the Lord. We're going and doing, studying this lesson, and rushing to the next task. But, friend, I ask myself and I ask you the same question: When do we ever stop and just think? In the stillness and quietness of being with God, our thoughts become established, our goals are made clear, and there is peace so that we can hear His voice.

I encourage you today: take time, sometime today, just to be still and think.

SEPTEMBER 11

Growing Every Day

In 1 Peter 2:1–3 we read, "Rid yourselves of all malice and all deceit, hypocrisy, envy, and slander of every kind. Like newborn babies, crave pure spiritual milk, so that by it you may grow up in your salvation, now that you have tasted that the Lord is good."

Peter is speaking of a divine command that must be obeyed if we as Christians expect to have a real hunger for God's Word. He is saying, "Rid yourself once and forever of all sin, for until a complete break is made with sin, you cannot expect to have a hunger for God's Word."

The word *deceit* means to "to catch with bait." We are not to be crafty, sly, or underhanded, but open, sincere, accomplishing our purposes by fair means. *Hypocrisy* comes from the Greek word used in reference to one who impersonates another. As believers ,we are not to pretend we are something that we are not.

We are cautioned against slander, which literally means "running down someone." We are admonished to "crave" or "intensely desire" the pure milk of God. God's Word is not like so many human teachings filled with some ulterior motives. But it is pure and unblemished, and that's the only way it can work; that's the way it brings blessing to the one who puts faith in it. *Grow* is literally "to be nourished up," to make progress" in your salvation.

That's what the writer is talking about. Sin in any life destroys the appetite for the Word of God. When sin is put away, the normal result is an intense hunger for God's Word. Then, when we feed our souls upon God's Word, we will make progress and grow in our salvation. Let's make up our minds to grow every day.

SEPTEMBER 12

The Principle of the Next Mile

In 1 John 1:7 we read, "If we walk in the light, as he is in the light, we have fellowship with one another." Fellowship with one another and fellowship with God are supremely important to us—and all we have to do is walk. Doesn't that sound easy?

Just walk! Then why does the journey at times seem so long, the task so overpowering?

I remember hearing an interesting story that lodged in my memory. As I recall paratroopers had to bail out of a plane that had been damaged. The soldiers ended up parachuting into a desolate, mountainous area. It was many weeks before an armed relief expedition could reach them. It was late summer, with sultry heat and downpours of rain. The hundred plus mile trip was treacherous and potentially life threatening.

As the march began a soldier felt a sharp object penetrating his foot. It was a boot nail that had pierced his foot. He marched on in spite of the pain. By evening he had large blisters on both feet. He and many other soldiers were sure they could never survive the ordeal. However, they found if they could somehow stumble to the next friendly village they could gain strength to carry on for another mile, another day. And really that's all they needed was to put one day after another that would eventually lead them to home and health. It was a tremendous demonstration of fortitude and a mindset to never give up. The entire event was characterized by the words, 'the principle of the next mile,'

When the going gets tough, don't fret about tomorrow, next week or next year – always remember the 'principle of the next mile' just take the next step.

SEPTEMBER 13

Are You on the Way God Has Chosen?

Abraham's servant was sent on a mission, and while he was carrying out his assignment, the Lord gave him direction. The New King James Version records Genesis 24:27 in these brief but blessed words: "Being on the way, the Lord led me." The NIV reads, "The Lord has led me on a journey."

Some people indicate by their attitude that God's will is a frustration to them, or perhaps I should say that their struggle to find God's will is a constant source or fretfulness. To be serious about God's will, we must be serious about God's Word. However, even studying God's Word must be done in balance. We must recognize the two sides of God's Word: His side and our side. Our side is merely to be "on the way." To be on the way we must be surrendered to God, to do His will His way.

This "being on the way" is for the person who puts himself or herself where they can be led. It is then God's responsibility to lead. Our desire to know God's plan ahead of God's timing brings much of our confusion. If we do our part, we can rest in the confidence that God is doing His part.

There may come times of doubt and wondering such as the servants of Abraham possibly experienced. Yet, obedience was the direction of the servants' lives, and guidance was the outcome.

Whatever decision you are making, just make sure you are "on the way" God has chosen for you—and you can rest assured in His guidance.

SEPTEMBER 14

Leaves but No Fruit

Is His fruit in your life? In Matthew 21:18–22 we read that early one morning with His disciples, Jesus was heading for Jerusalem. Jesus, the Master teacher, did some of His instruction in seemingly incidental situations. Evidently He was hungry and was looking for fruit but found an empty fig tree—all it had was an abundance of leaves.

At that moment the fig tree became a good illustration. Jesus spoke to it and said, "May you never bear fruit again!"

> Immediately the tree withered. When the disciples saw this, they were amazed. "How did the fig tree wither so quickly?" they asked. Jesus replied, "Truly I tell you, if you have faith and do not doubt, not only can you do what was done to the fig tree, but also you can say to this mountain, 'Go, throw yourself into the sea,' and it will be done. If you believe, you will receive whatever you ask for in prayer." (Matthew 21:19–22)

Could this be a picture of many Christian lives: full of leaves but lacking in fruit? We may have a positive outward appearance, but no love, no joy, no inward peace or power, no real desire to help others find Jesus—just barren trees.

Scholars indicate that this was an accurate picture of the Jewish world at the time of Jesus. It had all the outward adornment: daily services, lavish feasts, elaborate rituals, and rules by the hundreds—but no real fruit.

Today people long to see in you and me the genuine fruit of living and growing in Jesus. They long to see His love, His kindness, His patience, His life—living in us. Friend, never be satisfied with leaves. Ask God for His fruit to grow in your life.

SEPTEMBER 15

Loneliness

Billy Graham once said, "I can go anywhere in the world and speak on emptiness and loneliness and know that I am speaking to a felt need in any crowd." Jesus knew His followers would face temptations to lonely feelings, so some of His final recorded words in Matthew 28:20 were "Surely I will be with you always, to the very end of the age."

Loneliness is a major social concern today. Yet God never intended for people to feel lonely. God loves to fill the lonely heart with His joy, His peace, His presence. Jesus drew His disciples to Himself. One reason no doubt was to fellowship with them. We have biblical records of God's desire that we should not be lonely but that we should have fellowship with the divine.

Enoch walked with God. Moses met with God, Abraham was God's friend, and God promised Joshua, "I will be with you." The writer of the twenty-third Psalm could face "the valley of the shadow of death" because God was with him. Christ was so concerned about the disciples sensing His presence that He said, "Even though I am going away, I am sending another Comforter who will be with you forever." There is a difference between solitude and loneliness. We each desire and need those special times when we can get away and be alone (solitude)—but loneliness needs not be a part of our lives.

SEPTEMBER 16

Connecting with People

What would you do to win someone to Jesus? I mean, how much would you break out of your comfortable pattern to reach out to another person? How much discomfort would you allow in your own life if it would bring comfort and salvation to somebody else?

In 1 Corinthians 9:22 Paul wrote, "I have become all things to all men, so that by all possible means I might save some." Paul did not mean that at times his conduct was unprincipled or appeasing, depending on his crowd. At times Paul could be very stern and unbending in following the course of action that was essential to the gospel. But in nonessential things he accommodated those he was with.

The person who can see only his or her own point of view, who lacks any sympathy for others, and who never makes any attempt to understand the mind and hearts of others, will never have a lasting spiritual impact on their lives.

One of the great needs facing Christians today is getting close enough to people that they then have a right to speak to them about their spiritual lives. But the trouble so often is that they don't even try. Think about it, friend: Do you have anyone at all whom you are being "all things to, that by all possible means" you might help him or her be saved?

Building relationships with people, without compromising your Christian character, is part of doing all you can do to eventually share Christ with them. Is there anyone you are intentionally trying to connect with as Jesus would do?

SEPTEMBER 17

Believe Jesus and See Him Work

In Ephesians 4:30 Paul gives the church a solemn warning: "Do not grieve the Holy Spirit of God." This prohibition is also a promise in disguise. For what God commands He enables us to perform. The believer who seeks to live in step with the Spirit will find within himself or herself the power to live according to God's will. Thus we have assurance that we can live without grieving the Holy Spirit.

When Paul tells us in Romans 14:23 that "Whatever is not of faith is sin," he is giving us a basic principle. There is a reminder here that we play a key role in Jesus working in our lives. Is there anything in your life that Jesus is waiting for you to believe Him for? The great secret of the true Christian lies in daily, unceasing faith in Christ and His enabling whatever the situation.

It's great to have a history of trusting God and walking in victory. However, nothing grieves the Holy Spirit as much as unbelief. When this happens, Jesus is prevented from showing His power and glory in working out His deliverance in any situation. In Mark 6:5–6, when Jesus went to His hometown, "He could not do any miracles there, except lay His hands on a few sick people and heal them. He was amazed at their lack of faith."

Guard yourself today. Do not grieve the Holy Spirit by not believing that Jesus can make a difference right now in your life.

SEPTEMBER 18

Growing in Christ

Are you relaxed in your Christian walk, or are you on edge? Do you really rest, confident that God is working out all that needs to be done in your life?

In Philippians 1:6 Paul tells the Christians, "He who began a good work in you will carry it on to completion until the day of Christ Jesus." The Philippians had been a support group to Paul in his missionary endeavors, and he anticipated their continued support. But here Paul is also bringing a word of encouragement. Just as he advised the Galatians in Galatians 6:9 to "not become weary in doing good," so he underscores the fact that while they are being faithful to God, He is being faithful to them. God, who brought them to spiritual life, is leading them in their growth in grace.

A child does not get up every morning pulling on his or her legs and arms hoping for growth to take place. No, a child who takes in the proper nourishment and gets proper exercise will naturally grow. Growth is a by-product of healthy living for the child.

In our Christian life we cannot force growth. We simply take in nourishment through the Word and prayer and reach out in service to others—then the natural by-product of healthy Christian living is growth. Today I encourage you to keep on doing, trusting, and resting, and God will see to it that growing takes place.

SEPTEMBER 19

Speak When You Have Been Spoken To

In Philippians 1:9 Paul wrote, "This is my prayer: that your love may abound more and more in knowledge and depth of insight." Paul desired these believers to develop their knowledge and depth of spiritual understanding.

"Knowledge" generally conveys the idea of a mental grasp of truth, but the biblical sense of knowing God is an intimacy made possible by His self-disclosure, received by faith. A better knowledge of God and His ways will promote greater harmony with any fellowship of believers.

The "depth of insight" (discernment) is the application of the knowledge we have. These two Christian qualities have always been necessary in any group. Later in Philippians 4, Paul deals with some specific problems at Philippi that were threatening the unity of the local church. So here Paul prays for them before he proceeds with admonition and corrections.

Here is a good lesson for us all: the most effective way to influence another person is to pray for him or her. And if a word of rebuke or correction has to be spoken, let it be prayed over first, and then spoken in love. You may have someone at work, at home, at school, or even at church who is threatening the unity of the fellowship. Don't try to enlighten the person until the Holy Spirit has touched you in prayer about that person. Then and only then, speak a word of love.

Speak when you have been spoken to by the Holy Spirit.

SEPTEMBER 20

Discernment

Today Paul continues his prayer for the Philippian Christians in 1:10 by mentioning his desire that they "may be able to discern what is best and may be pure and blameless until the day of Christ."

The Greek here for *discern* permits two possible translations. Either approving what is best or testing things that differ—that is distinguishing between good and evil, or between what is good and what is better. In either case, Paul is focusing the prayer on what is essential in religion. It is a call to excellence.

The word *pure* is an interesting word that also has two possible meanings—first, it could refer to a purity similar to that derived from sifting something, a continual shaking-down until all impurities are gone. Second, it could be taken from a word that means "sunlight." In Bible times when pottery was made, a flaw in the pottery was sometimes filled with a waxy substance that could not be detected. However, if the vessel was held up to the light, the sunshine would illuminate the spots that were inferior, (the spots filled with wax).

Paul is praying for these believers that they will be found genuine, not covering over their faults but literally living transparent lives. Isn't it wonderful to know that you can live without hiding anything from anyone? What a way to live! What a way to die!

SEPTEMBER 21

Christ's Reputation

In Philippians 1:20 Paul writes, "I eagerly expect and hope that I will in no way be ashamed, but will have sufficient courage so that now as always Christ will be exalted in my body, whether by life or by death."

In Paul's difficult position as a prisoner of the Roman Empire, there was a danger of failure on his part to maintain his bold and fearless testimony, which was a habit all through his missionary career. This testimony had to do here not only with his spoken words but also the way he was responding to the pressures. You see, his testimony while under pressure said something that his preaching could not say. Your testimony when under pressure always says something about you.

The New English Bible translates Paul's desire by saying that "Christ will shine out clearly in my person." This is perhaps the ultimate truth to underscore in our minds. That is, the gospel is being communicated through your person, even through your personality. Here lies the awesome responsibility of every Christian. Once we have chosen Christ, once we have become members of His church, by our lives, by our conduct, we bring either glory or shame to Jesus. You see, a leader is always judged by his followers, and Christ is judged by us.

Psalm 23:3 says, "He guides me in paths of righteousness for his name's sake." What kind of a reputation are you making for Christ?

SEPTEMBER 22

To Die Is Gain

In Philippians 1:21 we have one of Paul's most familiar statements. It would be an excellent verse for you to memorize: "For to me, to live is Christ and to die is gain."

Since Paul was a prisoner when he wrote these words and was awaiting his trial, he had to face the fact that it was quite uncertain whether he would live or die. And in reality, to him it seemed to make no difference. As a matter of fact, when you stop to think about it, Paul really had no actual choice in whether he lived or did die; the Roman Judge would decide that. Paul was simply living in the middle of two possible verdicts: life or death. This adds more depth to his conviction that "to live is Christ and to die is gain." They were not idle words—they were very real possibilities.

The phrase *to die* is more accurately translated "to have died." The tense denotes not the act of dying but the consequences of dying, the state after death. Death itself would not be a gain to Paul, but to be in the presence of the Lord after death, in glory—that would be real gain. One of the benefits of living for Jesus is that not only do we have peace in this life, but at any time, at any moment—think of it, friend—we could be ushered right into the presence of Jesus. As Paul said in 2 Corinthians 5:8, "To be absent in the body, and at home with the Lord" (NASB).

We should live each moment with the reality that we could be in His presence before breakfast!

SEPTEMBER 23

Take It for Jesus

In Philippians 1:29 we read, "It has been granted to you on behalf of Christ, not only to believe on Him, but also to suffer for Him." Paul combines a couple of interesting thoughts when he writes, "It has been granted to you to suffer for Him."

Do you ever think of your pressures or sufferings for Christ as something that was *granted* to you? Here we have reference to suffering, which is no accident, nor is it a mark of divine punishment (as though God were angry with us). The exact opposite is true. Those who believe and yet suffer are shown great favor by God. It is actually a gift. The word translated "granted" in the Greek is a word from which we get our word *grace* or *favor.* What an eye-opener to all believers who suffer any hardship, any pressure relative to their faith! To suffer as this verse reads on behalf of Christ is actually a privilege given by God.

We must be careful not to draw the wrong conclusion. Suffering of its own sake is no privilege. But what a privilege suffering is *for Christ's sake*! You know, friend—there may be some things you face right now that are not right, they should not have happened, they should not be, you just should not have to take them. But let me ask you this: Could you be a witness through it all, could you take it for Jesus? Could God be "granting" something to you in the midst of it all?

Someone is being influenced by the way you respond, let that response bring glory to our Lord.

SEPTEMBER 24

One in Spirit

In Philippians 2:1–2 Paul writes, "If you have any encouragement from being united with Christ, if any comfort from His love, if any fellowship with the Spirit, if any tenderness and compassion, then make my joy complete by being like-minded, having the same love, being one in spirit and purpose."

When Paul uses the word *if,* he is not making a conditional statement but is stating a reality. His meaning may be clearer if we substitute the word *since* for the word *if.* Paul is not speaking of things that might be a part of their lives in the future. But he is referring to what *already* has taken place.

Paul is saying that since you believers are united because of Christ, since you are living in His love, since there is tenderness and compassion in your life—keep my joy full by keeping these characteristics you already have. Paul is not making a selfish plea. He knows whatever fills him with joy will also be for their good.

Later in Philippians, Paul deals with some things that threaten their unity. He knows the devil loves to create factions or cliques among God's people and thus disrupt their unity. Today, friend, keep close to Jesus and you will find you are closer to everyone in your life who knows Him. You indeed will be "one in spirit" with them.

SEPTEMBER 25

Work Out Your Salvation

Paul writes in Philippians 2:12, "Therefore, my dear friends, as you have always obeyed—not only in my presence, but now much more in my absence—continue to work out your salvation with fear and trembling."

As is always the case with Paul, his words are carefully chosen. The words *work out* are the translation of a Greek word that means "to carry out to the goal, to carry to its ultimate conclusion." For example, we may say that a student "works out" a problem in algebra. That is, he or she carries the problem to its ultimate conclusion. That is what Paul is exhorting these Philippians to do. They are to continue to work; they are to continue doing their part in their own salvation.

Here Paul is emphasizing what we are to do as Christians—but this is not a lopsided thing. It is not a suggestion that by our works we earn our way to heaven, for verse 13 says, "It is God who works in you to will and to act according to His good purpose."

The Greek word Paul uses for *works* and *to act* are the same word. There are two significant things about this word. First, it is always used in describing an action of God. Second, it is always used of effective action. The whole process of salvation is the action of God. In verse 12 we have human responsibility, in verse 13 divine enablement. Now there is a principle for life. Whatever God calls us to be or do, He gives us the power to accomplish. The choice is ours!

What are you choosing these days?

SEPTEMBER 26

Older than Jesus

In Philippians 3:10 Paul gives us five words that can be read so quickly that the depth of their message could be lost. He simply writes, "I want to know Christ."

It is clear that in this aspiration is a craving to know the person of Jesus. Paul wants to know the person of Christ. And to know a person is much more than knowing *about* a person. This distinction must always be kept in mind when talking about Christ.

A Jesuit priest by the name of John Powell tells of his prayer time with Jesus. In his mind he can remember a trail through a lightly wooded area. When he thinks about it, it brings warm, restful feelings to his heart and mind. And sometimes in his mind he goes back to that place. It is there in the recesses of his imagination that he meets with Christ daily. He pictures himself walking down the trail, and looking ahead, he sees Jesus walking toward him, and there in the serenity he and Jesus talk together.

One day as he walked through this scene that was so embedded in his mind, this Jesuit priest saw Christ coming to him. He looked at Jesus more intently and then said, "Jesus, I am older than you are." Now that may sound very strange to you today, but think of it. Here was a believer who had become intimately acquainted with the thirty-three-year-old Christ who fills the gospels. This priest, this man of God, had become so filled with this thirty-three-year-old Christ that his mental "prayer walk" with Jesus one day opened to him the realization that he was now older than thirty-three himself. As he looked at the person of Jesus, Jesus was so real that he was actually seeing Christ in a brand-new way. And he saw himself as a senior to Jesus.

Friend, how real is the person of Jesus to you today? Jesus will be as real to us as we really want Him to be.

SEPTEMBER 27

Is Your Stomach Your God?

Paul gives us some cutting words in Philippians 3:18–19: "Many live as enemies of the cross of Christ. Their destiny is destruction, their god is their stomach, and their glory is in their shame. Their mind is on earthly things."

Who do you think Paul is calling "enemies of the cross"? These are not people who are denying that Jesus is the Christ, the Son of the living God. These are not people who say they do not believe in the great doctrines of the church. The context reveals that these are people who have been identified with the church of Jesus Christ. They are those who rejoice in the liberty they have. However, they have turned liberty into license. They are part of the crowd who says, "Hey—if it's God's grace that's applied to our lives because of our sins, then let us commit more sins so that we can have more grace!" Paul says, "Their god is their stomach." That is just another way of saying they have turned pleasure and self-indulgence into their god.

Today it is a great privilege to serve God in the freedom of holiness. But we must never allow our freedom to become perverted. Let me ask you a question: Is there anything you do not do, not because it is evil but just because it may dull your sensitivity to spiritual things? Are you reading and watching things that add to your Christian walk? Is your "stomach" your god? Think about it.

SEPTEMBER 28

Praising and Forgiving

In Philippians 4:5 Paul writes, "Rejoice in the Lord always. I will say it again, rejoice. Let your gentleness be evident to all. The Lord is near."

Here Paul sets before these Christians two important qualities of their lives. First is the quality of *joy.* "Rejoice," says Paul. "I will say it again, rejoice." It is as if he said, "Rejoice"— and suddenly there flashed across his mind all that was to come. He himself was lying in prison with almost certain death awaiting him. The Philippian Christians were somewhat new in the faith, but difficult days, dangers, and persecutions inevitably lay ahead. So Paul is saying, I know what I'm talking about. I have thought of the worst that could happen and still I say, "Rejoice." Christian joy is independent of all things on earth, because Christian joy has its source in the presence of Jesus.

The second quality Paul speaks of is *gentleness.* He says, "Let your gentleness be evident." Gentleness is that quality that knows not only the letter of the law but also knows how to balance it with love. It is exactly what Jesus expressed when the woman who was caught in adultery was about to be stoned. According to the law, she should have been stoned—but Jesus gave her love and forgiveness. He gave her gentleness.

Today let us be like Jesus more than ever before. Is there anything you need to praise God about? Is there anyone you need to forgive? (Maybe even yourself)

Today do the praising thing and do the forgiving thing. You'll be glad you did.

SEPTEMBER 29

God Wants to Make You Strong

In 1 Peter 5:10 we have a very interesting passage: "The God of all grace, who called you to His eternal glory in Christ, after you have suffered a little while, will Himself restore you and make you strong, firm, and steadfast."

The word for *restore* is a word commonly used for setting a fracture. It means to supply that which is missing, to mend that which is broken, to restore that which is lacking. The definite suggestion here is that it takes a little time. Sometimes we hear it said or implied that when Jesus comes into your life, you are established immediately. But that is not necessarily so. Here Peter is saying that after you have suffered a while, then the healing, the growing, the mending take place.

You see, suffering, if it is accepted in humility, trust, and love, can add to a person's character that which is lacking. It can repair the weaknesses and add greatness to life. Peter says that suffering, if responded to appropriately, will help make you strong, firm, and steadfast.

I encourage you today to look at your pressures as a potential help and not a hindrance. God wants to make you stronger.

SEPTEMBER 30

Barrier in the Skies

Isaiah was very concerned about the people of God. It seemed the Lord was so far away. It seemed there was a barrier in the skies. So in Isaiah 64:1 he prays, "O that you would rend the heavens and come down." The Contemporary English Version says, "Rip the heavens apart!"

Have you ever had a day when you could have prayed that prayer? Do you ever feel as if there were a barrier in the skies? I know I have. Perhaps you too have had days when you sought His help and instead of waiting patiently for the answer, you said something like, "O God, if you really love me, please help me—right now." Does that sound childish? Maybe, but even the most mature feel as needy as a child at times, especially in hours of great need.

I'm finding that Satan can cause me to forget about miracles that are even less than a week old. That's one reason we've had a prayer book at our house. We write down our prayer requests and what God says. It's a blessing to look back and see what God has done.

Today would be a good day for you to start a prayer book, whether you are a single adult or married, teenager or parent, young adult or senior adult. You'll be blessed to see your answers to prayer right before you. Who knows? Maybe the barrier in the skies has been a blessing in disguise.

OCTOBER 1

We Are the Salt of the Earth

In Matthew 5:13 Jesus said, "You are the salt of the earth. But if the salt loses its saltiness, how can it be made salty again? It is no longer good for anything, except to be thrown out and trampled by men."

In the Old Testament times salt was used in many ways. It was used to season tasteless food, to purify a spring in Jericho, as a symbol of permanent friendship, and to preserve food.

The hearers of Jesus's words were well aware of the symbolisms wrapped up in salt. The words of the Master were directed to those who were already following Him. But His words were and are still a corrective for effective Christian living today.

Do you ever think of yourself as "the salt of the earth"?

We are to be an example of tasteful living. Do you think you have a zeal for life that most do not have? Christians have something, or rather *someone*, to live for.

We are to be a purifying element in our community. Are you making any conscious effort to clean up your town? Have you ever gone in to a drug store or convenience store and talked to those in charge about the pornographic books on display? I have. What other things could we (with a good attitude) speak for or against in the place where we live?

Our influence is to be used to support that which is good and holy and righteous and against evil where we see it. Today look for ways where you can be "the salt of the earth."

OCTOBER 2

Correcting the Drift

The writer to the Hebrews gives us a needed warning in Hebrews 2:1, where it is written, "We must pay the most careful attention, therefore, to what we have heard, so that we do not drift away."

In the Greek the word that means "to drift away" is used to describe a river that flows outside its normal channel, in the sense of flooding or moving outside its banks.

This word was also used of something slipping from one's memory or of a ring slipping from one's finger or of food going down the wrong way. It was also used in reference to a ship drifting off course. Here is a picture for us to learn from.

Most of the time those who know Jesus and eventually turn away from Him do not do so overnight. It is not an immediate change of direction, but generally it is a little bit at a time. It is a "drifting" more than a conscious rebellion. But both drifting and rebellion end up in the same place if they are not corrected.

What about you today, friend? Are you making allowances for things you now do that not long ago you would have avoided? Are you maturing or are you drifting? Think about it.

Is it time to correct the drift?

OCTOBER 3

Angels

In Hebrews 1:14 we read, "Are not all angels ministering spirits to serve those who will inherit salvation?"

From the throne of God, commands are given to angels to work on behalf of and for the benefit of believers. Angels are "ministering spirits"—they obey and serve God (of course, I am referring to the angels who did not fall). Even archangels, including Gabriel and Michael, are sent by God to work in the interest of Christians.

The angels make up a numberless host. In Revelation 5:11 John wrote, "Then I looked and heard the voice of many angels, numbering thousands upon thousands, and ten thousand times ten thousand. They encircled the throne."

The Greek here suggests that the angels are constantly being sent out to aid the saints. Jesus is sitting by the Father today and is dispatching His angels, and think of it—as you work, as you play, as you jog, as you eat and sleep—in all you do Jesus knows when to send an angel to minister to you. We're not talking about ghosts or make believe—we're talking about the holy angels of God.

Friend, think of it: we have the Father, Son, and Holy Spirit, and on top of them, millions of angels and all of them ministering to us every day. Glory to God!

OCTOBER 4

Disciple-Making

Jesus gave us a pattern for making disciples when He said in Matthew 4:19, "Follow Me." Later Paul continued the same pattern in Philippians 3:17 by saying, "Follow my example." Every Christian has the responsibility of becoming a pattern by which others may mold their lives. Oh, I know we are to keep our eyes on Jesus, but often the way we see Jesus is in the context of another believer's life.

Discipleship is not the result of a formula, seminar, or educational institution, but the work of Jesus Christ. We indeed are to be discipled by Jesus through His Word and often alongside another believer. What we are lives on much longer than what we say. In a sense, we are making disciples all the time. They are being made or unmade constantly by watching us. In addition, we can make a purposeful plan by which to intentionally disciple another follower in Christ. Ask Christ who it is that you could be discipling.

What is it you do as a Christian that you want your children, your spouse, and your friends to do? What is it that you do that every Christian would benefit from doing?

Think of it—you are a disciple-maker whether you want to be or not. Be sure you make the right kind of disciples.

OCTOBER 5

He Is with Us

In Hebrews 2:18 we read, "Because He Himself suffered when He was tempted, He is able to help those who are being tempted."

The Greek tense here emphasizes that though the temptation Christ suffered in the flesh was a thing in the past, its impact is permanent. The effect of His compassion and understanding applies to us right now.

The author to the Hebrews is underscoring the fact that Jesus's humanity was genuine. It was so real that He was actually tempted. Christ personally experienced the power of evil when Satan confronted Him. He experienced hunger when tempted in the wilderness. He experienced thirst when He asked the woman at Jacob's well for water. He was weary when He slept while a storm raged on the Sea of Galilee, and He knew sorrow when He wept at the grave of Lazarus.

When we are tempted we can be assured of the active support of Jesus. He has perfect understanding, because He Himself suffered when He was tempted.

Whatever you are facing these days, always remember: Jesus has been there and He will be with you.

OCTOBER 6

Praying in Jesus's Name

In John 14:14 Jesus said, "Ask me for anything in my name, and I will do it."

Here the Lord gives us tremendous power in prayer, but only when we are praying about His business. This is not some general promise that I can get personal comfort and material success every time I feel a need. When the Lord opens this door of prayer, it is ultimately to advance *His* cause, not mine.

To ask in Jesus's name means to ask concerning what concerns Him.

Using the name of Christ in prayer immediately brings into my hands all that Christ is with the Father. Christ always prayed to His Father for the welfare of kingdom work on earth; but when Christ left, He gave that privilege and responsibility to us. We are now to use Christ's position with the Father to carry on the work He left for us to do. We must not abuse that trust. We cannot make selfishly ours what is His. Christ's work—through us—must be our first concern. Whatever brings glory to God must be primary in our lives.

Today, believer, why not evaluate your prayer life? How much of your praying is about your financial needs, your physical needs, your concerns, and how much of your praying is about and for others, or simply about knowing Christ in a deeper way? Today pray in Jesus's name—which means for the things that glorify Jesus.

OCTOBER 7

Jesus Was Made like Us

In Hebrews 2:17 we read of Jesus that "He had to be made like His brothers in every way." That is like you and me. The scripture continues: "in order that He might become a merciful and faithful high priest in service to God and that He might make atonement for the sins of the people."

We must be careful not to put ourselves at a distance from Jesus Christ. If we're not on guard as we read of His mighty works, teaching, preaching, and living, we can be tempted to say as a kind of an excuse for ourselves, "But He was God and we're not."

True, He was and is the Son of God, but if I put too much distance between Himself and myself because of His unique relationship with the Father, I have missed the point of the New Testament.

Christ lived His earthly life in the strength and power of the Holy Spirit. He triumphed over the sins, ills, and woes of man by dependence upon the Holy Spirit, not by reverting to His innate deity. He stripped from Himself every other dependency except faith. He did this to live as we have to live, that He might demonstrate that victory is possible in the very center of our human condition.

Jesus Christ is not a tantalizer—He is a Savior. The works He did, He said we can do (see John 14:12). The peace He enjoyed we may enjoy. The joy that characterized Him can also characterize us.

The Bible says He is the author or the pioneer of our faith. As such, He shows us what victory really is. But He is also the finisher or the perfector of our faith. As such, He shows us how to attain that victory. You see, what Christ was, He is able to recreate in each of us. What Christ did, He is able to redemonstrate through us.

We deny who Christ really is if we keep insisting that He is only a heavenly person instead of a person from heaven who invaded humanity by taking flesh upon Himself. Once Jesus Christ became flesh, He forever undercut my excuses for failure. I must now accept Him for who He truly is—a Savior who begins on my level.

He really was a flesh-and-blood baby. Oh, the miracle of our Savior's life!

OCTOBER 8

Making Him Known

In 1 John 5:4 we read, "Everyone born of God overcomes the world. This is the victory that has overcome the world, even our faith."

We must not deny that there are good influences in the world. And yet we must take seriously the biblical warnings that being the world's friend is actually being God's enemy, according to James 4:4.

The world offers me an opportunity to toughen my spiritual fiber if I use it properly. The Israelites in the Bible, according to Exodus 23:30, were to conquer Canaan little by little. Victory was to be gradual so that people would not become too exalted or too proud.

That gives me a clue as to how I must relate to the world. I must use the world as an opportunity to develop my spiritual muscle, or else why all the training and discipline? Soldiers do not make themselves battle-ready only to enter a state of peace and rest.

In using the world as the proving ground of my battle readiness, I must do it little by little. If not, the world proves too much for me, as it did for Israel. It is working day by day for the kingdom that makes a difference.

I must never treat the world with anything less than respect, for indeed, it can contaminate, it can seduce, but Jesus confronted the world aggressively and defeated it according to John 16.

By Jesus's help I must do the very same thing. My life must cause the world to look seriously at Jesus Christ and His claims. I must always be on the offensive, never yielding to the world's charms for a moment but always pressing the battle into its own territory. That way I shall grow stronger little by little until Christ is well known in an alien land.

Let's make Him known today in our part of the world.

OCTOBER 9

Keep a Steadfast Heart

In Psalm 57:7 the psalmist simply writes, "My heart is steadfast, O God. My heart is steadfast." It was as if David said, "I have an anchor in my soul."

The word *heart* appears over a thousand times in the Bible. It denotes a person's center for physical, emotional, intellectual, and spiritual activities.

My heart is the center of my being and I must keep it strong if I hope to be triumphant. I cannot afford to make a mistake in my heart. That's where the real issue is. It's bad enough to err in my ways or in my mind, but if I make a deep error in my own heart I will begin to sow the seeds of ultimate defeat. To err in the heart is to be unpersuaded, unconvinced by God's Word. It means that God speaks in vain and His words carry no weight. He might have just as well remained silent. If I ignore God's message, before long I will become a firm unbeliever, which will in turn lead to hardness of the heart.

Peter made a terrible choice—he denied Christ. Once repentant, though, he found restoration with his Lord. By contrast, Judas allowed Satan to enter into him and ignored the teaching of Jesus, developing a resistance to the forgiveness Jesus offered and hardened his own heart.

I can't presume that because I am saved, I'm in no danger of developing spiritual heart trouble. The many New Testament warnings were uttered not just for their sound but also to make me a disciple with a clean heart, to keep me from regarding God's words as something trivial. And they were given to make me realize every message from God is of primary value to my own heart.

The most restless, discontented people are not the poor or the overworked, but the hard of heart.

OCTOBER 10

Childlike Trust

In 2 Chronicles 19:7 we read, "Now then let the fear of the Lord be upon you; be very careful what you do, for the Lord our God will have no part in unrighteousness" (NASB).

If the Israelites had one main fault in history, it was a sense of false security. Despite the fact that they had passed through the Red Sea, had been guided by the miraculous cloud, and had been fed manna, the miracle food, they still lusted after evil things, as recorded in 1 Corinthians 10. You see, they had every reason not to fall, yet they did fall. It was as if their past blessings had become sedatives instead of stimulants.

The best way for me to live is on the razor's edge of failure. I mean, I must be insecure enough to cling to the everlasting arms. If God blesses me as He did the Israelites, I do not become immune to future problems. I have no guarantees of perpetual bliss. I must appreciate my blessings and use them correctly.

Living on the razor's edge does not mean that, "Oh, I had better be careful or I may fall into sin," but it is rather a healthy appreciation that this security we have in Christ is conditional on our continual faith.

You see, success has a way of dimming my spiritual eye and slackening my spiritual grip. Being in Christ is no assurance whatever that I will be immune from the lashings of Satan, the tantalizing things of the world, or the rigors of God's disciplinary grace. I will be safe only as I run scared, in a sense, scared enough to be a child in my dependence upon God.

Psalm 40:4 states, "Blessed [fortunate, prosperous, and favored by God] is the man who makes the Lord his trust" (NLT).

OCTOBER 11

Making Things Happen for Jesus

In Matthew 12:43–45 we read these words of Jesus:

> When an evil spirit comes out of a man it goes through arid places seeking rest and does not find it. Then it says, "I will return to the house I left." When it arrives it finds the house unoccupied, swept clean, and put in order, then it goes and takes with it seven other spirits more wicked than itself and they go in and live there. The final condition of that man is worse than the first. This is how it will be with this wicked generation.

I asked myself, How can this be? And the reason it can be is because to merely conquer a bad habit, to win over an alienated friend, or to drive doubt out of the heart is not sufficient in itself. I must follow up these triumphs with being more than a conqueror who is seizing the territory so the enemy cannot recapture it.

When the Israelites conquered the Amorites, they followed up their victory by occupying the land, according to Numbers 21. This made any counterattack by the enemy virtually impossible. You see, we too must nail down our victories in such a way that effective counterattacks are impossible. Otherwise, as Jesus stated in our scripture, the end could be worse than the beginning. The only way to conquer hate is to replace it with love. The way to conquer bitterness is not by confessing it, but we must replace it with praise and thankfulness.

What I am saying is that there must be no vacancy where there has been victory. If you've gained victory over a bad habit, replace it with a good habit. If you've been a discourager, fill that void by becoming an encourager. Our Christianity is not passive, as in "Let's see what happens." It's active, as in "Let's trust Christ and make it happen."

Today, friend, make something happen for Jesus.

OCTOBER 12

Go On

In Hebrews 6:1 we read, "Let us leave the elementary teachings about Christ and go on to maturity" (CSB).

The leaving spoken about here does not mean disregarding or abandoning the elementary teachings. Oh, no—basic understanding of the death, burial, and resurrection of Jesus will always have a high place in our biblical understanding. The point here is that the beginning of biblical knowledge is not a stopping place but rather the door to progress and the springboard to achievement.

Do not allow yourself to be satisfied with only memorizing John 3:16 or Psalm 23. Rather, as the scripture says, "Go on." Go on—memorize passages that will help you in the time of temptation. Go on—study and learn about prayer, holiness, heaven, and a hundred other things. Do not stop, friend—*go on.*

The Greek here rendered "go on" has within it the idea of being carried along. The suggestion is a personal surrender to an active influence. In other words, God is desiring, God is attempting, God is doing all He can to help us to grow up spiritually.

Why not take spiritual inventory today?

Is there anything that has come your way lately that you have questioned? Have you wondered why God allowed it or why nothing seems to be working out at all? Could it be that it is God's way of saying to you, "Go on, go on, *go on* to maturity"? Think about it.

OCTOBER 13

Equipped to Do His Will

Toward the end of the book of Hebrews the writer prays a wonderful prayer: "May the God of peace...equip you with everything good for doing His will" (Hebrews 13:20–21).

Here we have reference to what God desires to do *in* us— so he can work *through* us. He wants to equip us so that we can do what is good, so we can carry out His will.

The word *equip* actually means "to make someone complete." It suggests the act of restoring, perfecting something. Some translations read, "May the God of peace...make you perfect." God strengthens us so that shortcomings may be overcome. He supplies us with every good thing so that we may be able to do His will.

It should encourage us to know that whatever God wants us to do is not only good but also possible. You see, God places within us the ability to do what we need to do.

Is there anything God wants you to do? Does it look too difficult? Are you tempted to say, "Hey, God—you've got the wrong person"? God's Word indicates that if it's a good thing, we *should* do it, and if we *should* do it, we *can* do it. Go ahead—God's already given you what you need to carry out His will. Your job is simply to trust Him and follow through.

OCTOBER 14

Praise God Anyway

Have you made any sacrifices lately? I'm not asking if you've given up anything—I'm asking if you've made any *biblical* sacrifices. Can you name a biblical sacrifice that we're admonished to give? Of course, in the Old Testament era animals were given in sacrifice to God, but now we no longer do that. So what is it we can give? Hebrews 13:15 says "Through Jesus, let us continually offer to God a sacrifice of praise."

Throughout our lives we have certain expectations about how things should be. It's common to want healthy children, a measure of comfort in living, personal health, safety, and a sense of purpose. However, sometimes things don't go as they should or as we would have them go. As a result, the temptation to complain or even doubt God may come.

Here is the precise point where the believer can offer a sacrifice of praise to God. In a sense it is as if I give up my right to a certain thing and praise God anyway. For example, a person might give up his or her right for health and choose to praise God anyway.

This passage continues by saying that this praise is the "fruit of our lips," so I challenge you today: with your mouth, in prayer, give up your right to some things that have escaped your reach, and praise God anyway. Yes, today offer a sacrifice of praise.

OCTOBER 15

His Death, Our Life

In Hebrews 13:12 we read, "Jesus suffered outside the city gate to make His people holy through His own blood." I want you to see four things in this passage:

First, *the person.* It was *Jesus,* the Son of God. It was not some substitute, but He was the best God had. And it was this person, Jesus, the sinless one, who became sin for everyone.

Second, *the price.* There is no way with my limited vocabulary to express to you the depth of *suffering* that Christ endured on the cross. But the fact remains that He did, and we are the recipients of countless blessings because of His sacrifice.

Third, *the place.* Jesus's sufferings "outside the city" underscored the shame that criminals experienced in New Testament times. The Christ was treated like a common criminal and was made to feel a total outcast.

Finally, *the purpose.* In order "to make His people holy," Jesus invites us as believers to present our bodies, our lives, as living sacrifices (Romans 12:1).

Jesus gave His life and died so that when we give our lives to Him, we can live!

OCTOBER 16

God Really Does Love You

John 3:16 says, "God gave His only Son." You know I have a son, and I could hardly stand it when he had to have a shot. It really bothered me the time he was six years old and cut his head open, and I had to help hold him while the doctors put in the stitches. I could hardly stand it. I wonder: Would I give my son to save the life of a stranger or an enemy? Would I? Could I?

You know God allowed Abraham to give his only son, Isaac. At least Hebrews 11:17 says Isaac was Abraham's "only son." But you remember God said, "No, Abraham—stop. You have proven you trust me. Do not take the life of your son.

In my mind I can see Jesus and the Father looking down from heaven as Abraham stops just short of killing his own son. I can imagine Jesus looking at the Father and saying, "One of these days, just like Isaac, I am going to be placed on the altar, and just like Isaac, my life is going to be threatened—but unlike Isaac, you are not going to stop my execution. Isn't that right, Father?" And God looks to His Son and says, "Yes, Son. I am going to let them take your life. I am going to let you die."

Friend, if you ever wonder how much God loves you – just remember the cross—that's how much God loves you.

OCTOBER 17

Close to God

In Micah 6:8 we read, "What does the Lord require of you? To act justly and to love mercy and to walk humbly with your God."

It seems that the Lord's requirements are pretty simple. Although scholars can never understand a tenth of the complexity wrapped up in God, a child can know God in a real way. When God relates to people, He meets them in utter simplicity.

When Jesus met a religious official, He did not try to debate theological issues. He simply said, "You must be born again" (John 3:7). It seems the Lord always comes back to the basics, though He challenges the greatest minds.

The Laodicean church was a model organization, filled with those who thought they knew so much, but they were dead. We can become so structured, so bound to tradition that God has trouble telling us anything new, simple as it may be.

God reserves the right to break in, change habits, start new directions, and just basically make life a living adventure. God is not finicky, but He does understand human nature and does not want us up tight, majoring on minor issues.

Friend, do you find that your life it too hectic? Is there no time to be quiet before God? I find the closer I get to God, the simpler my life becomes.

OCTOBER 18

Meekness

In Matthew 5:5 Jesus said, "Blessed are the meek, for they will inherit the earth."

Can you think of anyone you know who is meek? Is meekness something you want in your life? The Bible seems to put a premium on meekness—so it must be something we Christians should cultivate.

The Greek word for *meek* means "gentle," "humble," "considerate," or "courteous." Meekness is essentially a true view of ourselves, expressed in our attitudes and conduct with respect to others. Meekness is not *created* by what we do—it is *revealed* in what we do. Meekness first has to happen in our mind and spirit before it is ever expressed in action.

The meek person is genuinely grateful to God and others for everything that comes into his or her life.

It's easy to take things for granted: our homes, our cars, our families, our health, and our church, and sometimes even God.

Meekness is often defined as "power under control." The road to meekness is paved with love to God and genuine appreciation for others around us. Meekness, according to the Bible, is humility and gentleness toward others and submission and obedience to the Lord.

In a very real sense meekness has to do with how we think. It is humble-mindedness. Are you a meek person?

OCTOBER 19

Grumbling

Look what Paul said to the Philippian Christians: "Do everything without grumbling or arguing" (Philippians 2:14). The Amplified Version says, "Do everything without murmuring or questioning [the providence of God]." The Message says, "Do everything readily and cheerfully—no bickering, no second-guessing allowed!"

Have you grumbled or complained today? Do you ever think that when you grumble about life you are often grumbling against God?

There may be many things you're not happy about. You could be unhappy with school, your home, your job, your marriage, your church, or __________ [you fill in the blank]. What does it take to make you grumble or express your feelings of discontent?

If you asked three people who know you fairly well, "Do you ever think of me as a grumbler?" what do you think they would say? How would you describe yourself?

Look again at what Paul said: "Do everything without grumbling or arguing." He doesn't leave much wiggle room when it comes to complaining. And notice this is not a suggestion but a clear command.

I know you have had much happen that you could complain about, but brace yourself as you read some of what Paul faced, which he described in 2 Corinthians 11:23–29:

> I have worked much harder, been in prison more frequently, been flogged more severely, and been exposed to death again and again. Five times I received from the Jews forty lashes minus one. Three times I was beaten with rods, once I was pelted with stones, three times I was shipwrecked, I spent a night and a day in the open sea, I have been constantly on the move. I have been in danger from rivers, in danger from bandits, in danger from my fellow Jews, in danger from Gentiles; in danger in the city, in danger in the country, in danger at sea; and in danger from false believers. I have labored and toiled and have often gone without sleep; I have known hunger and thirst and have often gone without food; I have been cold and naked. Besides everything else, I face daily the pressure of my concern for all the churches. Who is weak, and I do not feel weak?

To these Philippians he said in Philippians 4:11, "I have learned to be content whatever the circumstances."

Ask yourself this question: What does God owe me in this life? He really does not owe us anything, but we owe Him everything. Grumbling is saying that God owes us something that He is not presently providing!

Grumbling is a slow-acting poison. It poisons you and the people you share it with. Here is some good advice if you are a grumbler: *stop it!*

OCTOBER 20

God's Discipline

In Hebrews 12:5–6 we have some words that are not easy to accept: "My dear child, don't shrug off God's discipline, but don't be crushed by it either. It's the child he loves that he disciplines; the child he embraces, he also corrects" (MSG).

Here the writer is telling believers to be sure to see and feel the hand of God in all their difficulties. The use of the expression "don't shrug off" suggests that they ought to view discipline as coming directly from God. Discipline is a privilege that God extends to those He loves. This almost sounds contradictory until we see that discipline is not extended to the ungodly. They receive His judgment. Discipline is a sign that God accepts us as His children.

I remember as a child that my dad and I would see a child trample over some other person's flowers or abuse their dog or any of a hundred different other possible infractions. Then I would hear him say, "If you ever did that..." in other words, I knew that if I ever did *that,* I would wish I hadn't. But why didn't he correct the neighbors' kids? Because they were not *his*—that's why. You see, he loved me as he loved no other child in all the world. You see, he loved me as if I were his only child, (which indeed I actually was).

Friend, God loves you as if you were His only child also. So today, look for the good side. Look for the loving side of His discipline.

OCTOBER 21

Do What He Tells You

In Matthew 7:13–14 Jesus said, "Enter through the narrow gate. For wide is the gate and broad is the road that leads to destruction, and many enter through it. But small is the gate and narrow the road that leads to life and only a few find it."

The narrow road is a road of discipline, our Lord warns. The devout life of a disciple is not a dream but an on-purpose decision that calls for the use of all our powers. No amount of sheer determination can make me right with God. That is His gift to me when I am born again. Where discipline and determination come in is in the letting that new life work itself out according to Christ's standard.

We must always keep clear in our minds what God will do for us and what we need to do for ourselves. We cannot save ourselves or cleanse ourselves or give ourselves the Holy Spirit. Only God can do that. Confusion occurs when we try to do what God alone can do.

Or we want God to do what *we* should be doing. For example, we pray that God will make us walk in the light. He will not do it. *We* are the ones who must walk in the light. Oh, God will grant us the power to do His will, but we must choose to use that power.

Friend, check your prayer life today. Have you been asking for God to do some things that He has already given you the power to do? Do what He has told you and He will take care of the rest.

OCTOBER 22

Doing Good to All People

In Galatians 6:10 we have an important word: "As we have opportunity let us do good to all people, especially to those who belong to the family of believers."

Christians are to do good to all people. We are to treat others just as Jesus would if He were here in the flesh. This means that in our ethics, our business transactions, in all we say and do, we are to be representatives of Jesus. It would not be a bad question to ask ourselves every day simply, "What would Jesus do now?" Before you give that word of chastisement, ask, "What would Jesus do now?" Before your neighbor receives a good piece of your mind, ask, "What would Jesus do now?"

Jesus in shoe leather, in your shoe leather (or tennis shoes) that is what the world needs to see today. That is what we all need to see. But note, our scripture not only admonishes us to do good to all people, but it also has the special emphasis on those who belong to the family of believers. What is this additional word from Paul all about? Why did he add that phrase?

Paul probably added this phrase because we must make a special effort not to take Christian friends for granted. When did you last thank God for your pastor and family, for the staff and families of your local church? When did you last write a person in your church a note or email of appreciation? How about the board members, the ushers, the nursery workers, or the custodian? Let us do good, friends, especially to the family of believers.

OCTOBER 23

A Witness for Christ

In Matthew 28:19 we have the familiar words of Jesus "Go and make disciples of all the nations." The word *disciples* means "followers" or "learners." Are you doing anything about following Jesus's command? Are you a witness or are you just a testimony? Does that sound like a strange set of words to use as a contrast, a witness, or a testimony? Is there a difference between the two? I think there is.

The early Christians did not try to build the church on their testimony. Paul did not say, "I have given my life to Jesus; I am different now." No, he did not try just to base the authority for his faith on some spiritual experience. Oh, without a doubt, Paul and others gave personal testimony to their experiences and that will always be a vital part of living.

But testimony is only a small part of what a witness is about. Witnessing goes a step further. Witnessing goes on to talk about Jesus, His death, His resurrection, His ongoing life. In other words, our strongest authority is not just our testimony. Honestly, people who have been in Weight Watchers, Eastern religions, or even the occult give impressive testimonies about changes in their lives. But the Christian faith is more than a testimony. It is also a witness to the fact of who Jesus is and what He came to do.

My admonishment to you today is to go ahead—give your testimony. But be sure you give a *witness* as well.

OCTOBER 24

Count the Cost

In Luke 14 Jesus has been talking about a life commitment to Him. And then in verse 28 He says, "You must sit down and count the cost" (KJV) A more literal reading would be, "Calculate the cost." The NIV says it well: "Estimate the cost." You know there is no real way to count what it will cost us to serve or not to serve Jesus. There is no way to see the hurt, the separation, and the total estrangement that many unsaved people experience.

There is no way to see the continual areas of surrender a Christian might be called upon to make. However, you can sit down and think or estimate the cost of going the direction you are going. Ask yourself, "If I live the next year the way lived the last year, where will I be spiritually?" That's a good question. If I really do put God first, I would calculate, or I would "estimate," that His dreams for me far outstrip all my own aspirations.

Look at your life. Would you have dreamed ten years ago, five years ago, or maybe even last year what God has done in your life? Would you have dreamed one-tenth of all God has done in, with, and through you? Me neither.

OCTOBER 25

God's Perspective

In Colossians 3:1–2 Paul writes, "Set your hearts on things above, where Christ is seated at the right hand of God. Set your minds on things above, not on earthly things."

The throne of God is the headquarters of the universe, thus the headquarters for every Christian. I must always keep the channels of communication clear with the divine command station. You see, heaven is the nerve center of everything that controls my life or the life of the church. Just as a soldier follows the leadership of his or her commanding officer, so I must follow the leadership of God.

Our commander in chief leaves no room for independent activity. We are continuously and totally dependent on Him. There is a tendency to misinterpret the signals from headquarters, not because they are not sounded, but because we are not listening.

Too often in essence we tell God what we are going to do and then ask Him to bless it. You see, patience to wait for direction from the heavenly control tower is sometimes lacking. Sometimes the things that occupy our emotional and physical energies are of little eternal value.

Today ask yourself this question: "How much of what I am doing this day is really important from God's perspective?"

OCTOBER 26

The Week the Lord Has Made

In Psalm 118:24 we have the familiar words "This is the day the Lord has made; let us rejoice and be glad in it."

I think one of the greatest things about praising God is that it happens right now. The moment you praise Him, at least two things take place. First, God's heart is warmed by our adoration for Him. Second, we find the sense of His presence and power that we do not have when we fail to praise Him.

As Christians, most of us have better plans than we do actions. We plan on having time for real Bible reading and thinking on the Scriptures. We plan on getting away for a time of prayer and communion with God. We plan on committing to memory some of God's Word. We plan, we plan, we plan—but how much do we *do*?

I have an idea for you. Why not try a spiritual experiment for seven days? For seven days actually read the Bible till God makes a passage come alive for you; actually pray till you have truly connected with Him. Why not actually (for one week) do the spiritual disciplines you have planned on in the past? Maybe you will need to fast television for a week, or some social media that eats away at your time. Wouldn't that be a tragedy?

In other words I'm saying, friend, why not live one week as you think you would if you were at your best, disciplined, spiritual self? Yes, this is the day the Lord has made. Let this be the week when you are at your best. Indeed, this will be the week that the Lord has made.

OCTOBER 27

Our Strengths

It is true that Satan attacks us at our weakest points, but sometimes it is even more true that he attacks us at our *strongest* points.

Now think of it: How did he cause Peter to fall? By striking him where the disciple thought he was strong. His ability to lead, to be the hero, to be the star, to be the one to speak up—that was a strength of his. Remember what he said in John 13:37: "I will lay down my life for you." But just like Samson, Peter's strength was his weakness. And Satan knew it.

Have you ever felt the same thing? In the place where you felt so strong and bulwarked—that's where Satan tripped you up. Or the place you felt most confident in—there he caused you to stumble.

I think of Jesus, the Son of God. It was in His very Sonship that Satan tried to dislodge Him. In Matthew 4:3 he said, "If you are the Son of God, command these stones to be made bread." Satan knew Jesus was God's Son. Acting on that knowledge, he tried to shrewdly twist Jesus's strongest element into something devious. He attacked Jesus at the strongest part of who He was.

I must not think of Satan as only a serpent who sneaks around nibbling at my exposed weaknesses, but I must see him as a frontal foe who hammers hard at my very strengths. That means I must be careful not to allow my strengths to blind me to my vulnerability. I am assured that because Christ is in me, I can be bold in standing my ground against the evil one. Remember James 4:7: "Resist the devil and he will flee from you." Then my strengths can remain my strengths through the victorious one, Jesus Christ.

OCTOBER 28

God Goes Before You

God has a special kind of blessing for some of His choice disciples. It is a blessing that goes on ahead of the disciples as they follow His way. God said to the Israelites in Exodus 23:27, "I will send My fear before you" (NKJV). You know, if I obey God fully, He will not only go with me but will also go ahead of me—in advance—and in going before me He will prepare and condition the hearts of the people who I am to meet.

One of the unique features of the ministry of Jesus was that the people were prepared to meet Him. We know John the Baptist helped to prepare the way for Jesus. In Mark 2:1 the people knew that Jesus was in the house; they had been talking about the coming of this Jesus. Because of His complete obedience to the Father, Jesus became as it were perfume in God's hands, which He spread all over Palestine.

The perfume of Simon Peter's life reached as far as Joppa, according to Acts 10. Paul's floated across the Aegean Sea, according to Acts 16. May God make you and me that kind of a disciple. I pray that He will. There will be people in our future who will need the touch of God that we are preparing for even now. You see, by walking the disciple's path now, we are preparing for a future meeting God has planned for us. And God is preparing the people to whom we will go.

My goal as a disciple should be to achieve the kind of obedience that sends God before me. Sometimes we hear it said of a Spirit-anointed person, "His [Her] very presence was a blessing to us." Just the person's spirit, their presence, was a blessing to others. No doubt the Lord had gone before this believer.

If I look for victory on the spot every time, I may be disappointed. You see, victory comes the way a garden grows. First sow the seed and then reap the harvest. By walking closely to my heavenly Father, I am now sowing seeds of a victory to be harvested later. Not only do I benefit, but that victory may be far beyond the bounds of my present location.

Yes, as God goes before us, He is preparing us for our greatest moments of usefulness.

Knowing that God goes before you, ask yourself: What is God preparing me for right now?

OCTOBER 29

What Concerns God?

Years ago the game Trivial Pursuit took the country by storm. It was a table game, an Internet game. as well as a television game show. Trivia is by no means new, and things that we call trivia God has been calling a part of His knowledge since time began. According to Luke 12:6–7, God notices the sparrows that fall and counts the hairs on our heads.

God not only works with trivia, but at times He also seems to major in it. He created the massive details of the universe and watches over it all. He also is the architect of the trivia in our lives. He knows our mood swings, our personality types. He knows our interruptions and the thousand other things that impact our lives.

Remember that Luke 15 says that God is concerned about one lost sheep. He is concerned about one lost coin. He is concerned about one lost son. And when they are found, He rejoices in each one. As a loving parent, God is interested in the cuts and scratches that invade our daily existence.

What concerns you concerns God. It is no bother to Him when you pour out your heart's trivia on Him. He really does care for you. If God knows how many hairs are on our heads, there is nothing is too small for Him to care about.

OCTOBER 30

Be Jesus to Someone Today

In Colossians 2:9–10 we read, "In Christ all the fullness of the deity lives in bodily form, and in Christ you have been brought to fullness. He is the head over every power and authority."

I must at all costs avoid the deadly delusion of focusing on self-fulfillment. I am hounded on all sides to be the person I was meant to be, to realize my full potential, and to explore the possibilities within me. You see, even Christians have succumbed to this idea. But in this passage I am told that in Christ I will be able to fulfill myself as God intended—in contrast to being self-fulfilled by the world.

The error in all this is that nowhere does the Bible talk about self-fulfillment. The only fulfillment the Bible talks about is the fullness we have in Christ.

Many times self-fulfillment is only another form of pride, and it can hardly be differentiated from the sin of Lucifer many years ago. We progressive moderns, however, have so covered the term with attractive clothing that it no longer appears to us as sin but an inherent right of personality.

Self-fulfillment is expressing *my* full self, achieving *my* glory, carving out *my* niche in life. Its ultimate goal is the coronation of self. Further, it is a fatal contradiction. How can everyone fulfill himself or herself? The total exaltation of everybody would result in racial mania. The *fulfillment* of all my desires usually means the denial of someone else's. You see, as a disciple I must talk of *His* fulfillment in me.

When I received Christ, I received *His* fullness. As I live out His fullness, I flesh out His presence on this earth.

Let Jesus be seen in you today.

OCTOBER 31

The Power of God's Word

Our last devotional for this month is going to be a little different. In all the other months I have never done one just like this. But I want you to join me in reading a large portion of Psalm 139. I know this chapter will generally speak to us all, but I also believe in my heart that there is someone reading this who will find the scripture speaking specifically to him or her.

> O Lord, you have searched me and you know me. You know when I sit and when I rise, you perceive my thoughts from afar. You discern my going out and my lying down; you are familiar with all my ways. Before a word is on my tongue you know it completely, O Lord. You hem me in—behind and before. You have laid your hand upon me. Such knowledge is too wonderful for me, too lofty for me to attain. Where can I go from you spirit? Where can I flee from your presence? If I go up to the heavens you are there. If I make my bed in the depths, you are there. If I rise on the wings of dawn, if I settled on the far side of the sea, even there your hand will guide me, your right hand will hold me fast. If I say, "Surely the darkness will hide me and the light become night around me," even the darkness will not be dark to you, the night will shine like the day, for darkness is as light to you. For you created my inmost being, you knit me together in my mother's womb. I praise you because I am fearfully and wonderfully made; your works are wonderful, I know that full well. My frame was not hidden from you when I was made in the secret place. When I was woven together in the depths of the earth, your eyes saw my unformed body. All the days ordained for me were written in your book before one of them came to be. How precious to me are your thoughts, O God! How vast is the sum of them. Were I to count them, they would outnumber the grains of sand. When I awake I am still with you.... Search me, O God, and know my heart. Test me and know my anxious thoughts. See if there is any offensive way in me and lead me in the way everlasting.

What did God say to you?

NOVEMBER 1

Is God Calling You?

In John 1:42 Jesus said to Peter, "You are Simon, son of John. You will be called Cephas"—which means "Peter."

You probably are aware of the fact that *Peter* means "Rock." However, in the gospels Peter was anything but a rock. He showed very little stability and was always acting without thinking.

In the book of Acts, Peter did become a pillar of the early church. Jesus named him not for what he was but for what he would become. I guess you could say that Jesus is the Lord of "what is to come."

Are you sensing that the Lord is leading you into an uncertain assignment? Do you see a responsibility coming that appears too much? Has the Lord allowed something in your life that you feel ill-equipped for?

Well, cheer up. You're not alone. He has been calling people for years to do what they thought they could not do. At times it seems God specializes in calling people who cannot do what needs to be done. That must be one of His ways of creating dependence upon Him.

Whatever it is that God has permitted to come your way, remember: He knew about it a long time ago, and He has been preparing you for it, even though you did not know it. And best of all, He promised He would be with you forever. Always remember the often-repeated truth "God does not call the qualified, but He qualifies the called."

NOVEMBER 2

Jesus Washes the Disciples' Feet

In John 13:1–12 we have the record of Jesus in the upper room, shortly before His arrest, trial, and crucifixion. He knew what was coming. He knew the disciples would all flee during His arrest (Mark 14:50) and yet He washed all twelve disciples' feet—and yes, even the feet of His betrayer, Judas.

Verse 3 says that "Jesus knew that the Father had put all things under His power." So Jesus was not a bystander here, simply accepting the situation, powerless to change things. Far from it—the Father had given Jesus "all power" and yet Jesus surrendered His power to fulfill the purpose for which He had come.

Jesus's washing of the disciple's feet was much more than a cultural accommodation to the day in which He lived. Verse 1 says Jesus was showing His disciples that He "loved them to the end," meaning eternally. There was something far deeper than foot washing going on here.

In verse 4 we read that Jesus "laid aside His garments." And verse 12 says, "When He had washed their feet and taken His garments, [He] reclined at the table again."

These words *laid aside* and *taken* are identical to those He uses when He earlier speaks of His own death as the Good Shepherd: "I lay down my life that I may take it again" (John 10:11, 15, 17, 18). This is an act of incredible humility when Jesus voluntarily does the menial work of a slave, but more importantly, it is a parable depicting the sacrifice of His own life.

Behind Jesus's actions there is always a deeper meaning. I wonder: What His actions in your life are meaning today?

NOVEMBER 3

Is God Guiding You?

I'm finding that the Lord is not as committed to procedures as He is to people. Sometimes we're guilty of trying to systemize God's dealings and directives in our lives.

In Romans 11:33 we read, "Oh, how great are God's riches and wisdom and knowledge! How impossible it is for us to understand his decisions and his ways!" (NLT).

It's a dangerous thing for us to try putting God in a corner, because try as we may, it can't be done. "Oh," you say, "I would never do that." Well, did you ask God's will about the car you bought, the house you moved to, or the job you took? Did you take time to search God's Word? Did you think to stop and just listen in your prayer time? Or did you ask God His will and then acted as you pleased and assumed that since it worked out, it must have been right? God does not want to override us—He wants to guide us. Is He guiding *you*?

There's nothing wrong with developing biblical patterns to discern God's direction, but never become so narrow that God has to direct you the same way every time. Through prayer and honest communion with Him, be alert to God's creative ways of communication. I wonder how He wants to speak to you today.

NOVEMBER 4

When Jesus Seems like a Stranger

Does Jesus ever seem like a stranger instead of a Savior to you?

In Matthew 15:21–28 a Canaanite woman came to Jesus, asking Him to heal her daughter. But He seemed to treat her like a stranger. At first He did not answer her, but then He said, "I came to help others" and then said a strange thing about not giving children's food to dogs.

After Jesus's strange words, I'm surprised that the woman did not leave in utter disgust. She did not, and no doubt Jesus wanted her to stay, for immediately He commended her for her great faith—and then granted her request.

Do you ever feel Jesus treats you like a stranger? Are there times that He seems to reward your moments of desperation with silence? Are there times that He seems to be helping everyone but you? Do you ever have trouble interpreting what He is teaching you in a given situation?

Evidently the Lord wants us to trust Him as Savior—even when He seems like a stranger. I'm sure Jesus is not allowing our struggles for no reason. He's never really a stranger. It just seems that way occasionally.

When the time was right, Jesus rewarded the Canaanite woman. Continue being faithful, for the stranger is really your Savior. Never confuse His silence with His absence.

NOVEMBER 5

Make the "Rejoice Choice"

When was the last time you really rejoiced? By definition, *rejoice* means to feel joy or great delight. Can you remember the situation that occasioned that moment in your life?

In Psalm 118:24 we read, "This is the day the Lord has made. Let us rejoice and be glad in it."

Here the psalmist is not referring to some special feast or holiday. Nor must we limit this to Sunday or some rare occasion. Any day and every day is the day the Lord has made. Therefore, any day and every day is the day in which to rejoice and be glad. It's true that not all days are alike in their trouble or their blessing. But something more important than a certain day is in mind here. The important thing is not the day—but the God who made the day.

Here's one of the key reasons Christians can give thanks in everything. Because regardless of the things that come our way, God is still good. Regardless of the difficulty of the day, God still deserves praise.

Let us choose today, and every day, to rejoice in the day that the Lord has made.

NOVEMBER 6

Obey Regardless

In Philippians 2:8 we read how Jesus was "obedient to death."

All true obedience is unto death. But too often obedience is given with conditions. In essence someday I will obey *if* I agree and *if* it does not cost me too much. I will obey *if* it fits with my plans. I will obey *if* it makes sense to me. The *if* basically means I must be assured of having my own way.

But that is not the obedience outlined in the Bible or in the life of Christ. His was not an "obey *if*" but an "obey *regardless*."

True obedience is always successful because it always accomplishes God's will. The moment we choose to obey, success is automatic. But it must be remembered that we are talking about God's success, not ours. At least there are times when our personal immediate good is not apparent. But ultimately we will see that God's way is always the best way.

That is one of the reasons we walk by faith and not by sight.

Regardless of what you are facing these days, always—yes, always—continue instant in obedience and if need be even unto death.

NOVEMBER 7

Have You Seen Jesus Today?

When did you last see Jesus?

Jesus had died. He had been buried and now was raised from the dead. In Luke 24:13–31 we have the record of two of His followers walking to a village named Emmaus. They were discussing everything that had happened to Jesus. As they were talking, a stranger joined them—and that stranger was the resurrected Christ Himself. He asked them what they were talking about and what things had happened.

The men related to Jesus (the supposed stranger) all the events so fresh in their minds. I'm sure they registered their disappointment in their hopes that this "Jesus" would redeem Israel. But He obviously had not, and furthermore, "Today" they said, "is the third day, and some of our companions went to the tomb and found it empty, but Him they did not see."

Isn't it interesting that not only did those who went to the tomb not see Him, but the very ones speaking to the Christ did not see Him either? Finally, however, in Luke 24:31 we read, "Their eyes were opened and they recognized Him."

I wonder if sometimes our eyes need to be opened. Do you ever see Jesus at work, at home, in the backyard, down the street?

Let us be careful today not to be so caught up with the *facts* about Jesus that we fail to actually *see* Him.

NOVEMBER 8

Moving Mountains

In Matthew 17:20 we find some familiar words from Jesus: "I tell you the truth, if you have faith as small as a mustard seed, you can say to this mountain 'move from here to there' and it will move—nothing will be impossible for you."

Here we come face to face with the word *faith*—a word everyone knows and nobody totally understands. But without it, nothing really happens.

When Jesus spoke about moving mountains, He was using a concept that the Jews easily understood. In Jesus's day, a great teacher who could expound and interpret scripture and who could explain and resolve difficulties was commonly called an "uprooter" or even a "pulverizer of mountains." "To tear up," "to uproot," and "to pulverize mountains" were all common phrases for removing difficulties.

Jesus's emphasis was not on actual mountains. For honestly, an ordinary person seldom finds any necessity to remove physical mountains. What He *was* illustrating is this: if you have faith, all your difficulties can be solved and even the hardest tasks can be accomplished. Faith in God is the instrument that enables people to remove the hills of difficulty that block their paths.

What mountain does God want to *pulverize* for you?

NOVEMBER 9

Thirst for God

One day David was in a desert. The heat and thirst of the moment turned his thoughts toward God. In Psalm 63:1 he wrote, "O God, you are my God, earnestly I seek you. My soul thirsts for you, my body longs for you, in a dry and weary land where there is no water."

I want you to ask yourself something today: "Do I honestly long for God? Do I have an unquenchable thirst for Him?"

Any spiritual discipline that stops short of connecting with God always stops far too short. We can be so focused on the means that we forget the end.

Reading the Bible and or going to church may bring you spiritual insight. You may lay down your Bible or go home after church with a comfortable sense of a duty well performed—but do you find your heart (like David's) *seeking, thirsting* for God Himself?

Prayer is also a means to an end. We may get spiritual satisfaction out of praying that makes the act of praying an end in itself.

Feelings, experiences, reading, church attendance—with all these we may still stop short of God, finding spiritual satisfaction perhaps but actually stopping short of God. In all your seeking today—take time to seek God Himself.

Paul expressed the longing of his heart in Philippians 3:10: "I want to know Christ."

As you look at the longing of your heart, fill in the blank: "What I really want to know is ____________."

NOVEMBER 10

Keep Your First Love

In the book of Revelation Jesus gave a word of correction to the church at Ephesus. Here was a church that had struggled and succeeded at keeping a proper belief—yet in Revelation 2:4 to the church in Ephesus Jesus said, "You have forsaken your first love."

Although their struggle with false teachers had made no inroads into their sound doctrine, it had had a serious impact on their Christian conduct. They had abandoned the love they used to have. Sound doctrine does not guarantee right actions.

The Ephesians' labor to stay pure in doctrine had apparently brought about hard feelings and harsh attitudes toward one another. Their doctrinal purity was taking the place of love for one another—and thus love for God.

Do you ever wish you could return to the simple days of your early walk with Jesus? Remember when it was easy to trust Him and easy to share with others His presence in your life? Remember the simple, childlike faith you had? Your love for Jesus was three feet thick.

I once asked the founder of Campus Crusade For Christ, Bill Bright (with twenty-six thousand employees), what the key was to his decision-making in ministry. He quickly said, "I have kept my first love for Jesus."

I'm not saying to stop learning, reading, investigating new truth. No, I'm not making a case for ignorance, but always be sure to gage the appropriateness of whatever you do by how it affects your love for God and for others.

NOVEMBER 11

Lukewarmness

Yesterday we talked about losing our first love for Jesus. Related to that is what happened to the Laodicean church in Revelation 3—they had no doubt lost their first love also and had moved on to what Jesus called lukewarmness. He said in Revelation 3:16, "Because you are lukewarm—neither hot nor cold—I am about to spit you out of my mouth." Here is how the Amplified Version says it: "So because you are lukewarm (spiritually useless), and neither hot nor cold, I will vomit you out of My mouth [rejecting you with disgust]."

Here is a further step away from God: first a lack of love for one another, then a lack of love for God, and then a general lukewarmness to all things spiritual. This is a very subtle danger we all face. Satan knows we probably will not commit some great sin today—we're not going to murder anyone, rob a bank, or commit adultery—so Satan suggests that we compromise, and before long we forget we are compromising, we change our priorities, and then we become spiritually cold. We are then more susceptible to doing things we never thought we would do.

I imagine you've heard of the legend concerning a frog in hot water. The frog is placed into a pan of water that's put onto the stove. As the water gets hotter and hotter, it does not scare the frog, who could easily jump to freedom. The frog's body temperature adjusts with the heating of the water. He's unaware of the danger and remains in the boiling water—until he dies. The problem is that *he got used to the hot water.* Though this is just a story, it illustrates an important truth.

As spiritual beings we can be impacted by evil little by little until it is spiritually fatal. How would you rate your spiritual temperature? Are you on fire for God, lukewarm, or flat-out cold? Let us not allow Satan to cause our spiritual thermometer to get used to lukewarmness. Jump to freedom while there's still time.

NOVEMBER 12

Knowing *about* Him vs. *Knowing* Him

A historian by the name of Gibbon talks about Christianity back in the tenth century and describes its followers as those who "handled the literature and spoke the language of the spiritual, but knew not the life." He continues: "They held in their lifeless hands the riches of their fathers without inheriting the spirit which had created such a heritage."

The Pharisees of Jesus's day handled the things of God, read the Scriptures faithfully, kept the letter of the law, and were separated from the world—but publicans and harlots went into the kingdom before them.

Being raised in a Christian home today is a great benefit to any person. But there are some dangers that must not be ignored. One is to take for granted the things of God. Because we are constantly around the Bible, prayer times, preaching, teaching, and the general life of a congregation, we are tempted to replace *His* presence with *their* presence.

Indeed, we can take God for granted. You can know a lot *about* God and not *know* God. James 4:17 says, "Anyone who knows the good he ought to do and does not do it, sins." Be careful not to fall into sins of omission by taking God for granted.

Doing spiritual things does not make us spiritual people. We have to be in relationship with Him and walk in obedience.

How well do you know Him?

NOVEMBER 13

Resisting the Devil

Yesterday James 4:17 indicated that we should act upon what we know. Today James 4:7 gives us something to act upon: "Submit yourselves to God, resist the devil, and he will flee from you."

As Christians we can and must do more than say *yes* to God—we must also say *no* to the devil. We're not really submitting to God unless at the same time we're resisting the devil.

The devil is too strong for us to handle. Our victory begins with surrender to God.

We fight with spiritual weapons, but we do still fight. We express not only passive submission but also active resistance.

Some people make the mistake of mere submission without a positive stand against the tempter. Others resist without submission, and then they wonder why the devil does not flee. Here James clearly gives us a double-barreled admonition.

This verse is referring to what we must choose to do. When we submit to God's will, then we can, by the grace He gives us, resist the devil.

Resist is a military term, and when used in a spiritual sense, it can be used to urge Christians to stand their ground against Satan's attacks. We resist the devil when we refuse to surrender to his enticement to sin.

If we obey these commandments, God promises that the devil will flee from us. Christ's resistance of Satan in His wilderness temptations provided the devil no foothold in His life and eventually forced the devil to flee (Matthew 4:1–11).

Today as you cooperate with God's will, be sure to actively resist the devil. It's exciting to see him run.

NOVEMBER 14

Look for God's Answer

In James 1:6 we read that when asking the Lord for wisdom, the believer "must believe and not doubt, because he who doubts is like a wave of the sea, blown and tossed by the wind."

The word *doubt* here refers to vacillating, hesitating, or wavering. These are hindrances to God working in our lives.

Have you ever watched the ocean waves? They churn and toss about, driven by the wind. The person who will not trust God and believe is as unstable as "a wave of the sea."

When you ask God about something, is it easy or hard to believe for the answer? Do you anticipate an answer? Are you surprised if it is delayed? We often get what we expect.

It's amazing how our thought patterns affect the outcome of our everyday existence. Thinking you will get a certain job done helps to make it happen. Thinking you will win the soccer game helps make it so. Thinking you will make new friends helps to bring it to pass.

If that is true in everyday positive living, how much more is it true in everyday Christian living?

The basis for our faith is knowing in advance what God has said in His Word. So if today you're struggling with faith, stay in the Word and make decisions according to it. Then look for God's answer.

NOVEMBER 15

When God Says, "Not Now"

In Daniel 3:17–18 the three Hebrew young men said, "Our God is able to deliver us. . . . But if not, we will not bow down."

Shadrach, Meshach, and Abed-Nego knew God had the power to deliver them, but they left the results with Him. God's ability was not in question here. They knew God was able to deliver them, but "if not" now, they knew in His perfect timing He would.

Do you have "if not" religion? Oh, I know we're all excited when someone testifies to how God came through in the nick of time. But what if we are *not* healed, what if the loved one is not spared, what if the job does not work out?

Where is God in the "if nots" of life? He is at the same place he was when Stephen was stoned to death. He is at the same place he was when His Son was ridiculed and killed.

You see, God always has a higher plan, and His "if nots" are not eternal "if nots"—they are really "not nows." So remember: God always has a higher purpose. Your temporary problem is preparing the way for an eternal blessing.

NOVEMBER 16

Can God Trust You to Trust Him?

Hebrews 11 is the great faith chapter of the Bible. If you haven't read it for a while, read it today. It's rich, referring to Abel, Enoch, Noah, Abraham, and many more champions of the faith. It talks of those who conquered kingdoms, shut the mouths of lions, and escaped the edge of the sword. It continues by saying that their weakness was turned to strength, they were powerful in battle, and women received back their dead, raised to life again.

I can feel the goose bumps on my back as I see in my mind this procession of heroes. But not all believers end that way, for suddenly the chapter changes, and a different procession passes by. In verse 35 we read, "Others were tortured, chained and put in prison, stoned, sawed in two, put to death by the sword, persecuted and mistreated."

From this it is obvious that faith is not a sure road to deliverance from harm and danger.

The main note is sounded in verse 39, talking about both groups, those delivered and those *not* delivered: "They were all commended for their faith." Whether we're delivered or not is not the issue—the real issue is that we be faithful.

You may be facing something right now that makes no sense to you. Trust God's faithfulness. He who brought you through in the past will bring you through again.

Can God trust you to trust Him?

NOVEMBER 17

Never Take Your Spiritual Life Easy

Have you ever thought, "One of these days I'm going to take life easy"? in Luke 12:19 one man said to himself, "I have plenty of good things laid up for many years. I'm going to take life easy now."

This man is often referred to as a "rich fool," but he was apparently no fool when it came to farming—he was quite a success. He evidently was religious because the Greek says he spoke to his "soul" and said, "I have plenty." A lot of people seem not to know that they even have souls.

"Take it easy" is a familiar parting word today that everybody hears and nobody obeys.

When it comes to spiritual things, however, we must never "take it easy." Paul said to the Ephesians, "Wake up, O sleeper, and rise from the dead." God does not come to give a soul a *vacation*—He comes to give a soul a *vocation.*

The song writer said, "We'll work till Jesus comes."

There's never a time when the Christian goes off duty. Oh, it's fine to pace yourself, but *never* take your spiritual life easy.

There's always something to do for God. What would He have you do today? (If you have no idea, ask Him)

NOVEMBER 18

Taking Hold of God

Isaiah proclaims God's vengeance and yet the hope of redemption. Then he turns to prayer, and in Isaiah 64:7 he says, "There is no one who stirs himself up to take hold of God" (KJV).

Here the prophet is not saying people are not stirred up. Rather, he says they are just not stirred up about the right things.

Even today there is enough stirring going on in the church world that would suggest that something is going on. But that's just the problem: some things are going on that are ends in themselves. They do not cause us to "take hold of God."

The justification for all valid stirrings is in the fact that they draw us closer to God.

Ask yourself, "Is what I'm doing at church drawing me closer to God ? Am I more aware of His presence as a result?" If not, it does not mean you should quit your activity—it means you need to change your motivation for what you do.

Are you doing what you do for Jesus—or for a church? Think about it. There's no need to change churches; just change your focus. And take hold of God.

NOVEMBER 19

Something Is Happening

In James 5:11 we read, "You have heard of Job's perseverance and have seen what the Lord finally brought about."

After all Job went through, God turned his situation around and blessed his life more than before.

Have you lived long enough to look back and see "what the Lord finally brought about"? A friend of mine said that God is a snail. He was not being critical of God, for he loves the Lord dearly. But he was expressing a common feeling among honest people that sometimes God seems to take His time in helping us.

God's purpose is not so much to explain our suffering as to sustain us while we're going through it. God does not always restore our lost prosperity or broken dreams, but He does desire to be with us.

Don't pine away in your time of adversity, seeking explanation and restoration of all things. Seek to know God and enjoy Him for Himself—regardless of the circumstances.

One day we'll all look back and see "what the Lord finally brought about." We'll realize that when it seemed nothing was happening, *something* was actually happening.

NOVEMBER 20

Believing and Receiving

In Mark 11:24 Jesus said, "Whatever you ask for in prayer, believe that you have received it, and it will be yours."

Now that's the language of faith! James 1 tells us to ask for wisdom, but after we ask, verse 6 says we must believe and not doubt.

Do you ever feel as if faith is often trying to talk yourself into believing something? Without doubt, it does call for effort, but not a forced, artificial something. Faith has a natural flow to it.

We must not only believe that we receive, but we must *believe* that we *believe.* Though it's a well-worn saying, it's still true: we must believe our beliefs and doubt our doubts. Too often, though, we doubt our beliefs and believe our doubts.

To always be examining our faith is to destroy it. There is an unhealthy approach to faith that so questions everything that nothing can be known for sure. There are some who are ever learning yet never able to come to the knowledge of truth (2 Timothy 3:7).

Why not try to trust the Lord as simply as a child would? Just choose to trust today—and see what happens.

NOVEMBER 21

Trust When You Cannot See

In John 20:19 we read, "On the evening of that first day of the week, when the disciples were together, with the doors locked for fear of the Jews, Jesus came and stood among them." In verse 26 we read, "A week later His disciples were in the house again, and Thomas was with them. Though the doors were locked, Jesus came and stood among them."

Are you living behind any closed doors these days, doors bolted against some nameless dread or fear? Is it fear of people, of tomorrow, or of a future failure?

Remember: the Lord is with you, not visibly as in the accounts in John, but as He told Thomas on this same occasion, "Blessed are those who have not seen and yet have believed."

You may remember that *blessed* means happy. Think of it. Happy, contented, at rest, and secure are those who have not seen and yet have believed.

You are in store for something great if you keep on believing during the dark times of life. Regardless of your closed doors, look up—Jesus is about to "stand among you."

NOVEMBER 22

God Is Working in Your Life

Do you ever feel that God has forgotten about you? Did something unpleasant ever happen to you for no apparent reason and it seemed God had somehow forgotten to intervene?

In Philippians 1:12 Paul was in prison, his life was in danger, yet he says, "I want you to know brothers, that what has happened to me actually served to advance the gospel."

I believe Paul is giving us a principle for life. He was convinced that whatever happened to him could turn into an "advance of the gospel." As Christians, we are not just freewheeling through life without the watchful care of God. We are not helpless victims suffering for no reason.

You know that scripture you memorized in Romans 8:28: "We know that in *all things* God works for the good of those who love Him" (emphasis added). Note that it is not just for the gospel's good but for our good too.

Today why not personalize Romans 8:28? Whatever you're going through must be a part of God's "all things"—so just put your concerns in the "all things" file. Say, "God is working in my lost job for good, "God is working in this fractured relationship for good." Indeed, God is working in whatever situation you face, for good."

Glory to God! He really is. You have His Word on it.

NOVEMBER 23

Catching Men Alive

In Luke chapter 5:1–10 Jesus was standing by a lake with people crowded around him. Here at the edge of the water he saw two boats belonging to fishermen who were now washing their nets.

He got into the boat belonging to Simon Peter and asked him to move out a little from the shore. Then Jesus taught the people from the boat. After His teaching session, He told Simon to move out into deeper water and let down his nets for a catch. Peter had been fishing there all night and had caught nothing, but he obeyed the Lord anyway and caught so many fish that he had to get some men with another boat to come help him.

The suggestion here is clearly to a lifestyle of evangelism—whether it's a brother getting another brother and bringing him to Jesus or a person influencing his or her entire household to know the Christ he or she knows.

Evangelism is not just an event—it's also a lifestyle. It can happen at church but also needs to happen where people live. We meet people where they are in life, build relationships with them, then win them to ourselves, after which we can more easily win them to our Christ.

Verse 10 records Jesus saying, "From now on you will catch men." The word *catch* in our passage is a powerful word but does not clearly express the Greek meaning here. The actual Greek word Jesus used means "to take alive or to catch alive, as taking animals alive for a zoo or circus." It's a much more accurate image of what Jesus was talking about. Jesus was promising those early disciples that they would be taking people alive for the kingdom, and that's exciting business. The verb tense used here describes an ongoing process. It's not like deer hunting, in which you get your limit for the season and quit until next year. Taking people alive for Jesus speaks of a continuous and never-ending endeavor.

As you move through your world today, be conscious of winning people to yourself, that you might "take them alive" for Jesus.

When you catch fish, soon they are dead. But when you catch people for Christ, He helps you catch them alive and at that moment they take on new lives.

Who is it in your life that Christ wants you to catch alive today?

NOVEMBER 24

Lifestyle Evangelism

Yesterday we talked about lifestyle evangelism and how winning people to Jesus is done not only at church but also where people live, preferably by those who have a relationship with them already. But there's a prerequisite to lifestyle evangelism: revival.

In Psalm 51:12–13 we read, "Restore to me the joy of your salvation and grant me a willing spirit to sustain me. Then I will teach transgressors your ways, and sinners will turn back to you."

Ask yourself, "When someone sees me, does he or she see the joy of the Lord?"

Here in Old Testament language is the difference between revival and evangelism. David is saying, "Make me right, and then I will be able to help someone else." We have to *be* what Christ wants in order to *do* what Christ wants. Too many Christians do not have the joy of Christ, and thus they have nothing to share.

Renewing of priorities, confessing of failures, cleansing, and a right spirit are all part of revival. Evangelism, soul winning, personal work, and the conversion of sinners flow from revival.

If you are not in a spiritual condition to make others want what you have, then tarry until the Spirit of God reveals to you where you are and where you need to be.

Walk in the light of God and you'll be ready to "take people alive" for Jesus. And you'll be able to spread that life to others.

NOVEMBER 25

You Will Understand Someday

Jesus was humbling Himself before the disciples in John 13. For here it was that He washed their feet. When he came to Simon Peter, the disciple asked, "Lord, are you going to wash my feet?" (v. 6). Jesus replied, "You do not understand now what I am doing, but later you will" (v. 7).

Jesus's word here to Simon Peter goes much further than the original application. Here we have a principle for life: there are many things we do not understand now, but we will later.

There's no way Stephen could have understood why, in the prime of his life, God would allow him to be stoned to death. For a moment I want you to picture Stephen and Paul in heaven. Paul, of course, had been a mighty voice for God and had won thousands. Upon his entrance to heaven, I can imagine Jehovah God saying something to Stephen like "Stephen, you would have won hundreds if I had stopped your stoning, but here stands Paul—he was influenced by your death to win multiplied thousands for me. Yes, it was your death that caught his attention. That's why I let it happen." (We know that thirteen of the twenty-seven books of the New Testament were written by Paul.)

Without doubt, all your questions will be satisfied when you get to heaven. You may not realize now what God is doing, but when you get to heaven you will. Mark it down: you're going to see why God allowed what He allowed—and you will understand.

NOVEMBER 26

Growing Up

In Ephesians 4:14 Paul tells the Christians to grow, writing, "No longer be infants."

It is true according to Matthew 18:3 that we are to be childlike—but we are not to be childish.

The Bible encourages us to use our minds and not just meander through life, never thinking, never growing, and never knowing what maturity is all about.

It is true that starting out with Jesus is childlike, and in many respects childlike faith, even among mature Christians, is a welcome sight. But childishness is not a proper Christian adjective.

It's childish to wonder why you were not selected to sing in a certain group or teach a certain class—and then pout about it. Come on! The kingdom of God is much bigger than that. So what if you're not on the church board next year? Is that why you're part of the church, to have influence and visibility? No, that's a long way from being like Jesus.

I think I can hear Jesus saying, "Come on—grow up!" When the disciples said, "Show us the Father, and that will be enough," Jesus replied, "Have I been with you so long and you still do not even know who I am?" Is the Lord telling you to "grow up" in some area of your walk with Him? Is He asking: Don't you remember who I am?

NOVEMBER 27

A Change in Plans

In Acts 3:1–2 we read, "One day Peter and John were going up to the temple at the time of prayer—at three in the afternoon. Now a man who was lame from birth was being carried to the temple gate called Beautiful, where he was put every day to beg from those going into the temple courts."

That morning Peter and John did not have the needy man written down on their agenda for the day. When they started toward the temple for prayer, they never dreamed what was ahead for them. The man did not know it was to be his very special day either. Peter and John's unscheduled event became the main event of the day. Sometimes an unscheduled event in our lives is indeed the main event of our day.

Often when we're busy doing the things of God, He invades our agenda with unscheduled events. Peter and John could have easily passed over the man, but thank God—they didn't. They were alert to a change in their plans.

How alert have you been to agenda adjustments in the last seven days? Could it be the very thing that you've been complaining about, that thing that disrupted your plans, could it be that it was part of God's agenda for you? Think about it.

NOVEMBER 28

Your Miracle Today

In Matthew 14:13–18 we have the familiar story of Jesus feeding the five thousand. He had told the disciples to feed the crowd, but their resources seemed totally inadequate. In verse 17 the disciples said, "We only have five loaves of bread and two fish." Jesus replied, "Bring them here to me."

The loaves of bread were not like our loaves today. They were round cakes, more like pancakes, meager morsels to say the least. What deserves the emphasis is verse 17. Here we see that the disciples were not answering in faith—but utter despair. They were literally saying, "We do not have *anything* here except loaves and fish."

Like many of us today, the disciples were quick to see why the plan would not work. Jesus said, "Bring them here to me." Here is the contrast between the helpless doubt of the disciples and the confident courage of Jesus.

The very thing the disciples thought was an impossibility Jesus turned into a miracle.

Has the Lord asked you to do something for which you are inadequate, that would take a miracle? I hope so!

I wonder what your miracle could be today.

NOVEMBER 29

There Are Only Two Kingdoms

In Matthew 12:30 Jesus said, "He who is not with me is against me. And he who does not gather with me scatters."

With these solemn words Jesus draws a line of separation. He points out that *neutrality* is not an acceptable word when it comes to a Christian's vocabulary. The reason is that there are only two kingdoms. One is of God with Christ as the head. The other is of the world with Satan at the head. A person belongs either to one or to the other.

Consequently, if we are not in active association with Christ, "we are down on Him," as the Greek literally says—that is, we are against Him. To be with Jesus means to gather. To be "down on Him" means to scatter. To be with Jesus is to be instrumental in gathering people to be His followers. To be against Him means to be unwilling to follow Him and His mission of gathering the lost.

Romans 6:16 says, "Don't you know that when you offer yourselves to someone as obedient slaves, you are slaves of the one you obey—whether you are slaves to sin, which leads to death, or to obedience, which leads to righteousness?"

The words of Jesus in Matthew 12 make it clear that there is no middle ground. Right now you are either a gatherer or a scatterer.

Ask yourself, "Am I a gatherer or a scatterer? Is anyone closer to Jesus because of my influence in the last six months?" If not, why not?

NOVEMBER 30

Jesus Promised

In Matthew 28:20 (the last verse of this gospel) Jesus says, "Surely I am with you always, to the very end of the age."

Here Jesus leaves us with no question about His future presence.

The word *surely* here is an emphatic word, meaning "Take note," Pay close attention," "Listen to what I'm saying."

When Jesus said, "I am with you," the pronoun *I* is almost underlined in His expression, as if Jesus said, "Take note; mark it down—no one less than I Myself am with you always."

The thought here is "I am with you daily" or more correctly, "I am with you day by day." The picture here is of days passing one by one, each with its own trials, troubles, and difficulties, but each day also accompanied by His presence.

I have no idea what this month has brought into your life. I'm not sure what blessings or burdens you're facing. But I know for sure the Lord is with you. He promised He would—and He always keeps His promises.

DECEMBER 1

Forgiveness

In Luke 7:36–39 we read of a Pharisee named Simon (not to be confused with the disciple bearing the same name) who invites Jesus to dinner. A woman in that town hears of Jesus's visit and comes to Him. Jesus is reclining at the table with His feet extended behind Him. She stood behind Him and began weeping. She was a sinful woman, probably a prostitute. She began washing His feet with her tears and drying them with her hair; she then anointed His feet with expensive oil.

If the woman had touched the host Pharisee, he would have no doubt slapped her and had her removed from the house. He would have felt contaminated, with no forgiveness in his heart for the woman.

Those with a lack of forgiveness fail to realize how much they have been forgiven of and are undoubtedly self-righteous. If you struggle to forgive someone else, chances are that it reveals an area of self-righteousness in your own life.

Those who recognize they have been forgiven much find it easier to forgive others. Friend, remember that Christ died for you while you were still a sinner. Did you deserve forgiveness? Me neither.

Forgiveness is "for-giving." In other words, we're to give the gift of forgiveness to others. Is there anyone you need to give the gift of forgiveness to today?

Don't Worry When You Can Wait

In Matthew 6:28–30 Jesus said, "Why do you worry?...God clothes the grass of the field, which is here today and tomorrow is thrown into the fire. Will He not much more clothe you, O you of little faith?"

If God ever did things by accident (which He doesn't), I would say, "God accomplishes more by accident than we do on purpose."

We've all heard the old cliché "Haste makes waste." I guess one reason those three words are passed on from generation to generation is that they're so true.

It seems that every time I get in a hurry, frustration comes in and peace is disrupted, and it never goes as smoothly as I had hoped. However, if I simply pray, read the Word, and follow the signs as God gives them, the frustration is gone, the peace level rises, and it turns out better than I imagined.

Another common phrase is "Why worry when you can pray?" I would also say, "Why worry when you can wait?"

Are you following God's signs today, or are you so busy making something happen that you don't have time to let God work? Are you worrying or are you waiting? Is your agenda so important that you can't wait on God?

If that's you, then you're too busy. Step back, take a breath, and give God time.

DECEMBER 3

The Holy Spirit

When you hear the word *Pentecost,* what do you think of? I hope you think of Acts 2:4, but what else do you think of? The one hundred twenty people in the upper room, the sound of a violent wind, flames of fire dancing upon their heads, or the miracle of languages. What do you think of? I hope you think of the coming, as never before, of the Holy Spirit.

Here God reached out as far as possible to the human scene. Christ had been with the disciples, but now His Holy Spirit was within them. Think of it: the presence and power of God actually dwelling in His followers.

He dwelt among us in the incarnation, but now, in the person of the Holy Spirit, God Himself moves into the hearts of His followers.

Think of it, friend: today, through the infilling of the Holy Spirit, you can personally be aware of the presence of the divine.

It's wonderful to hear about the good things God has done, but to know His power and presence in everyday living is joy beyond words. Walk with confidence, believer. The God of all the universe is living in you—right now!

DECEMBER 4

Doing the Right Thing

James 4:17 is one of the best definitions of sin in the entire Bible: "To him who knows to do good and does not do it, to him it is sin" (NKJV).

Here James is warning us against the sin of omission. Without a doubt, this is one of the most difficult forms of sin with which to deal.

Sin is literally missing the mark by not only doing wrong, but by failing to do what is right. Again, James is urging us to be *doers* and not only *hearers* of God's Word.

To know what is right and then not to do it is disobedience, and disobedience is sin. The Lord gives us a commandment, and we either ignore it or simply fail to do it. When we fail to follow this knowledge, we commit a sin of omission. God holds us accountable for more than merely *knowing* the right—He wants us to *do* the right.

As Christians, we are more concerned about *His* plans for us than we are about *our* plans for us. God wants us to study His Word, pray, share our faith, and live in constant obedience.

Some people have the mistaken idea that to follow God's will is a path to misery and discontent. Just the opposite is true. Simply look at the lives of those who choose their own way.

Proverbs 14:12 says, "There is a way which seems right to a man, But its end is the way of death."

It's always better to do the *good*—which is *right* thing.

DECEMBER 5

Quench Not the Holy Spirit

In Mark 3:28–29 Jesus said, "All the sins and blasphemies of men will be forgiven them. But whoever blasphemes against the Holy Spirit will never be forgiven; he is guilty of an eternal sin."

Those listening to Jesus were saying He was possessed by the devil. To blaspheme against the Holy Spirit was to say that the spirit that was in Jesus, the Holy Spirit, was an unclean spirit, the Lord of filth.

Today if any person is wondering if he or she has blasphemed against the Holy Spirit, that person can be sure he or she has not. For if the person had committed the unpardonable sin, he or she would not be troubled, with a guilty conscience. I personally know of no one who has committed this sin, though Jesus says it is indeed a possibility.

Today we would be wise to do what is said in 1 Thessalonians 5:19: "Quench not the Spirit," or more literally, "Do not put out the Spirit's fire."

Though I have never met anyone who has committed a single act that would be called the unpardonable sin, I have met many who have quenched the creative power of Holy Spirit in their lives. They have been fearful and at times self-seeking, and as a result, the Spirit's fire has gone out. Be careful not to let the Spirit's fire go out in your life.

DECEMBER 6

Keeping in Step with the Spirit

Instead of the coming of the Holy Spirit being an isolated event happening at Pentecost, it brought us to a relationship with the Holy Spirit. Jesus did not come to do away with the law, but to finish or make up where it lacked. A religion of the law is viewed as an immature and childish kind of arrangement, whereas a religion of the Spirit is a maturing, growing, dynamic life.

Paul was very concerned about the Galatians living in the power of the Spirit. He was troubled that they were turning from an inner surrender to an outer struggle.

The key thought in Galatians 3:1–3 is Paul's question in verse 2: "Did you receive the Spirit by observing the law, or by believing what you heard?" In essence he was asking, "Did you receive the Spirit by struggling to keep all the details of the law, or by surrendering to the power of God?"

Do you live by the law, or by the freedom of the Spirit? Oh, there's a place for dos and don'ts—I know that—but if our freedom in Christ is not a daily reality, then we're trusting in something less than the grace of God.

It's good to begin in the Spirit, but it's even better to *stay* in the Spirit. Ask yourself: "Am I keeping in step with the Spirit?"

DECEMBER 7

More and More like Him

The freedom of the Spirit is beautifully expressed by Paul in 2 Corinthians 3:17–18: "For the Lord is the Spirit, and wherever the Spirit of the Lord is, there is freedom. So all of us who have had that veil removed can see and reflect the glory of the Lord. And the Lord—who is the Spirit—makes us more and more like Him as we are changed into His glorious image" (NLT).

Note that with the "veil removed"—that is, with no cover-up, hidden conflicts, or unsurrendered areas—we are to reflect the Lord's glory. That is making Jesus Lord of every area of our lives. As a result, we are made "more and more like Him." That is, we are becoming like that which we are constantly gazing at.

Just like a husband and wife who take on characteristics of each other (habits, mannerisms, and even facial features), so we take on the likeness of Christ. The scripture continues: "The Spirit makes us more and more like Him as we are changed into His glorious image." That is endless growth.

All of this comes from the Lord, who is this inner working Spirit. He is the inner agent of the soul, forming within us the image of Jesus.

When the Holy Spirit is free to work within us, then we are the ones who are set free. Friend, you are not only free in Christ—you are free indeed!

DECEMBER 8

His Leadership

In Romans 8:14 we read, "Those who are led by the Spirit of God are sons of God." Here we have a state of Christian living that many Christians never seem to attain. They are not led by the Spirit. In their daily conversation you never hear them talk about something God said to them in devotions. Many Christians never indicate that God has told them to do or give anything; they are led by self-interests. They seem to know little if anything about conversation with the Spirit.

God leads us through Scripture, prayer, Godly counsel, and the inner voice of the Holy Spirit.

To cultivate a Spirit-led life, a life that is guided by the inner voice of God, we must cultivate the art of listening. Do you ever listen when you pray?

And then, when we hear an inner voice, we need to check it, or test it, with the Word of God. If it's God's voice, it will always be in harmony with God's Word.

A wise old Christian once asked a young disciple, "Have you heard God speak lately?" The answer was a hesitant "No, I haven't." The mature Christian said, "You must have forgotten to be still." The Bible says, "Be still and know." Too often we are not still, and too often we don't know His presence.

Take time to be still today. He's closer than you think.

DECEMBER 9

Spirit-Led Prayer

In Romans 8:26–27 we read, "The Spirit helps us in our weakness. For we do not know what to pray for as we ought, but the Spirit himself intercedes for us with groanings too deep for words. And he who searches hearts knows what is the mind of the Spirit, because the Spirit intercedes for the saints according to the will of God" (ESV).

Here we have the focal point of the Spirit's work in our lives. That is, He helps us to pray. Our weakness is often right at this point—a weakness in prayer. If we are weak in praying, then we are weak in all other areas of Christian living. There is a good chance that weakness in the Christian life is found in our prayer habits more than in any other area.

It's a wonderful thing to have the Spirit so much a part of our lives that He draws us to prayer. We then have the Spirit of prayer.

The Holy Spirit inspires us to pray. It could be that we are about to do something we've planned on, like a trip to the store, watching a television program, making a phone call, or spending time on the Internet. But for apparently no reason we are drawn to prayer. If we are faithful to that inner voice, it will come again, but if not, chances are that God will not trouble us again for some time.

The Spirit-led prayer is the Spirit-answered prayer. This is why it is so important to be led by the Spirit. He knows who needs prayer in the next sixty minutes. He knows who is close to making a decision. He knows how we could make a prayer difference for someone.

If we were more faithful to prayer, God would give us more to be prayerful for.

DECEMBER 10

Making the "Rejoice Choice"

In Romans 8:37 Paul said, "In all these things we are more than conquerors through Him who loved us."

It's noteworthy to remember the context of Paul's words. "In all these things"—what things was he referring to? According to verse 35, they were the kinds of things that could upset and even destroy: "trouble, hardship, persecution, famine, nakedness, danger or sword." A worse combination of events is hard to imagine. And yet the writer says that in all these things we are not only conquerors but *more* than conquerors. We are conquerors with room to spare. We are not only conquerors who are victorious but also conquerors ready for another attack.

As you read this scripture, underline the word *in.* Paul says this victory, this conquering, is *in* all these things. This is not a victory that looks back after the conflict is over and says, "I've made it, the battle is over, I'm on the other side of the problem, and now I'm victorious."

No, here we have a suggestion of victory in the heat of the battle. Here we find the picture of Paul, who, while behind bars, said in Philippians 4:4, "Rejoice in the Lord always. Again I say rejoice." Here is a picture of victory in all these things.

What "thing" are you in right now? Are you choosing to rejoice? By the way, "choosing" is indeed a choice and not a feeling. It's the "rejoice choice."

DECEMBER 11

God Is Working for Good All the Time

Let's look again at Romans 8:37: "In all these things we are more than conquerors through Him who loved us."

God has a purpose for each believer and is working on it all the time. Yesterday we talked of how *in* all things we are more than conquerors. Some of the things we meet in the *ins* of our lives are evil things. How can we get victory, not just through difficult things but also through evil things? Romans 8:28 helps us. Here we are reminded that "God works in all things for the good of those who love Him."

Note the thing itself may not be good—its source and content may be evil—but God works in that evil to turn it out for good.

The cross of Christ is an excellent illustration. The cross was evil—a place of unjust punishment, Satan's attempt to defeat God's plan—but God was working in it all the time. You see, the cross was evil and yet God worked in it to make redemption possible.

Now there is a principle for life: if we love God, He works in the very thing that threatens our existence and makes it the very springboard of our growth.

Whatever you're facing today, I challenge you to look to God. He is not gone and you're not alone. He is working, right now, on something very, very good.

DECEMBER 12

Minister to Someone Who Can't Pay You Back

Do you consciously reach out in an attempt to minister to others? Think back over the past few weeks. Whom have you reached out to? Have you helped anyone lately who could never pay you back?

In Philippians 1:3–7 Paul was thanking God for the Philippians' ministry to him while he was in prison. He could do nothing for them. He could not repay them. He simply thanked those who had ministered to him.

Ananias one day ministered to Paul. In Acts 9:17 he laid his hands on Paul's blind eyes and Paul saw again. Ananias had nothing to gain. As a matter of fact, Paul had a notorious reputation for killing Christians at the time. So Ananias had nothing to gain and all to lose. But he ministered to Paul anyway. He even called Paul "brother."

Is there anyone you are reaching out to these days who can do nothing for you? Oh, I'm not saying that you should never let someone do something for you. But who are you consciously reaching out to—just to minister to them at the point of their need?

Today look for someone to help who will probably never be able to do anything for you. There's someone who needs you to reach out to him or her. Ask the Lord to show you when that person crosses your path.

DECEMBER 13

Urgency

In John 9:4 Jesus said, "As long as it is day we must do the work of Him who sent me. Night is coming when no one can work."

Both *we* and *must* are important words in this passage. Jesus is speaking not only of what *He* must do, but also of His followers and what *we* can do. Here Jesus is concerned about people believing on Him who God had sent. That is also one of our great concerns: to persuade others to believe Jesus and to turn to Him as their Savior and Lord.

The word *must* reminds us that this is not simply what is advisable or just a good idea. Rather, here we have a sense of urgency, even a compelling necessity.

John, the writer of this gospel, emphasizes over and over that God sent Jesus. John 3:16 is sort of a theme for the book, and John never loses sight of that fact. God's love was demonstrated in His sending of Jesus.

Here we have a reminder that the works in question do not originate here on earth. They are heaven-sent works that we must do. And there is a need to do them *now*, for the opportunity will not always be present. This verse says, "The night is coming"—a sobering thought and an awesome warning.

We all have vocations. You may work in an office, a hospital, or attend a school. You may have a responsibility to maintain a home and care for children. We all have tasks to perform. However, no matter what our vocational attachments, we all have a Christian calling. We are to spread the news of Jesus.

Today take time to tell someone of Him. Tell someone of an answer to prayer. Tell this person of His presence in your life. Do it today! Tomorrow may be too late.

DECEMBER 14

Being Fed by Jesus

In John 6 we have the familiar story of Jesus feeding the five thousand. What a miraculous time it must have been, and now with the miracle food perhaps even still in the people's mouths, Jesus said in John 6:35, "I am the bread of life. He who comes to me will never go hungry, and he who believes in me will never be thirsty."

When Jesus said, "I am the bread of life," everyone could envision what He was saying. They had been fed with physical food, but now they could see there was a higher food in focus: food for life, spiritual life—Jesus Himself.

Many of the people wanted to make Jesus their king. They thought here was someone who could set up a breadline anywhere, anytime. But Jesus was more concerned about a *life*line.

As bread feeds a person and gives him or her strength and energy, so Christ meets a person's basic needs. He gives the Christian an ever-abundant supply of faith, joy, love, peace, patience, goodness, and truth. These things, like ordinary bread, are essential to health and happiness.

In The Lord 's Prayer we say the words "Give us this day our daily bread." Daily we must eat and be filled. Also, daily we must partake of God's Word and be fed.

It's sad, but I'm afraid often true, that people spend their efforts in storing up spiritual food from Sunday services rather than having daily nourishment for themselves.

How much of your spiritual nourishment comes from your alone time with Jesus? Take time to be with Him today.

DECEMBER 15

Your Account with God

When Paul talked to the Galatians about trusting God, He referred to an Old Testament character: Abraham. In Galatians 3:6 we read, "Consider Abraham, he believed God and it was credited to him as righteousness." In other words, Abraham entered into his particular blessing by realizing that he could do nothing himself—he simply believed God. He confessed his need of God, throwing himself onto God and counting on God to do what he himself could not. That is the paradox of faith, as true for us as for Abraham. It was by ceasing to try doing anything for himself and by accepting this position of humble and utter dependence that Abraham was justified.

Paul said Abraham's faith was credited to him as righteousness. The Greek word for *credit* means "to count, to reckon, to set to one's account." Abraham believed God, and his act of faith was placed in his account; it was put on deposit; it was reckoned to be so.

Abraham put himself in the place where a righteous God could offer him salvation and work in and through him. God, therefore, put righteousness to his account. He evaluated Abraham's act of faith as that which made it possible for Him to give him salvation.

Think of it, friend. God counts, reckons, and credits to your account righteousness by your faithfulness to Him. Our acts do not save us, but our confession and obedience allow Him to save us.

Righteousness is credited to your account as you daily live by faith. What is being credited to your account these days?

DECEMBER 16

Jesus Speaks to the Father about Us

In 1 John 2:1 we read, "I write this to you so that you will not sin. But if anybody does sin, we have one who speaks to the Father in our defense—Jesus Christ, the Righteous One."

The words *one who speaks* are taken from the Greek word often called "comforter" or "advocate." The verb form of this word refers to the act of calling someone to one's side in order to help him or her. The noun form refers to the one who is called upon to render aid. In the broadest sense of the word it means a helper, one who aids another. In this passage the Lord Jesus is the one who comes alongside, the one who speaks for us.

Jesus pleads our cause before our heavenly Father. The plan of God is that we live without sinning, but if we do sin, we are not cut off, and we are not thrown out.

Jesus immediately comes to the rescue. He comes before the Father and represents us. He presents our case.

I can almost hear Jesus talking to the Father when one of His children falls. Jesus might say, "Father, you've never been down there, but I have. I know what it is to be tired, to be temped, and to be alone. Father, this child is one of ours. He [She] loves us and is sorry for his [her] sin."

I can hear the Father reply, "Well, Son, if that's how you feel about Tom [Sue, John, Mary, Bill, Alice (put your name in there)], so do I. Let's be sure to stay close to them, strengthen them, and help them."

Be confident that Jesus represents you well and is presenting you to the Father. Think of it: Jesus is talking to the Father about you.

DECEMBER 17

Access to the Father

In Romans 5:1–2 we read, "We have peace with God through our Lord Jesus Christ, through whom we have gained access by faith into this grace in which we now stand."

The word *access* is an interesting New Testament word, made up of the words *to go* and *toward*. It was also used in a technical sense for "a landing platform." It is thought that it was used as a nautical term referring to the approach of a ship to a haven or harbor where it could safely land. So the total thrust of the word would be access into a rest, a haven, or a harbor.

The Old Testament temple worship with its outer court, the Holy Place, and the Holy of Holies is part of the background here. For it was only the high priest who had access to the Holy of Holies and only once a year. But now all believers can go, can move "toward," can find a safe "landing" in the presence of God.

The word was also used to describe a person who brings another into the presence of a third party.

Think of it, friend: because of Jesus, we now have access to the God of the universe. We can actually draw near to the very presence of God Himself. Jesus is the one who brings us into the Father's presence.

Take advantage of your "access" opportunities today.

DECEMBER 18

The Family of God

In Romans 8:15 we read, "You have not received a spirit that makes you fearful slaves. Instead, you received God's Spirit when He adopted you as His own children. Now we call Him, 'Abba, Father'" (NLT).

The words "adopted you as His own children" literally are one word in the Greek. That is adoption. *Adoption* is a compound word meaning "a son" and "to place." The compound word means "to place as a son."

This was a term used in Roman legal practice. It referred to a legal action by which a person takes into his or her family a child not born to him or her but taken with the purpose of giving them all the privileges of any child. This practice was common among Greeks and Romans.

This custom is used in the New Testament as an illustration of how God brings us into His family. *Abba* was a term much like our affectionate word *Daddy*. Here again we find that God makes Himself accessible to us (as we discussed yesterday) and actually makes us a part of His family by adoption.

All Christians are adopted by the same Father, and then as a result, really are brothers and sisters in Christ.

So to you, my brothers and sisters who read this devotional, have a great day today. Remember that we are family.

DECEMBER 19

Don't Be Afraid—Just Believe

The synagogue ruler's name was Jairus, and his heart must have sunk within his chest when the messenger said in Mark 5:35, "Your daughter is dead—why bother the teacher anymore?"

They were telling him, "It's hopeless. Don't bother Jesus. No one, not even Jesus, can help her now."

Have you come to a place where the case seems hopeless, where the prospects seem bleak? Maybe someone for whom you have prayed seems worse off and farther than ever from God and salvation. Your hope has perhaps turned to despair.

But Jesus held no funerals. When the world says the issue is as dead as a corpse, remember that Jesus can break up funerals. We are so prone to give up and attend the funeral of our hopes— when God desires to raise the dead.

Jesus said to the troubled father in Mark 5:36, "Don't be afraid—just believe."

And that's what He says to us today: "Don't be afraid—just believe." When human logic says, "It's too late. Don't trouble Jesus with it. Just let it go and make the best of it"—you can cry out, "It's *not* too late! I'm not afraid. I do believe!"

Remember—Jesus changed every funeral He ever attended.

DECEMBER 20

Let Him Carry Your Hurts

In Psalm 41:9–10 we read, "Even my close friend, whom I trusted, He who shared my bread, has lifted up his heel against me, but you, O Lord, have mercy on me, raise me up."

We might as well face the facts that some of us suffer great hurts at the hands of our friends. The follower after God needs to always remember that although God never fails, sometimes God's people do.

We must all answer this question for ourselves: "Am I going to trust God or not?" People will fail me, my best friend may forsake me, but God will make up any deficits in His own way. Either we continue following Him with childlike trust, or we become sour, suspicious, and disheartened.

It's better to be wronged once in a while by people we trusted than to grow cynical after the pattern of this world. When it's all over, we will find that God was faithful to us and took care of us, even though some of His people failed us.

We don't have to carry our hurts—He can carry us and our hurts at the same time. Let Him.

DECEMBER 21

No Darkness Can Penetrate His Goodness

Have you been conscious during these past few days of God as the giver of every good and perfect gift?

In James 1:17 we read, "Every good and perfect gift is from above, coming down from the Father of Lights, who does not change like shifting shadows."

The word *shadow* in the Greek has various meanings. It can refer to the shadow cast by an object, as in an eclipse, or it can mean the act of overshadowing or can have the meaning of a reflected image. God's benevolence is like a light that cannot be extinguished, eclipsed, or overshadowed in any way at all.

The thought is that nothing can block God's light, interrupt the flow of His goodness, or put shadows over us so that we are out of His reach.

What a comfort that is to my soul today, to know that every good thing I have in my life is from God and that He is not a temporary influence in my life. Rather, He is as enduring as eternity. There is no darkness so dark that His light cannot penetrate. There is no situation so desperate that He cannot work in it for good.

Today walk in confidence that the God of the universe is working right now for you for good and forever.

DECEMBER 22

Glorifying God

In Genesis 1:27 we find a familiar verse of Scripture: "God created mankind in his own image, in the image of God he created them; male and female he created them."

No intelligent businessman ever puts a product on the market unless it meets a need or supplies a requirement. Similarly, God created the universe and everything in it for a purpose: to testify to His power and His glory.

Man was created as the crown of all creation, made in God's very image. He reflected God's glory on earth and ruled over God's creatures. But man ceased to fulfill the purpose for which he was created. This is why there is such chaos and failure in human lives and in society today.

Do you know why you were created? Relatively few people know why they were created. That's why, in spite of all their efforts, they fail to find satisfaction.

We can be at peace only when we are fulfilling God's purpose. The Bible says that in all we do we are to bring glory to God. That is our purpose in life—to glorify God.

Ask yourself this question: "Am I glorifying God by the way I speak, dress, spend my money, treat my parents, and live?" Think about it.

DECEMBER 23

He Runs to Our Aid

In Hebrews 2:18 these words from the Amplified Bible are found: "Because He Himself (in His humanity) has suffered in being tempted (tested and tried), He is able (immediately) to run to the cry of (assist, relieve) those who are being tempted and tested and tried."

There are two reasons Jesus became man: to destroy the devil (v. 14) and to deliver people from bondage (v. 15). He came to destroy the power of Satan by conquering death. His death on the cross was for all humanity, and as a result Satan was defeated.

In John 12:31 we read, "Now is the time for judgment on this world, now the prince of this world will be driven out."

The remedy for all sin was forever settled at the cross. Although Jesus defeated Satan by His death, He delivered humanity by His risen life.

He delivers us when we acknowledge His presence in our hearts, live in obedience, and commit our problems into His hands by faith.

Remember that our scripture says that Christ will immediately run to our aid. This means that whenever we have a test or trial, immediately Christ is there. Whether we feel Him or not, He is with us today in the good and in the bad. Let's look for Him.

DECEMBER 24

Humanity Needs to Worship Something

In Romans 1:24 we have the sobering words "God gave them over in the sinful desires of their hearts."

In the first state of perfection in the garden, God had given bountifully out of His heart of love to His creation. After the fall, when people chose to walk in independence of God, we find God gave again—only this time He gave them over to their own lusts.

People wanted independence, so God gave it to them. They wanted the knowledge of good and evil, so God gave it to them. People would be wise to be careful about what they want, because chances are they'll get it.

In verses 29–31 of Romans 1 we have a terrible picture of what people are filled with when not filled with God. They no longer worship and serve God; instead, they have exchanged the truth of God for a lie and now worship the creation more than the Creator (v. 25).

Humanity needs to worship something. Sometimes it's their country, sometimes a hero, sometimes sex, self, sports, position, drugs, money—the list goes on and on. People know what to expect as a result of such sins, but still they continue and even find pleasure in others committing them (v. 32).

Remember, Christian friend: you are capable of any of the sins Paul referred to. He warned the Corinthians in 1 Corinthians 10:12 to "be careful that you do not fall." We would all be wise to heed that warning.

DECEMBER 25

Don't Be like the World

In Romans 12:2 we read, "Do not conform any longer to the pattern of this world, but be transformed by the renewing of your mind."

The Greek word used for *conformed* refers to the outward form, a form that varies from year to year and day to day. A person's "form" is not the same at age seventeen as it is at age seventy. An automotive technician's outer form (the way he or she dresses) is different at work than when attending church on Sunday. A person's outer form or dress is constantly changing.

So Paul says, "Don't try to match your life to all the fashions of this world. Don't be like a chameleon, which takes its color from its surroundings. Don't go with the world, and don't let the world decide what you are going to be like."

The Greek word used for *transformed* means not the passing changes of a person but rather the unchanging shape, the very DNA of the person's life. If the world controls your thinking, you are a conformer; if God controls your thinking, you are a transformer.

Paul is saying that to worship and serve God, we must undergo a change, not of our outward form but of our inner being. What is that change? It is basically a change from self-centered living to Christ-centered living. That's the real change.

I think the Phillips translation says Romans 12:2 as well as could be said: "Don't let the world around you squeeze you into its own mold."

Are you feeling the "squeeze" of the world? Draw near to God, through prayer and the Word, and He will draw near to you.

DECEMBER 26

Satan Brings Division to the Church

Christians need to be very wise these days. Satan is subtle and he loves to confuse, bring questions, and especially disrupt a group of believers.

Paul admonishes the Romans to beware of such people whom Satan would try to use. Listen to Romans 16:17: "I urge you to watch out for those who cause divisions and put obstacles in your way."

First, Paul talks of those who cause division among believers. Any person who disrupts the peace of the church has much to answer to God for. Someday this person will suffer heavy judgment from Him who is the king and head of the church. Don't ever create division in Christ's church.

Second, Paul talks of those who are a hindrance to individuals living a Christian life. The person who makes it hard for someone to live a Christian life will have much to answer for.

The person whose conduct is a bad example and whose influence is an evil snare will someday bear his or her own punishment. It will not be light punishment, for Jesus was stern to any person who causes someone to stumble. It is a wise person who lets God deal with such people.

Whatever you do, never cause divisions in the church or make it hard for someone else who wants to live for Jesus.

DECEMBER 27

Baptism

In Galatians 3:26–28 we read, "You are all sons of God through faith in Christ Jesus, for all of you who were baptized into Christ have clothed yourselves with Christ. There is neither Jew nor Greek, slave nor free, male nor female, for you are all one in Christ Jesus."

All of you, Paul says, who were baptized into Christ have clothed yourselves with Christ. In Roman society when a young person became old enough to be considered an adult, he or she took off their children's clothes and put on an adult's toga. This switch indicated that the person had adult citizenship and responsibilities. In the same way, the Galatians had laid aside the old clothes of the law and had put on Christ's new robes of righteousness. Having the Son in us means we are being made like Him.

Baptism was a very involved Jewish rite and custom. The man to be baptized cut his hair and nails and undressed completely. There was enough water to touch every part of the candidate's body. The man then made confession of his faith before three other men who were called "fathers of baptism." It was through baptism that he entered the Jewish faith.

By Christian baptism a person was to enter into Christ. Early Christians looked on water baptism as something that produced a meaningful union with Christ. Baptism plus repentance and faith demonstrated a right relationship with God.

In Paul's pre-Christian days he still was considered a religious person. No doubt he often prayed their common prayer that said, "I thank God that I am not a Greek, a slave, or a woman." But now in verse 28 Paul says that the distinctions between Jew and Greek, slave and free, male and female have been removed.

Think of it, friend: you have entered into Christ by faith. If you haven't been baptized, talk to your pastor about it. I have never been in a baptismal service that was not significantly blessed by the Lord's presence.

DECEMBER 28

Restoring a Fellow Believer

In Galatians 6:1 Paul writes, "Brothers, if someone is caught in a sin, you who are spiritual restore him gently. But watch yourself, or you also may be tempted."

Paul knew that problems would no doubt arise in any Christian society. The best of believers may slip up. The Greek word Paul uses for *sin* here does not necessarily mean a deliberate sin but rather a slip as might come to a person on an icy road. The danger of those who are Christian and really wanting to live for Jesus is that they may tend to deal harshly with the offender.

Paul says that if a believer slips, the real Christian duty is to get the person on his or her feet again.

The word Paul uses for *restore* is a word used for "making a repair," and it's also used for the work of a surgeon in removing a growth from a person's body or in setting a broken limb. The whole thrust of the word lays stress not on the punishment but on the cure.

I don't know if you're facing any slip-ups in your life, but I do know that God reaches out to us all and is constantly trying to draw us to Himself.

Picture today in your mind a God who is reaching out, longing to fellowship, and earnestly desiring your love. Because He really is.

DECEMBER 29

Reaping What One Has Sown

In Galatians 6:7 some serious words jump to our attention: "A man reaps what he sows." Each person decides what his or her harvest will be.

Here Paul states a grim truth. He insists that in the end, life holds the scales with an even balance. If a person follows the directions of the flesh with no concern for God, no disciplined spiritual living, in the end he or she can expect nothing but a harvest of trouble. But if a person walks conscientiously in God's will, he or she may have to be patient, but in the end God repays.

The Greeks believed that when a person did wrong, immediately a sort of curse was placed upon the person and sooner or later he or she would have to pay.

What we sometimes don't remember is this: although it's a blessed truth that God can and does forgive us of or our sins, even God cannot wipe out the consequences of unconfessed sin. If a person sins against his or her body, one day the person will pay with ruined health, even if he or she is forgiven. If a person sins against their loved ones, sooner or later hearts will be broken—even if the person is forgiven.

Friend, don't give up doing the right thing. Just because it's rough, be faithful. When payday comes, you'll find that you have reaped what you have sown.

DECEMBER 30

Don't Be a Complainer

In Philippians 2:14–16 we read these admonitions of Paul: "Do everything without complaining or arguing, so that you may become blameless and pure, children of God, without fault in a crooked and depraved generation, in which you shine like stars in the universe as you hold out the word of life."

Christians are to do all things without complaining or arguing. The word Paul uses for *complaining* is an unusual Greek word, with a strong tie to the Old Testament. It's the word used of the rebellious, faithless, complaining and murmuring children of Israel in their desert journey. In Exodus 15:24 the Bible says that the people "grumbled against Moses." In Exodus 16:2, "The whole community grumbled against Moses and Aaron." This complaining in Philippians 2 describes the low, threatening, discontented muttering of a mob who distrust their leaders and are on the verge of a rebellion.

The word Paul uses for *arguing* refers to useless and sometimes ill-natured disputing and debating, with doubting and wavering. The Christian life is to have a serenity and a certainty about it that springs from total submission to God.

Whatever you do, don't be a complainer, and don't be an arguer. Do you think you are a complainer or an arguer?

Here's a challenge for you: ask someone who knows you well if you are a complainer or an arguer. If so, face it—and make up your mind to stop it!

DECEMBER 31

Discerning What Is Best until the Day of Christ

In Philippians 1:9–10 Paul prays a wonderful prayer for the Christians at Philippi. "This is my prayer," Paul says, "that your love may abound more and more in knowledge and depth of insight, so that you may be able to discern what is best and may be pure and blameless until the day of Christ."

It was Paul's prayer for his people that their love would grow greater every day. And that love was not merely a sentimental thing. It was a love that was to grow more and more in knowledge, and more and more in sensitive perception, so that they would be increasingly able to distinguish between right and wrong. Love is always the way to knowledge.

If we love any subject, we want to learn more and more about it. If we love any person, we want to learn more and more about him or her. If we love Jesus, we will want every day to learn more and more about Him and about His Word.

I can think of no better desire or higher prayer on my part for you than Paul's words here in Philippians. Let me pray for you:

> Lord, for a year now I have had the privilege by way of this book to meet with many friends. In my mind I see them: husbands, wives, college students, single adults, teenagers, and children— people who love you and Your Word. I pray that their love may abound more and more and that they may grow in knowledge and depth of insight, so that they may be able to discern what is best until the day of Christ. In Your precious name I pray. Amen!

Scripture Index

ABOUT THE AUTHOR

Dr. Lenny Wisehart is an evangelist/pastor. For 30 years he pastored in Colorado, Indiana and Iowa. He and his wife Joy have been full time evangelists for many years, traveling across America and many foreign countries.

His passions for ministry include preaching and teaching the Word, reaching the lost and discipling the reached.

He grew up in Indianapolis and is a graduate of Olivet Nazarene University and Nazarene Theological Seminary. He completed post graduate work in preaching at Trinity Evangelical Divinity School.

Pastor Wisehart and his wife, Joy, have two children: Brady and Amy, and also four (outstanding) grandchildren. Joy is an ordained minister. She and Lenny often preach in a tag team style. Joy is sought after as a speaker in various retreat venues.

He loves a certain football team (Colts)… enjoys competition, golf (disc and ball), fishing and boating… and (some say) 'makes the best fudge ever.'

His preaching is filled with the Word, humor and daily application to life's joys and sorrows.

If you would like to book the Wiseharts for future meetings please contact them at: lennywisehart@yahoo.com